Multilingualism and Gendered Immigrant Identity

MULTILINGUAL MATTERS

Series Editors: Leigh Oakes, *Queen Mary, University of London, UK* and Jeroen Darquennes, *Université de Namur, Belgium.*

Multilingual Matters series publishes books on bilingualism, bilingual education, immersion education, second language learning, language policy, multiculturalism. The editor is particularly interested in 'macro' level studies of language policies, language maintenance, language shift, language revival and language planning. Books in the series discuss the relationship between language in a broad sense and larger cultural issues, particularly identity related ones.

All books in this series are externally peer-reviewed.

Full details of all the books in this series and of all our other publications can be found on http://www.multilingual-matters.com, or by writing to Multilingual Matters, St Nicholas House, 31–34 High Street, Bristol, BS1 2AW, UK.

MULTILINGUAL MATTERS: 174

Multilingualism and Gendered Immigrant Identity

Perspectives from Catalonia

Farah Ali

MULTILINGUAL MATTERS
Bristol • Jackson

DOI https://doi.org/10.21832/ALI2071
Library of Congress Cataloging in Publication Data
A catalog record for this book is available from the Library of Congress.
Names: Ali, Farah, author.
Title: Multilingualism and Gendered Immigrant Identity: Perspectives from Catalonia / Farah Ali.
Description: Bristol, UK; Jackson, TN: Multilingual Matters, 2022. | Series: Multilingual Matters: 174 | Includes bibliographical references and index. | Summary: "This book examines the intersectionality of gendered, religious identity among Muslim women in Catalonia, and illustrates how this identity is brokered through language use in a multilingual and diasporic context. It offers a unique lens through which we can further our understanding of the role of language in the acculturation process"—Provided by publisher.
Identifiers: LCCN 2022026106 (print) | LCCN 2022026107 (ebook) | ISBN 9781800412071 (hardback) | ISBN 9781800412064 (paperback) | ISBN 9781800412088 (pdf) | ISBN 9781800412095 (epub)
Subjects: LCSH: Women immigrants—Spain—Catalonia—Social conditions. | Muslim women—Spain—Catalonia—Social conditions. | Catalan language—Social aspects. | Group identity—Spain—Catalonia. | Intersectionality (Sociology)—Spain—Catalonia.
Classification: LCC JV8258 .A46 2022 (print) | LCC JV8258 (ebook) | DDC 305.48/892764046—dc23/eng/20220809
LC record available at https://lccn.loc.gov/2022026106
LC ebook record available at https://lccn.loc.gov/2022026107

British Library Cataloguing in Publication Data
A catalogue entry for this book is available from the British Library.

ISBN-13: 978-1-80041-207-1 (hbk)
ISBN-13: 978-1-80041-206-4 (pbk)

Multilingual Matters
UK: St Nicholas House, 31–34 High Street, Bristol, BS1 2AW, UK.
USA: Ingram, Jackson, TN, USA.

Website: www.multilingual-matters.com
Twitter: Multi_Ling_Mat
Facebook: https://www.facebook.com/multilingualmatters
Blog: www.channelviewpublications.wordpress.com

Copyright © 2023 Farah Ali.

All rights reserved. No part of this work may be reproduced in any form or by any means without permission in writing from the publisher.

The policy of Multilingual Matters/Channel View Publications is to use papers that are natural, renewable and recyclable products, made from wood grown in sustainable forests. In the manufacturing process of our books, and to further support our policy, preference is given to printers that have FSC and PEFC Chain of Custody certification. The FSC and/or PEFC logos will appear on those books where full certification has been granted to the printer concerned.

Typeset by SAN Publishing Services.
Printed and bound in the UK by the CPI Books Group Ltd.

Contents

	Acknowledgments	vii
1	Introduction	1
	Dispatches from Barcelona	1
	Gendered Immigrant Identity in Catalonia	4
	Islam and Muslim Speech Communities	6
	Overview of Chapters	8
2	Language Use and Language Policy in Catalonia	11
	Introduction	11
	Languages of Catalonia: Present Day and Historical Overview	12
	Shifts to Democracy, Shifts in Ideology and Policy	15
	Migration and Immigrant Languages in Catalonia: Maintenance and Shift	20
	Conclusion	27
3	Acculturation and Negotiating Identity	28
	Introduction	28
	Discursively Negotiating Gendered Identity	28
	Intersectionality: Gender and Religion	31
	Linguistic Identity Among Immigrants in Catalonia: Adopting Catalan and Spanish	35
	Acculturation, Investment and Language Learning	38
	Acculturation and Immigrant Identity	43
	Conclusion	45
4	Research Design	46
	Introduction	46
	Setting	47
	Researcher Positionality and Informant Recruitment	47
	Informants	49
	Data Collection Tools	51
	Questionnaire	52
	Interview	53
	Method of Analysis	54
	Notations	56

5	Spaniard on Purpose: Narratives of First-Generation	
	Informants	57
	Introduction	57
	Connections to the TL Community: Navigating with Catalan, Spanish and Other Local Languages	58
	Disconnect from the TL Community: The Role of Linguistic and Cultural Differences	64
	Connections to Immigrant Communities	70
	Additional Comments	76
6	In Two Worlds: Narratives of Second-Generation Informants	79
	Introduction	79
	Connections to Immigrant Communities: Heritage Language Use	80
	Connections to the TL Community: The Role of Catalan	90
	Heritage Languages and Racism: The Role of TL Community Attitudes	92
	Multilingualism and Dual Identity	99
	Additional Comments	101
7	Catalan, Spanish and Heritage Languages: Reported Language Use and Attitudes	104
	Introduction	104
	Reported Language Use	105
	Language Attitudes: Likert-Scale Statements	110
	Language Attitudes: Speaker Traits	115
	Connecting Reported Language Use to Attitudes	120
8	Implications for Sociolinguistic Research	125
	Introduction	125
	Immigrants' Experiences with Societal Multilingualism	125
	Intersectional Identities in Sociolinguistic Research	129
	Future Directions	131
	Conclusion	134
9	Implications for Language and Immigrant-Targeted Policies	135
	Introduction	135
	Language Policy in Practice: Informants' Perspectives	136
	Problematizing Language Policy and Planning	138
	Final Remarks	143
	Appendix A: Questionnaire	145
	Appendix B: Interview Questions	155
	References	157
	Index	164

Acknowledgments

First, I am thankful to *Allah, subhan ahu wata'ala* (God, the Glorious and Exalted) for blessing me with the ambition and work ethic that carried me through to the completion of this project.

I would also like to acknowledge the various sources of support I received throughout this lengthy journey: the study that is detailed in this book could not have been completed without the funding I received as a doctoral student at the University at Albany, SUNY. This includes funding from the Graduate Student Association (research grant), Benevolent Association (research grant) and Initiatives for Women (Karen R. Hitchcock New Frontiers Fund Award). I am also grateful to my dissertation committee members – Dora Ramírez and Elizabeth Lansing – for providing me with helpful feedback when this book was still a dissertation, along with my advisors: the late Maurice Westmoreland, who served as my dissertation adviser until his untimely passing, as well as Megan Solon, who graciously stepped into that role and directed my work until I graduated. I am incredibly thankful to them both for their support and guidance, particularly during a time when achieving this goal seemed insurmountable.

As I worked toward transforming the dissertation into a book, so many others contributed either directly in helping me develop my manuscript, or otherwise offered various other forms of support to me. I appreciate the anonymous feedback that I received on my first draft, and so I wish to offer my thanks to whomever is responsible for providing me with so many helpful comments, suggestions and encouragement. I also want to thank my colleagues and friends who offered publishing advice, moral support, inspiration (academic and otherwise), reasons to always be excited about sociolinguistics and, most importantly, reasons to smile and laugh. Many thanks to these colleagues and friends: Sahar Ejaz, Carol Ready, Sherez Mohamed, Rochelle Compaoré, Marina Scatolin, Melissa Potts, Monique Mendoza, Daniela Orozco, Paul Johnson, Carmen Eugenia Nieves Rosado and Caleb Rivera-Bloodworth.

I'd also like to acknowledge two significant mentors who shaped my academic and professional trajectory: first, the late Flore Zephir, whose mentorship, unwavering support and sunny smile will never be forgotten. Second, a special thanks to John Zemke. No professor has played a more significant role in my professional development, nor invested so much in my well-being. I would not be where I am today without his mentorship and friendship.

There are also people who have simply been in my life for so long; their love and support pre-date the conception of this book and will continue well after its publication. I am grateful to and cherish my family, the whole unruly bunch: *Ami* (mom), *Daji* (dad), *Nani* (granny), Sarah, Jawad, Abrar, Nimra, and especially the newest and undoubtedly most beloved members: Abdullah and Hasan.

Lastly, I want to express my gratitude to the 34 women who participated in this study. These women invited me into their homes, even took me in as a lodger, fed me, connected me with their friends and made me feel welcome whenever I was in their company. I thank them for sharing themselves with me.

This book is dedicated to those women, and to all of the brave and resilient souls who are searching for a place to belong.

1 Introduction

Dispatches from Barcelona

I was a seasoned reader of research, if not a seasoned researcher, when I first conducted fieldwork for my doctoral dissertation. At the time, my theoretical knowledge of sociolinguistics born out of coursework, textbooks and journal articles seemed like sufficient preparation for my first major research endeavor. As it turned out, this was most certainly not the case. As a Spanish-speaking Muslim woman, the task of taking up a brief residence in Barcelona in order to connect with and collect data from other Muslim women did not seem like a daunting one at the onset. Upon arrival, I had a few initial contacts who were Muslim and therefore had faith that it would not take long to gain momentum in terms of gaining informants for my study. As it turned out, meeting other Muslims who were willing to participate in my study was a formidable quest, as one contact was a male grocery store manager named Hassan,[1] who did not know many Muslim women apart from a middle-aged Egyptian shop owner woman named Mona with whom he had put me in contact because she had a room available for me to rent for part of my stay. Mona, in turn, had declared to me on many occasions that she made a point not to socialize with other Muslims and preferred to keep to herself, often criticizing the majority-Moroccan Muslim population for being overly prying and intrusive to her taste. Since my initial contacts were unable to introduce me to potential informants – not only due to a lack of connections, but also due to a lack of time, as their respective jobs kept them extremely busy throughout the day – I began working through my list of strategies for reaching out to other Muslim women on my own. I remember my first encounter with the first informant of my study: I had approached Aisha, a 47-year-old Moroccan woman, in the produce section of Hassan's grocery store, and could recall her nervous demeanor. While she ended up being receptive to meeting with me later to complete my questionnaires and sit for an interview, she was initially shy and hesitant, and I had the distinct impression that she had drawn up the same barriers I myself would have raised had I been accosted by a stranger.

While Aisha was the first person I had approached on my own during my first week in Barcelona, I experienced many failed attempts at connecting spontaneously with Muslim female informants. On the streets and in shops, they were bustling about, running errands, tending to their children and, more often than not, they simply did not seem comfortable with talking to a stranger. During this initial period in which there was a dearth of available informants, I was advised to try connecting with Muslim men and getting data from them as well, not only because it was better to have some data than no data, but also as a way of gaining entry into a somewhat enclosed speech community. To those who had advised me, Muslim men were considered the gatekeepers to the female constituents of the Muslim community, and connecting with men would allow me greater access to female informants. The prospect of changing recruitment and data collection plans so early on in this study was both frustrating and bewildering to me. How could it be so challenging for me? After all, I was a Muslim woman and wore a *hijab*, which to me had strongly signaled not only my religious identity, but my universal membership in any Muslim community that I came upon. This did not seem like a wide leap of faith; I had been born and raised in the US, in a diasporic situation that I had considered to be not very dissimilar from that of Muslims in Spain, and part of that experience included a social norm among Muslims (both familiar and otherwise) to greet each other with wishes of peace, or at the very least, for those of us who are more timid – to acknowledge each other with a smile and a nod of solidarity when we came upon each other in everyday life.

It became clear early on that Muslim diaspora in Spain, or at least in Barcelona, was not entirely like that which I had been accustomed to in the US, and thus neither were some of the social norms I had previously taken for granted. Greeting and acknowledging passersby and other Muslim strangers in public spaces was not nearly as common as I had experienced in the American Midwest, and so small talk – which would have hopefully turned into recruitment opportunities – was difficult to come by. Perhaps we were less conspicuous as Muslims in Spain, and there was less of a need to show solidarity among each other; while there are over 3 million Muslims in the US (Pew Research Center, 2018) and a little over 2 million in Spain (Observatorio Andalusí, 2019), the latter is far more concentrated in a much smaller country. Moreover, reflecting on my own experience of being raised in St. Louis, Missouri, I was still hundreds of miles from any densely populated Muslim community (Chicago, Illinois), and still even further away from the US's largest Muslim community in New York City (Muslims for American Progress, 2018). Other nuances also became apparent as I navigated my way through this first foray into linguistic fieldwork. For example, while I initially had difficulty recruiting informants and had been convinced that it was nearly impossible to do so in my role as a complete stranger, I was fortunate to make a couple of additional contacts who were kind enough to reach out to friends of theirs, only to learn that a mere introduction on their part was all that was necessary to connect me with new informants. These introductions were never direct or formal, and typically consisted of my contacts sending text messages to their friends informing them that they had just met a Muslim woman who was looking for other Muslim women to speak to for her dissertation research and that they should contact me directly if they were interested in speaking with me. Through this simple invitation, responses to my request began to trickle in, with Muslim women of all ages sending me text messages letting me know that they were available and – in several instances – that I should come to their homes to talk to them.

It also became clearer that, contrary to the advice I had received, Muslim men did not hold the keys to this speech community and that male participation was not necessarily easier to solicit. In fact, this detour through Muslim male speakers proved to be a thorny endeavor. If approaching Muslim female strangers was complicated by a desire to keep one's distance from complete strangers (as is certainly the case with people of all backgrounds), approaching Muslim male strangers was an even more complex venture, as it was no longer about simply maintaining a socially appropriate distance from a stranger that one would attempt with any unknown individual. Other considerations entangled these interactions: would an unmarried Muslim man close to my age misinterpret my directness in accosting him as embedded in something other than research interests? (On one occasion, yes.) Would a Muslim man be offended or feel uncomfortable at my attempt to speak with him? Having been brought up, socialized and, to some extent, educated in an American Muslim community, I knew that outcomes would vary. Some men would find my intermingling inappropriate, while others would not. Ultimately, I was only able to interview a few men during my time in Barcelona, most of whom did not provide the additional contacts that I was told would come out of these interviews. More than that, the quality of the interactions was also different, and typically did not penetrate the layer of superficial formality that sociolinguists aim to avoid or minimize during interviews. This was also reflected in the differences in settings: I met male informants in cafes or other public spots. They did not invite me into their homes, and – given the considerations noted above – I would have been hesitant to accept such invitations. Yet hospitality was a common practice among female informants: inviting me to come to their homes, preparing food for me, complaining that I had not eaten enough and introducing me to others in their household.

Going into this project, I had already known from my own life experiences that gendered, religious identity can have a profound impact on how we interact with others, particularly in the case of Muslim female identity, and the recollections above prove that as well. Every interaction – successful and otherwise – was not merely serving a communicative purpose, but also a performance of identity. The languages I would choose to use (Spanish with most, Urdu with several first-generation informants, and occasionally English) reflected a desire not only to accommodate my informants but also to establish solidarity with them. Similarly, languages in which I had limited proficiency (e.g. Arabic and Catalan) and therefore could not rely on during interviews may have also played a role in positioning me as an outsider to some extent for some informants. In terms of register choice, the degree of formality I employed when speaking with female and male contacts was a gendered performance rooted in my own experiences and nonliberal upbringing as a Muslim, where formality in speech marked distance and boundaries between speakers. In short, though I was collecting data on gendered, religious identity and language use, I myself was constructing and negotiating my own Muslim female identity in every interaction. Yet social interactions consist of many different elements and functions. One key aspect, however, is language use. This can include the employment of specific linguistic features as well as code choice, whether it be distinct languages or distinct registers of the same language. Language use – and how it connects with the performance of Muslim, female identity – became the focal point of my research (though this was not the case in my doctoral dissertation, for which this data was originally collected) and is the broader topic that guides the discussions in this book. Specifically, how does language interact with Muslim, gendered identity in an immigrant context in which individuals have sociolinguistic structures and norms that they associate with their (religiously informed) heritage, as well as structures and norms that may be significantly different in the receptive society?

Gendered Immigrant Identity in Catalonia

This book examines the vital role that language plays in the acculturation process for individuals. Acculturation, which will be further discussed in Chapter 3, refers to the process of adapting to the socially dominant culture in a given society. This can often entail complete assimilation, where heritage identities and cultures are completely abandoned in favor of the socially dominant ones. In other cases (such that will be the focus of this book), acculturation can take on the form of integration, where individuals adopt these identities and cultures while still retaining their heritage identities and cultural practices. This process is a significant experience for immigrants settling into a new society, as well as for subsequent generations who are brought up in that society. Moreover, language use is a critical aspect of acculturation, whether it involves adopting one or more societal languages, or even a different variety of the same language. However, adopting languages or varieties is often far more complex than simply making the time and effort to learn them; rather, the ability and motivation to learn and make use of varieties beyond one's native/heritage tongue is also shaped by other factors, such as opportunities available to learners, the extent to which a language is instrumental to their lives and the extent to which others may readily engage with them in said languages. Ultimately, however, this is a critical topic of discussion because together, these factors – along with the overall experience of acculturation – not only shape individuals' identities and cultural connections, but also play a pivotal role in individuals' sense of belonging and acceptance in their environment. For this reason, my book focuses on the immigrant experience in Catalonia, an autonomous community in Spain that has drawn immigrants from all over the world, particularly in its largest city, Barcelona. However, the case of Catalonia is an especially interesting one, in that immigrants in this region – many of whom were already multilingual prior to relocating – are introduced to two socially dominant languages, Catalan and Spanish. Besides the long political history connected to these languages (see Chapter 2), another aspect that may inform attitudes and usage of these languages is the fact that both belong to the Romance family and are typologically similar, particularly with regard to syntax and phonology. Moreover, Catalan is commonly mistaken for a dialect of Spanish, either because of their structural similarities, confusion between 'Catalan' and the similar-sounding 'Castilian' (another name for Spanish), or even because Catalan is simply region-specific within Spain, much in the way that dialects are. Nonetheless, both languages have a presence in Catalonia, and many immigrants living in this region may juggle three or more languages in their everyday lives. Given that the interlocutors with whom they interact may not all have the same linguistic repertoires as themselves, these different languages are likely to serve different functions, be present in specific domains of language use and even have distinct attitudes associated with them.

The array of languages that may be a part of an immigrant's daily life is in itself a topic worth exploring. However, as noted in the anecdote at the beginning of this chapter, the languages that individuals employ in different communicative situations may not only reflect a need to fulfill certain functions or accommodate other individuals; rather, one's linguistic choices can also be performative of one's identity. Identity negotiation, as this process is often described, involves individuals establishing who they are in the context of specific relationships or social contexts, or interactions, and often signal membership in certain social or cultural groups. While heritage and ethnic identity have often been the focus of sociolinguistic research in an immigrant context, certainly other identities are tied to an individual's linguistic behavior. These multiple identities may be interconnected both in the manner in which an individual constructs or negotiates these identities, and also in terms of how these intersections create different modes of discrimination and marginalization. Certainly, immigrant identity by nature is multilayered, and an intersectional approach would be conducive to its examination, as different immigrant groups may have distinct experiences with how they are received in any given target language (TL) community, often depending on where they are from and other aspects of their background. This in turn can impact how immigrants negotiate their identities as they go through the process of acculturation.

In this study, I use this concept of intersectionality to argue that religion and gender are intertwined identities that are connected to language use and also that Muslim women reflexively and/or intentionally use language to perform these identities. Through this dual focus on identity and multilingualism, the study that I present over the course of this book has several specific aims. First, the linguistic behavior of immigrants in Catalonia is already an ongoing discussion in the field of sociolinguistics, and so this study aims to contribute directly to this dialogue by examining the language practices of Muslim immigrant women. Using informants' narratives and questionnaire responses, I will demonstrate that acculturation is a transgenerational process reflected in informants' self-reported linguistic behavior, as well as highlight the intersectionality of gendered and religious identity among Muslim immigrant women. Finally, this study will illustrate how this identity is brokered through language use and attitudes in a multilingual context.

Islam and Muslim Speech Communities

In this section, I provide a brief overview of Islam and the role of language in Muslim speech communities (for a more specific discussion of Muslim women, see Chapter 3). Islam is a monotheistic and Abrahamic religion that originated in the Arabian Peninsula and is now the second-largest religion in the world, spanning across the globe to the extent that its non-Arab followers well outnumber Arab followers. There are various denominations among Muslims, which are often region-specific; for instance, Shia Muslims account for a minority of the Muslim population and are predominantly in Iraq and Iran, while the majority of the Muslim population in other parts of the world are of the Sunni denomination.

From a social perspective, Muslim societies – including those where Muslims are minority communities and/or are in diasporic contexts – are typically collectivist and focus on the needs and values of the larger community, rather than the individual. Because of this, relationships within the Muslim community – both among family and friends – play a central role in everyday life. It is thus not uncommon for extended families to intentionally settle near each other in a diasporic context. This was certainly the case for several of the informants in this study, and in fact, these familial connections played a role in being connected with new informants, and even in contriving my living arrangements for part of my stay: one of the male contacts I had met early on had not only introduced me to some of his female friends that would serve as informants, but he had also put me in contact with his aunt, who would later offer me a room in her home for the second half of my stay, during which time I spent many evenings socializing in the homes of her relatives living nearby.

Beyond family ties, this collectivism among Muslims often entails being an active member of the Muslim community and attending prayer services and other activities at one's local mosque, where many relationships are first formed. In larger Muslim communities that may have the benefit of more affluent members, many mosques also establish Sunday schools for children to study Classical Arabic and Qur'anic studies, or even full-time schools where children may combine their religious studies with secular studies. However, while a mosque may serve as a social center for many Muslims, this particular setting can also assume a culture of its own with certain norms by which its members must abide. Because mosques are first and foremost religious centers, most mosque-goers expect each other to dress in a manner that is appropriate for performing prayers: for all individuals, this entails wearing clothes that cover the whole body, though in the case of women, this also includes wearing a *hijab* as a head covering. Additionally, mosque-goers are typically expected to cease their conversations during prayer times and generally avoid socializing in spaces that are specifically designated for prayer. Furthermore, Muslims typically observe gendered segregation at mosques, both in and outside of the prayer spaces. As such, women and men often do not socialize at mosques except in some common spaces (if there are any) such as a lobby or in the parking lot, and only do so sparingly.

Given the collectivist structure of many Muslim communities, it is unsurprising that social practices can be largely informed by social expectations that are rooted in Islamic principles. Going against such expectations, then, can be met with censure and even a disconnect from one's Muslim identity. In other words, Muslims who do not practice specific and commonly practiced elements of Islamic teachings (e.g. adhering to Islamic dietary restrictions that prohibit the consumption of alcohol or pork) may be regarded as less of a Muslim, essentially creating a 'good' Muslim/'bad' Muslim dichotomy between those who actively incorporate Islamic teachings in their daily lives and those who do not. Mixed-gender interactions (and the degree of intimacy involved in these interactions) are often part of these social expectations, and – as will be demonstrated in Chapters 5 and 6 – can play an important role in how some women construct Muslim identity.

The role of Arabic among Muslims is also worth noting, especially considering that the majority of the Muslim population is non-Arab and does not speak Arabic as a native or heritage language. As noted above, Arabic is studied by many Muslims regardless of ethnic or cultural background, as it is considered the vehicular language in specific religious contexts: besides being considered the original language of the Qur'an, daily prayers are typically performed in Arabic. Because of the significant presence of Arabic for many practicing Muslims who pray and read the Qur'an, Arabic is often associated with Muslim identity, regardless of an individual's cultural heritage. However, this usually takes the form of Classical Arabic (such that it is used in the Qur'an and in prayers), and at times Modern Standard Arabic (MSA), which is sometimes taught in Islamic schools. Neither of these varieties, however, are native to any Arabic speaker and are typically only accessible in religious and formal domains. Instead (or in addition to the above), many Arab Muslims speak colloquial dialects of Arabic, which are typically less accessible to non-Arab Muslims.

Finally, in addition to the many nuances that comprise social practices and identities of Muslims, those living in a diasporic context may have distinctive experiences from Muslims living in Muslim-majority societies. In a diasporic situation, the ideologies and practices of socially dominant groups can play a significant and often detrimental role in Muslims' sense of belonging. One practice that is especially pervasive and impacts many different minority groups is the act of racialization. Here, racialization refers to 'ascribing sets of characteristics viewed as inherent to members of a group because of their physical or cultural traits. These are not limited to skin tone or pigmentation, but include a myriad of attributes including cultural traits such as language, clothing, and religious practices. The characteristics thus emerge as "racial" as an outcome of the process' (Garner & Selod, 2015: 12). This process thus forms the basis of Islamophobia, whereby characteristics associated with Muslims (e.g. violence and misogyny) are viewed as innate qualities possessed by all members of the group (Garner & Selod, 2015), and are often attached to (in)visible cues that signal Muslim identities. Linguistic behavior is one such cue, such as an individual speaking Arabic, or even speaking the socially dominant language with an accent. Racialization may also be gendered, where Muslim women who wear a *hijab* are conspicuous and more easily identified as Muslim. More than that, socially dominant groups may impose specific identities on *hijab*-wearing women: victims of oppression who are in need of saving, and who have anti-feminist values incompatible with Western culture. (Selod, 2018). Among the cumulative results of perpetuating these beliefs is the perpetual othering of Muslims (particularly for those whose religious identity is visible), using such otherness to justify discrimination (Rodríguez-García *et al.*, 2021), and naturalizing the structural inequality experienced by Muslim migrants. These practices are certainly insidious across different diasporic contexts but are particularly notable in Europe (Perocco, 2018) and specifically in Spain (Rodríguez-García *et al.*, 2021).

Overview of Chapters

Chapter 2, 'Language Use and Language Policy in Catalonia', focuses on lending social and historical context to this study, and examines Catalonia's political history of linguistic normalization in a post-Franco era and its role in formulating language policies as well as social cohesion policies targeted at immigrant populations in the present day. This chapter also provides a broader overview of the linguistic situation in Catalonia and discusses the presence and status of various languages, including those spoken by immigrant populations, that comprise multilingualism in Catalonia. Chapter 3, 'Acculturation and Negotiating Identity', similarly provides a theoretical framework for this study and focuses on some of the existing scholarship that grounds this study relating to the acculturation process for immigrant populations, and how identity – specifically gendered and religious – is connected to language use. This chapter also delves into the notion of intersectionality as an important tool for reflecting on identity negotiation.

Chapter 4, 'Research Design', situates the present study and delineates my data collection process. This includes a description of the local setting of my data collection sites and the informant recruitment process. I also include here a reflection on my role as the investigator and positioning in the Muslim immigrant community, which presented various limitations and advantages in data collection. I also provide in-depth information about the diverse group of informants I worked with, a description of the data collection tools I used (questionnaires and interviews). Finally, I present my analytical approach, as well as a brief note about transcription conventions and other notations that will be helpful to observe while looking at data.

The next two chapters focus on narrative data from informants. Chapter 5, 'Spaniard on Purpose: Narratives of First-Generation Informants', focuses on my interviews with first-generation informants and narrates the experiences of women from diverse backgrounds, ranging from new to longtime residents, minimally to highly educated, unemployed and employed. This chapter describes these informants' self-reported language use, how they position themselves within Spanish and/or Catalan society, and reflections on the extent to which they feel they have acculturated. Informants also discuss their interactions with different groups of interlocutors – members of their heritage/Muslim community, those of the TL community – and how gendered and religious identity plays a role in these interactions. In a similar vein, Chapter 6, 'In Two Worlds: Narratives of Second-Generation Informants', focuses on second-generation informants, addressing the same themes found in Chapter 5. As such, this chapter is similarly structured in terms of its dual focus on informants' connections to immigrant communities and the TL community. While Chapter 5 establishes first-generation informants' positionality as individuals whose presence in Spain is intentional, as reflected in their positive attitudes and motivation to acclimate themselves to Spanish culture, Chapter 6 illustrates how this acculturation process shifts among second-generation informants, who straddle two different worlds that they were born into. Linguistic behaviors distinct from their first-generation counterparts also emerge, such as an affinity for Catalan that is not present among the former group. This chapter also examines the apparent shift in the role of gender and religion in their social interactions. Additionally, despite being native speakers of both Spanish and Catalan who personally identify with the TL community, several of these informants attribute the visibility of their religious identity as a reason for frequently being positioned as outsiders.

Having dedicated Chapters 5 and 6 to giving a voice to the informants included in this study and spotlighting their specific experiences, Chapter 7, 'Catalan, Spanish and Heritage Languages: Reported Language Use and Attitudes', provides supplementary quantitative data on reported language use and attitudes and relies on questionnaire responses from the 34 informants. The questionnaire tasks include (1) a series of various communicative domains for which informants indicated which language(s) they used, (2) a series of Likert-scale statements relating to language attitudes and (3) a series of speaker traits (such as 'educated' and 'friendly') that informants assigned to either a bilingual speaker of Catalan and Spanish, or a speaker of their heritage language(s). This chapter also includes a comparative analysis of the responses of first and second-generation informants.

Chapter 8, 'Implications for Sociolinguistic Research', transitions toward a conclusion and describes how this study contributes to the field of sociolinguistics. Specifically, this chapter briefly summarizes the findings from previous chapters and highlights the significance of better understanding immigrants' experiences in acquiring societal bilingualism. I also discuss the importance of acknowledging the intersectionality of identity in linguistic research in terms of how multiple, overlapping characteristics can collectively contribute to otherness and marginalization. Finally, this chapter also lays out points of future research, such as acknowledging the bidirectional nature of acculturation and a need for an examination of TL community members' attitudes toward immigrant communities, as they may also serve to provide a clearer picture of the setting in which immigrants are attempting to acculturate, and/or if members of the TL community have distinctive attitudes toward different immigrant communities and languages.

Chapter 9, 'Implications for Language and Immigrant-Targeted Policies', is dedicated to elaborating on how the findings from my study relate back to the language and immigrant-targeted policies discussed in Chapter 3. Here, I discuss the ways in which these policies – based on the observations from my study – do or do not appear to achieve their goals. From here, I problematize specific aspects of language policy and planning in Catalonia, and some of the limitations presented in current iterations of policies and plans. Finally, I will offer suggestions on how future iterations of these policies may be constructed to mutually and better benefit immigrant populations as well as the larger Catalan society as a whole.

Note

(1) Pseudonyms are used for both informants and any other individuals with whom I interacted for the purposes of this study.

2 Language Use and Language Policy in Catalonia

Introduction

As a socially situated practice, language use is often constructed by the politics and history that shape a community. This is certainly the case of Catalonia, where linguistic ideologies, policies and language use were and continue to be significantly tied to the region's political landscape, especially in terms of how it has been at odds with national politics. Furthermore, an understanding of this sociopolitical context shines light on how multilingualism exists today in Catalonia, and how its linguistic situation presents not only a unique setting for immigrant populations residing in Catalonia, but also a unique set of challenges as they try to negotiate different identities, including linguistic identities that involve more than one societal language beyond what they speak as heritage or native languages. Moreover, these challenges may also be in conflict with immigrants' own expectations of what moving to Spain might have entailed, as well as how they make decisions about their language education, and even how subsequent generations born and raised in Catalonia identify with the socially dominant languages as well as their heritage languages.

This chapter provides a panorama of Catalonia's present linguistic situation, as well as an overview of Catalonia's recent political history; specifically Catalonia from the Spanish Civil War to the end of Francisco Franco's fascist regime and shift toward democracy, as well as the language policies that shaped the language use in this region during that period. Next, I discuss how the transition toward democracy and the promulgation of a new national constitution also sparked a shift in language ideologies and policies in Catalonia that would ignite what would become decades of linguistic revitalization efforts. Here, I also discuss the implications of these policies for migrant populations, as well as specific policies geared toward migrant populations. Finally, this chapter briefly delineates Catalonia's history of migration and the maintenance of immigrant languages within this autonomous community, focusing specifically on linguistic practices. This overview thus serves as a premise for the subsequent discussion of how these linguistic practices relate to immigrant identity (see Chapter 3).

Languages of Catalonia: Present Day and Historical Overview

Societal multilingualism in Catalonia presents a unique linguistic situation; not only does this region's government officially recognize four different languages (Catalan, Spanish, Aranese and Catalan Sign Language), but there are also a multitude of immigrant languages[1] that have maintained a steady presence in Catalonia. Among them, Arabic and Romanian rank as the most widely used native languages of migrant populations, who account for 19.3% and 7.8% of the Catalan population, respectively (Generalitat of Catalunya, 2019a). Beyond these two, other notable immigrant languages include Galician, French, Amazigh, Russian, Portuguese, Italian, Chinese, English and German – languages spoken by both international and domestic migrants. Although data on the distribution of these languages or representative immigrant populations across different *vegueries* (territorial boundaries) is unavailable, it is worth observing the presence of international populations in all parts of Catalonia. Barcelona has the largest foreign-born population (769,878 in 2021), which accounts for 15.6% of its total population. However, Catalonia's other *vegueries* – which each reportedly have fewer than 200,000 foreign-born immigrants, also have comparable percentages: Comarques Gironines, 20.4%; Camp de Tarragona, 16.89%; Terres de l'Ebre, 16.9%; Ponent, 19.7%; Comarques Centrals, 13.9%; Alt Pirineu i Aran, 13.8% and Penedès, 12.8% (Generalitat of Catalunya, 2019a).

While the use of immigrant languages often diminishes and may even disappear altogether after even one generation, several of these languages remain prominent in various domains of language use in Catalonia, which I discuss at length later in this chapter. However, one critical distinction that must be made between groups of languages is that which relates to official status. In both Catalonia and more broadly in Spain, there are several speech communities that are referred to as 'large established communities' or 'historical communities', due to their long-standing presence in the country (Turell, 2000). In Spain, this includes Basque, Catalan and Galician, while in Catalonia, these speech communities include Catalan, Aranese and – to a limited degree – Catalan Sign Language. This distinction is a notable one: being granted certain linguistic rights in the Spanish Constitution and/or the Statute of Autonomy of Catalonia also allows these speech communities to enjoy some social, historical and economic rights and advantages (Turell, 2000). However, while this may lend a certain degree of legitimacy and protection to formally recognized languages, other minority languages – particularly those spoken by immigrant communities and therefore considered 'immigrant languages' – do not have such a status and therefore their speakers may not have access to the same rights and advantages.

While linguistic diversity is certainly evident in Catalonia, Spanish and Catalan remain the two socially dominant languages of this region. As the national language of Spain, the presence of Spanish (or Castilian/ *castellano*, as it is better known in Spain) is unquestionably present in Catalonia, not only because of its broader use all across Spain, but also because Catalonia's capital, Barcelona, is also one of the most popular city destinations in Europe and draws millions of tourists each year who often rely on Spanish for communication. Still, Catalan is reportedly used in all parts of Catalonia to some extent. In an annual language policy report produced by the Catalan government's (Generalitat de Catalunya) Ministry of Culture, Barcelona's population is reported to rely on Catalan the least, with 72.6% of the population reporting using Catalan to some extent, among which only 11.0% report using Catalan 'a lot'. Outside of this metropolis, however, Catalan use in other parts of Catalonia is comparably higher, with the following percentages of reported usage (which includes a range between 'a little' and 'a lot'): Comarques gironines: 84.5%; Camp de Tarragona: 77.4%; Terres de l'Ebre: 89.6%; Ponent: 83.1%; Comarques centrals: 88.9%; Alt Pirineu i Aran: 88.1% and Penedès: 80.6% (Generalitat of Catalunya, 2019b). In these cases, the frequency of use is also comparably higher, where the number of respondents who reportedly use Catalan 'a lot' range between 18.5% and 55.1%, a significantly higher proportion than the 11% reported from Barcelona, which also suggests that more frequent Catalan use likely comes at the expense of Spanish.

Besides Spanish and Catalan, Aranese – a dialect of Occitan – also has official status in Catalonia and is in fact the only variety of Occitan to have official status in any Occitan-speaking region, among those include Southern France, Northern Italy and Monaco. While its use is primarily confined to Val d'Aran (Aran Valley) in northwestern Catalonia near the French border, Aranese is widely used in this region: the percentage of the population in Val d'Aran (10,093) that can understand, speak, read and/ or write in Aranese is reported at 83.3%, 60.0%, 73.5% and 45.8%, respectively. Considering that Aranese was once regarded as an endangered language that was generally associated with older generations, these numbers not only represent a relatively steady increase in the past decade, but also an extension in its use among younger populations. Both of these changes signal growth in the overall linguistic vitality of Aranese and stability with regard to its maintenance.

Finally, Catalan Sign Language has had an official recognition since 1994, over a decade before the addition of Aranese. In 2019, the number of people in Catalonia identifying as deaf or hard of hearing is reported at 32,315, though this number does not necessarily reflect the actual number of signers residing in Catalonia. While the Catalan government's annual language policy report does not include data on how many users of Catalan Sign Language there are in Catalonia, it does provide an exhaustive list of programs, associations and universities that promote its use, offer interpreting resources and/or courses in Catalan Sign Language.

Among these languages, however, Catalan has perhaps had the most tumultuous history in Catalonia in terms of its development, suppression and revitalization. While a number of historical events have impacted the use and prestige of Catalan since as early as the 15th century – often negatively – much of what informs the present situation of Catalan dates back to the outcomes of the Spanish Civil War; namely, Francisco Franco's dictatorship from 1939 until his death in 1975. During this period, various ideologies shaped the Francoist regime, but none so much as Spanish nationalism, which was perhaps one of the cornerstones of Franco's dictatorship. This ideology pushed for a culturally and linguistically homogeneous Spanish population, where cultural traditions such as bullfighting and flamenco were promoted as national traditions (Balfour & Quiroga, 2007) (though it is worth pointing out that the latter is actually Andalusian in origin), while those that were not considered part of the Spanish cultural heritage were suppressed. This had severe implications for language use all across Spain, where regional languages were prohibited or discouraged, depending on the context. In the case of Catalonia, various official measures pushed the Catalan language out of the public sphere and into the confines of private use during the Francoist regime. In addition to declaring Spanish as the only official and national language of Spain, the Francoist regime also banned the use of Catalan in administrative contexts as well as in schools – both as a subject and as a language of instruction. Censorship of Catalan even extended to all forms of mass media and entertainment, such as films, books, magazines and radio (Siguán, 1992).

Another reason for Catalan's diminished use during the Franco regime relates to waves of domestic immigration during this time period, an indirect effect of Franco's rule. Residents from Andalusia in particular were a major source of immigration for much of the 20th century (1950–1975). Resulting from the widespread poverty that had plagued southern Spain during the Francoist repression, many Andalusian immigrants sought better economic opportunities in Catalonia, integrating into working-class Catalan neighborhoods in the process (Woolard, 1989). Domestic immigration, in fact, had been the main source of immigration in Catalonia up until the mid-1970s, and immigration from other countries – especially non-EU countries – did not become prevalent until the 1980s, a point to be further discussed in this chapter. While it has been argued that this immigration was far more directly related to the diminished use of Catalan in that it was supposedly imposed by Franco as a means of diluting the Catalan population and instigating a demographic destabilization of the region (Carner-Ribalta, 1995), the accuracy of such claims has not been borne out. Regardless of the intent, however, increased immigration during this time period resulted in an increase in Spanish-speaking – but non-Catalan-speaking – residents in Catalonia, many of whom did not know of or feel an incentive to learn Catalan. These factors collectively pushed Catalan into decline throughout the 20th century. Still, owing to its continued use in private, household contexts – as well as Spain's shift to democracy and implementation of new language policies – Catalan survived its period of suppression and has since seen a dramatic revitalization.

Shifts to Democracy, Shifts in Ideology and Policy

With Francisco Franco's death in 1975, Spain almost immediately began its shift not only toward democracy, but also toward more pluralistic political ideologies, much of which would play a crucial role in the development of language policies at the state and regional levels. At the national level, the promulgation of a revised constitution in 1978 was the most impactful policy for being a catalyst for linguistic change, particularly for multilingual regions in Spain. The new constitution re-established previously prohibited languages, thereby permitting multilingual autonomous communities in Spain to assign co-official status to other languages apart from Spanish. Articles Two and Three of the constitution recognize this right:

Artículo 2

(1) La Constitución se fundamenta en la indisoluble unidad de la Nación española, patria común e indivisible de todos los españoles, y reconoce y garantiza el derecho a la autonomía de las nacionalidades y regiones que la integran y la solidaridad entre todas ellas.

Artículo 3

(1) El castellano es la lengua española oficial del Estado. Todos los españoles tienen el deber de conocerla y el derecho a usarla.
(2) Las demás lenguas españolas serán también oficiales en las respectivas Comunidades Autónomas de acuerdo con sus Estatutos.
(3) La riqueza de las distintas modalidades lingüísticas de España es un patrimonio cultural que será objeto de especial respeto y protección.

Article 2:

(1) The Constitution is based on the indissoluble unity of the Spanish Nation, the common and indivisible homeland of all Spaniards; it recognises and guarantees the right to self-government of the

nationalities and regions of which it is composed and the solidarity among them all.

Article 3:

(1) Castilian is the official Spanish language of the State. All Spaniards have the duty to know it and the right to use it.
(2) The other Spanish languages shall also be official in the respective Self-governing Communities in accordance with their Statutes.
(3) The wealth of the different linguistic forms of Spain is a cultural heritage which shall be especially respected and protected.

(Constitution of Spain, 1978)

While the Spanish language retains primacy as the national language, the inclusion of other languages – and qualifying them as 'Spanish' and part of the nation's identity and cultural heritage – offers a legitimacy to these languages they had been previously stripped of during Franco's regime.

Moreover, in being granted the autonomy to self-govern and establish their own policies, the above ratification had now positioned Catalonia to stipulate their own language policies, ones that would attempt to counteract the effects of decades of linguistic suppression by promoting the use of Catalan as the vehicular language of Catalonia. Two laws in particular were instrumental in achieving this, the first being the *Linguistic Normalization Act [Llei de normalització lingüística a Catalunya]* (Generalitat de Catalunya, 1983) and later amended in 1998 as the *Language Policy Act [Llei de política lingüística]*. This law primarily aimed not only to recuperate the communicative space that Spanish had once dominated in previous years, but also to further legitimize Catalan's official status and connect it to Catalan identity. Specifically, this law:

> ...garantiza el uso oficial de ambas lenguas para asegurar a todos los ciudadanos la participación en la vida pública, señala como objetivo de la enseñanza, el conocimiento de ambas lenguas, las equilibra en los medios de comunicación social, erradica cualquier discriminación por motivos lingüísticos y específica las vías de impulso institucional en la normalización lingüística en Catalunya.
>
> ...guarantees the official use of both languages in order to ensure that all citizens may participate in public life, points to the objective of teaching, the knowledge of both languages, balances them in the media, eradicates any discrimination for linguistic reasons and specifies the channels of institutional thrust in the linguistic normalization of Catalonia. (Law 7, 1983)

While this law sought to promote the use of Catalan in all domains of public life, one especially crucial aspect is that it stipulates the requirement that Catalan be taught alongside Spanish in school, thus ensuring that students have equal competence in both languages. Additionally, in its original name, the term 'normalization' is used and becomes the operative word for expressing one of the central goals of language planning in Catalonia, which is essentially establishing Catalan as the center of Catalonia's linguistic norms, and that its use 'should become "normal" again' (Hoffmann, 2000: 429).

The second law that was significant to the promotion of Catalan was the *Statute of Autonomy of Catalonia (Estatut d'autonomia de Catalunya)*, first ratified in 1979 and later amended in 2006. With the goal of setting forth regulations as stipulated in the 1978 Spanish Constitution, this Statute defines the rights and duties of Catalan citizens, as well as the governing bodies and institutions that make up the government of Catalonia. With regard to the language use, the Statute includes knowledge of Catalan as one of the civic duties of Catalan citizens. Additionally, it is in this policy that Catalan Sign Language and Aranese are granted official status in Catalonia.

These laws have collectively seen a great deal of successful implementation: since these policies had intended for large sectors of Catalan society to learn Catalan (particularly those of non-Catalan descent) and all school-age children have been required for the past few decades to learn both Catalan and Spanish, the number of Catalan speakers has steadily increased since the passing of these laws (Roller, 2010). Additionally, the ideologies that come with these policies have also served to establish Catalan as a de-ethnicized, public language (Newman & Trenchs-Parera, 2015; Pujolar & Gonzàlez, 2013). Still, these policies have also been met with a good deal of criticism both in and outside Catalonia. Specifically, it has been argued that rather than becoming a language that represents inclusion for non-Catalan citizens, the Catalan language in fact marks exclusivity (Roller, 2010) by perpetuating ideologies that can distance racialized, lower class members of Catalan society from identifying with and using Catalan (Block & Corona, 2019). One of the ways by which this exclusion has occurred is Catalan's association with whiteness (Khan & Balsà, 2021) which in turn relegates Spanish – a language that in other contexts has represented colonialism – into the role of the language for foreigners and outsiders. It is at the intersection of native and migrant groups, then, that language policy and planning appears to fall short in their efforts to normalize Catalan use.

In light of this critical appraisal of language policy in Catalonia – as well as the unrelenting efforts to promote the linguistic normalization of Catalan – it is also worth noting that in recent years, the Catalan government has developed policies and plans geared specifically toward migrant populations residing in Catalonia with regard to language use. These policies reiterate and uphold the ideologies set forth in the previously mentioned laws, and additionally delineate how migrant populations contribute to the linguistic and cultural pluralism that is so central to the collective Catalan identity. Three policies/plans in particular are key here. First, the *Language and Social Cohesion Plan* [*Pla per a la llengua i la cohesió social*], (Generalitat de Catalunya, 2004) focuses on language education for migrant populations and emphasizes the importance of learning Catalan for the purposes of social integration in Catalonia. However, integration into Catalan society is also part of a greater goal, social cohesion:

> D'acord amb això, l'objectiu general d'aquest pla és potenciar i consolidar la cohesió social, l'educació intercultural i la llengua catalana en un marc plurilingüe. (2004: 12)
>
> Accordingly, the general objective of this plan is to strengthen and consolidate social cohesion, intercultural education and the Catalan language in a multilingual framework.

While this text suggests that immigrant languages and cultures also play a role in promoting social cohesion in Catalonia, it is clear that learning Catalan is a key element for achieving this goal. This is meant to be primarily accomplished through 'welcome classrooms' (*aules d'acollida*), where newly arrived immigrant students are to receive language instruction. It is uncertain, however, whether or not these programs achieve their goals in using language education to support social integration. Trenchs-Parera and Newman (2015), for example, point out that these classes signal marginalization in different ways; first, because classrooms are often situated in isolated areas of schools, and second, because many Catalan parents avoid enrolling their children in schools that have a significant number of immigrant students. Such realities not only result in fewer opportunities for immigrant Catalan learners to interact with native speakers, but further solidifies the divide between Catalans and non-Catalans and does little to encourage a sense of belonging for the latter.

More recently, the Catalan government ratified a law relating to migrant populations, *Act 10/2010, on the reception of immigrants and returnees to Catalonia* (*Llei/2010 d'acollida de les persones immigrades i de les retornades a Catalunya*). This law essentially formalizes and delineates the array of reception services to which immigrants are entitled upon arriving in Catalonia (some of which may be available in various immigrant languages), and further emphasizes that participation in these services and programs are the first step to social integration. Finally, the *Citizenship and Migration Plan, 2017–2020* [*Pla de ciutadania i de les migracions, 2017–2020*], (Generalitat de Catalunya, 2017a) a detailed integration plan consisting of 44 different programs meant to promote coexistence and interculturalism, and establishing social integration as a two-way process:

> Al mateix temps cal dir que, perquè la cultura pública comuna sigui comuna de debò (i no allò que els que van arribar abans imposen als que

arriben després) cal que la fem entre tots. Cal que tothom hi participi. Cal que tothom tingui prou competència en la llengua comuna per poder-ho fer. Cal que tots els espais públics siguin espais d'interacció entre catalans de tots els orígens.

And for the common public culture to be truly common – and not what the people who came before impose on those who arrive later – we need to do it together. Everybody must get involved. Everybody must have sufficient competence in the common language to be able to do this. Every public space must be a space for interaction between Catalans of all origins.

While language and social integration appear to be tightly linked, aspects of these various policies and plans have been problematized. Specifically, these texts do not assign any concrete role to immigrant languages in the various plans and programs; second, while social integration is emphasized as being a mutual effort to be undertaken by both Catalans and non-Catalans, language education responsibilities that do not allocate any space for immigrant language maintenance – paired with the general absence of any concrete roles assigned to native Catalans in terms of integration – would suggest that the burden of integration actually lies solely with immigrant populations, not with the host society. Collectively, these formulations suggest that much of the integration discourse in Catalan policies reconfigures the notion of *integration* to that of *assimilation* (Ali & Ready, 2021). Moreover, policy implementation has been shown to offer limited gains to immigrant populations. Often, there are few Catalan classes available to newcomers, some of which are instructed with minimal pedagogical training (Branchadell, 2015). These courses may also be approached with the mistaken belief that acquiring basic skills in a classroom setting are enough for navigating life in Catalan, and certainly enough for meeting the needs of immigrant populations. Together, these constraints amount to limited acquisition for immigrant learners, who are often blamed for their lack of linguistic uptake (Branchadell, 2015).

While the above policies and plans may have historical roots, current politics and political ideologies continue to play a central role in language use in Catalonia. Though separatism in Catalonia has been an ongoing movement in the region, the contemporary independence movement has gained momentum since 2005, and widely supported by a majority of the Catalan population (Crameri, 2014). This was certainly proven after the Catalan independence referendum of 2017; though this referendum was declared unconstitutional by the Constitutional Court of Spain, over 90% of the votes favored the secession of Catalonia as an independent republic (Generalitat de Catalunya, 2017b). While it has been argued that the ideologies of Catalan nationalism and separatism have shifted away from discourse on identity and language use and have more to do with concern over the political and economic welfare of Catalonia (Crameri, 2014), other empirical data suggests the contrary: in a study examining discourse in an online discussion thread that followed from an interview with a Catalan language activist, Atkinson (2018) notes that many posters in the discussion thread connected linguistic authority with linguistic officiality; specifically, Catalan as a sole official language was essential to linguistic authority, as well as for the survival of the language. Similarly, Stewart *et al.* (2018) examine social media discourse and illustrate that pro-independence discourse on Twitter is more likely to use Catalan than anti-independence tweets, pointing out the significant role that Catalan appears to play in expressing political identity.

It is worth noting here that the connection that Catalan has with nationalism may imply a connection with related ideologies. Secularism is a notably important element in nationalist ideologies in Catalonia and can be traced back – at least in part – to Francoist ideologies that collectively dominated Spain, such as Catholic identity and linguistic repression. As a result, Catholic identity is often perceived now as 'conservative, outmoded, and quintessentially Spanish' (Astor, 2020: 165). Such perceptions may play a key role in shaping attitudes toward religion in general: presently, Catalonia is the most secular region in Spain, with Leftist, progressive political discourse calling for a reduction in the role of religion in public life (Astor, 2020). This, in turn, may have linguistic implications: with secularism being associated with Catalan, and Catholicism (and possibly religion more broadly) being associated with Spanish, this raises the question of how immigrant populations – who may have religious affiliations (i.e. Muslim immigrants) – are perceived vis-à-vis their religious convictions and their compatibility with Catalan and/or Spanish social values. Not only that, this also puts into question the role of languages that are heavily associated with religion. As noted in Chapter 1, Arabic is strongly tied to the Islamic faith, both among Arabs and non-Arabs, and has a significant presence in Catalonia. However, its presence in an increasingly secular society may further perpetuate a sense of otherness among Arabic speakers.

Migration and Immigrant Languages in Catalonia: Maintenance and Shift

Like other countries in the European Union that are home to a number of metropolitan cities, Spain has seen an influx of immigrants in recent years. This is particularly salient in large cities such as Madrid and Barcelona but is also evident in nonmetropolitan areas across the country. Catalonia in particular has a reportedly large foreign population. According to data from the Generalitat's 2019 Language Policy Report, within a population of 7,675,217 residents, 64.3% of the population were born in Catalonia, while 16.6% were born elsewhere in Spain, both figures representing a decrease since 2018. Meanwhile, 19.1% of the reported population were born abroad, an increase from 2018's numbers. Although the immigrant population in Catalonia represents diverse nationalities from all around the world, the largest group is consistently those from Morocco (19.3% of the immigrant population), an unsurprising fact, given, among other reasons, Morocco's geographic proximity to Spain. While the next largest groups include immigrants from Romania (7.8%), and China (5.4%), it is also worth noting that immigrants from Spanish-speaking countries in Latin America collectively form 17.1% of the immigrant population. This breakdown provided in the Language Policy Report, however, only focuses on foreign nationalities, and statistics about migrants from other regions of Spain are not included. Still, Catalonia has a long history of domestic immigration from all over Spain. The first major wave of immigration (occurring between 1900 and 1930) consisted mainly of migrants from Aragon, Valencia and the Baleares, many of whom spoke Catalan (Gore, 2002). As mentioned previously, Andalusia also became a source of immigration later during the 20th century (1950–1975) during Franscisco Franco's regime, owing to widespread poverty that had plagued the south. As a result, many Andalusians sought better economic opportunities in Catalonia, and eventually integrated into working-class Catalan neighborhoods in the process (Woolard, 1989). Domestic immigration, in fact, had been the main source of immigration in Catalonia up until the mid-1970s. Immigration from other countries – especially non-EU countries – did not become prevalent until the 1980s. Similar to what motivated domestic immigration, many foreign-born immigrants of different backgrounds have been drawn to Catalonia for employment opportunities (Gore, 2002).

Resulting from the immigrant communities' diverse countries of origin, immigrant languages vary greatly, including typologically. While Latin American immigrants – whose numbers collectively approximate those of Moroccan immigrants – at first glance have a communicative advantage by being Spanish speakers, Latin American dialects vary greatly, and the overlap between their linguistic features and those of peninsular Spanish can also vary. For example, some features of Latin American Spanish may overlap with those of Andalusian Spanish (such as *seseo;* employed in some parts of Andalusia); however, some features may appear especially marked, such as the use of *voseo* or lexical Italianisms in Argentine Spanish (Moreno-Fernández, 2009: 126). Thus, while Latin American immigrants may face fewer communication barriers by sharing a language with the dominant Spanish-speaking community, their distinct dialects can still set them apart and position them as outsiders in their day-to-day interactions with the native Spanish/Catalan members of the community. In the case of non-Spanish-speaking immigrants, a number of different languages are brought over to Catalonia. Some of the largest immigrant groups bring the most typologically distant languages, such as

Chinese, as well as Berber languages and/or Arabic spoken by Moroccans; such linguistic distinctiveness can contribute to impeding intergroup communication if individuals from these countries of origin do not have any prior knowledge of Spanish or Catalan (Moreno-Fernández, 2009: 126). However, other languages such as Romanian and French (spoken by many Moroccans) are in the same linguistic family as Spanish, and therefore might somewhat assist immigrants in learning Spanish and/or Catalan.

A brief mention of how immigrant demographics may intersect with religious background is also relevant to the study I present in this book. Among the countries listed as the nationalities with the largest immigrant populations, three in particular – Morocco, Pakistan and Senegal – are predominantly Muslim countries (Pew Research Center, 2011) and likely provide a sizable influx of first-generation Muslim immigrants into Catalonia. While the previously cited language policy report does not provide data that specifies reported religious affiliations of this group of immigrants, the Department of Justice (Departament de Justícia) reports that Islam is the third most represented denomination in the region, with a total of 256 places of worship in Catalonia (Departament de Justícia, 2019).

As in any situation of prolonged language contact, one question that frequently arises is whether one language will supplant the other over the course of time, or if speakers will find a way to maintain their (typically less socially dominant) native or heritage language. In the context of immigrant language maintenance in Catalonia, there is a good deal of evidence that suggests that a variety of these languages play a prominent role in the day-to-day life of many immigrant populations and that this is sustained across generations. Fukuda (2017), for example, discusses linguistic vitality among the Japanese community in Catalonia and its interaction with Spanish and Catalan in family relations. Fukuda points to the presence of a full-time Japanese school and a Japanese language supplementary school that were established in the 1980s in Catalonia as active attempts at language maintenance on the part of the Japanese community. Additionally, Fukuda conducted a study looking at Japanese-Catalan-Spanish usage among Japanese families in Catalonia and found that Japanese retained a significant presence among families but that bilingualism was the most prevalent communication pattern between parents and their children, with Spanish and Japanese usage occurring with slightly greater frequency than Catalan and Japanese. However, Fukuda argues that while Spanish did have a stronger presence than Catalan (perhaps owing in part to the tendency toward monolingual Spanish usage between parents), this did not significantly affect the use of Japanese or Catalan at home. Fukuda also argues that the use of Japanese and Catalan can also be attributed to families in the study choosing to not establish a single common language and that the absence of one resulted in protecting the weaker languages (Japanese and Catalan) from being overwhelmed by Spanish (2017: 415).

While having specific linguistic domains and/or opportunities to use immigrant languages is certainly critical to language maintenance, is the availability of such resources sufficient? In an attitudinal study focusing on Romanian youth in Catalonia who participated in a heritage language maintenance program called Romanian Language, Culture, and Civilization (RLCC), Ianos *et al.* (2019) found that participants' attendance in the program did not appear to correlate with their language attitudes. While participants held the most favorable attitudes toward Spanish, Romanian followed closely behind, with Catalan as the least favored language. Still, while Romanian was valued for its connections to emotional and symbolic bonds and there were heritage language maintenance programs such as RLCC available, the authors indicate that Romanian would still be susceptible to effects of language shift. Even so, attitudes can certainly play an important role and motivating factor for language maintenance. In interviews with Quechua and Amazigh immigrants in Catalonia, Badosa Roldós (2020) indicates that – for immigrants who speak a language that is minoritized in their country of origin – the ability to relate to the similarly minoritized position of Catalan can contribute to forming positive attitudes toward their heritage/native languages and make active efforts to maintain it in the same way Catalan has been revitalized in Catalonia.

Despite the strong presence of immigrants in Catalonia who are of Muslim background (mainly, but not limited to those of Moroccan descent), much of what is known about the linguistic vitality of these groups stems from research focusing on other parts of Spain, such as Madrid and Andalusia, where there are also notably large immigrant populations of this background. These works typically focus on the maintenance of Arabic, which is not only strongly linked with Islam, but is also the native or heritage language of many of the informants in the present study. In particular, Madrid, as Spain's capital and an international, metropolitan center, has commonly been the setting of studies on Arabic maintenance. Mijares Molina (2006), for instance, focuses on the efforts made by the receptor community to respond to immigrants' needs, particularly within the context of the educational sphere. Mijares Molina examines the resources available to Moroccans in Madrid; specifically, the implementation of the language maintenance program, ELCO (Enseñanza de Lengua y Cultura de Origen), which was later renamed LACM (Lengua Árabe y Cultura Marroquí). This program was designed to teach Moroccan culture and the Arabic language to Moroccan immigrant students for the purposes of developing linguistic competence in Arabic and maintaining ties to their heritage identities. In practice, certain aspects of this program do not entirely comply with such objectives and have thus been subject to criticism; for example, this program has historically focused on teaching Classical Arabic (a nonnative variety of Arabic) to the exclusion of native dialects such as Moroccan Arabic, as well as other widely spoken Moroccan languages, such as Amazigh (Mijares Molina, 2006; Moscoso García, 2013). Still, the establishment of LACM suggests that social integration is viewed as a two-way process, wherein members of the receptor community recognize the value of multiculturalism and multilingualism and take on the responsibility of ensuring that Moroccan immigrants' experience of integration does not come at the cost of their heritage identities. This contrasts with similar programs found in contexts outside of Spain, particularly in communities where assimilation models are more prevalent than those of integration. In France, for instance, such heritage language maintenance programs were established with the goal of aiding immigrants in eventually returning to their countries of origin (Varro, 1992).

Moustaoui Srhir (2013, 2016, 2018, 2020) similarly focuses on the linguistic vitality of Arabic among Moroccan immigrants in Madrid through various approaches. In his (2013) study of the linguistic landscape of Madrid and the presence of Arabic within the local social space, Moustaoui Srhir notes the coexistence of Arabic and Spanish in the local signage of various Madrid municipalities. Specifically, Arab-owned businesses frequently used both Arabic and Spanish in their advertising, displaying both languages together in their signage. Despite this coexistence, however, Moustaoui Srhir points out that Spanish does appear to maintain its dominant position as the vehicular language in Madrid, given that it often appears more prominently, both in terms of its frequency of use, as well as in the physical lettering chosen for advertisements. Still, the use of both Arabic and Spanish allows for business owners to exercise their own legitimacy and membership in both linguistic communities (2013: 100). Furthermore, with such signage forming part of the public social space, individual business owners as well as Moroccans as a collective group can openly project their linguistic, social, ethnic and sometimes religious identities, allowing themselves to be integrated, included and made visible in a predominantly Spanish-speaking population, thus reorganizing the linguistic landscape in the area (2013: 105). Thus, while the public, social space of Madrid is a linguistic domain that is typically dominated by Spanish, the Moroccan speech community demonstrably maintains the use of Arabic in this sphere while still simultaneously integrating Spanish into it.

In other work that relies on interviews with Moroccan immigrants in Madrid, Moustaoui Srhir (2016) examines ethnolinguistic vitality among this population, as well as its connection to religious and linguistic identity. He argues that these two components are intertwined in the case of Arab Muslim immigrants, an observation that has been noted in other Muslim immigrant contexts (Mohamed *et al.*, 2019) and is further supported in the present study. Coming from the perspective that for many Muslims (both Arab and non-Arab) Arabic is a language associated with Islam, Moustaoui Srhir argues that interviewees construct Arabic as a superior language because of its religious importance.[2] Additionally, informants use Arabic as a marker of ethnic demarcation, creating a boundary between 'we' and 'them', where they position themselves separately from Spaniards. Additionally, this study suggests that these interviewees ultimately seek to resist total assimilation into Spanish culture by stressing the importance of using Arabic inside and outside the community and in passing Arabic on to subsequent generations. This is further substantiated in his subsequent (2020) work in which he examines family micro-language policies that mitigate language transmission among Moroccan families. Looking at both Arabic and Amazigh, Moustaoui Srhir found that the family environment favors the use of Arabic and/or Amazigh in the home environment, as a way of constructing cohesion, both among the family and the heritage community. Like his previous study, interviewees indicate that the transmission of Arabic is linked strongly to religious identity, as a means of achieving 'good Muslimness'. Interestingly, however, this particular ideological discourse is shown to be more present among fathers rather than mothers, who are notably more frequently associated with language transmission (see Chapter 3). Instead, mothers in this study connect language maintenance more to the maintenance of one's heritage identity, thus highlighting the important role that gender may play in language ideologies and practices.

While family dynamics certainly play a critical role in the maintenance of heritage languages, other factors may also be impactful, as evident in studies set in other regions in Spain. In a case study focusing on two first-generation Moroccan brothers in Granada, Ready (2021) argues that ethnolinguistic identity can be discursively constructed by different chronotopes, or discursive configurations of time and space. In the context of Ready's study, spaces such as Spain, Morocco, and – as a historical space – al-Andalus all function as chronotopes that play a role in constructing identity and informing linguistic practices of Moroccan immigrants in Granada. For one brother, Abdel, the chronotopes of Morocco and Spain come into conflict, mediating his preferred use of Spanish while still maintaining Moroccan Arabic as a marker of his identity. Meanwhile, his brother, Omar, identifies neither as Spanish nor Moroccan, invoking a combination of the two identities through al-Andalus as a chronotope. For Omar, this facilitates a historical connection that Arabic has with Andalusia, thus creating a link between Morocco and Spain. This chronotope allows him to construct an identity that steps outside of ethnolinguistic limits and that facilitates multilingual linguistic practices in an otherwise monolingual setting.

Multilingual practices can become even more complex in parts of Spain that have more than one widely spoken language, such as in the case of the present study focusing on Catalonia. In a study focusing on Moroccan and Algerian adolescents in Galicia, Moustaoui Srhir *et al.* (2019) demonstrate that the emerging translinguistic repertoire among these young participants certainly includes Galician and Spanish but that it is otherwise strongly rooted in Moroccan Arabic as a family language, with all but one participant indicating that it was the most important language for them. Like Ready's work, the authors here indicate that their participants indexicalize a broader 'delocalized' chronotope, where they essentially position themselves as deterritorialized, configuring themselves between Galicia and Morocco. Much as in the case of Ready's (2021) study, this delocalized chronotope can facilitate linguistic behavior, as evidenced by their use of hybrid communicative practices such as *Arabizi* – often referred to as an 'Arabic chat alphabet' – in which Arabic (typically colloquial varieties) are transcribed in texts using a combination of Latin script and Arabic numerals.

Multilingualism – particularly among younger populations – can also result in linguistic influences that extend beyond the written form. In a study set in Zaragoza that focuses on Moroccan children and adolescents with diverse linguistic backgrounds, Benítez Fernández (2019) examines linguistic leveling processes in Arabic as a result of inter-dialectal contact, as well as contact with Spanish. Leveling occurred at two levels: first, at the phonological level, with the realization of the uvular /q/; second, at the morphological level, with the construction of broken plurals, as well as through the bare construction of the present tense. Benítez Fernández considers various possible causes for these instances of leveling: exposure to mass media and the internet, the exposure to competing 'prestige' varieties of Arabic, as well as contact with Spanish as the socially dominant language.

Finally, while Arabic is certainly not the only language connected to the heritage backgrounds of Muslim immigrants in Catalonia (or more broadly in Spain), it is the most prominent one. This is not only due to the fact that – as illustrated above – Arabic has ties to religious identity for many Muslims, but also because of the long and significant history that Arabic has in Spain. With centuries of Arab rule that ceased in the 15th century, along with proximity to and close contact with North Africa, Arabic is uniquely positioned among immigrant languages, in that its presence in Spain predates any major waves of immigration, and indeed predates Spain's existence as a unified nation. As such, Plann (2009: 381) argues that 'Arabic is not merely a language of immigration: it is one of Spain's historic minority tongues, part of its "cultural heritage," and another "other Spanish language."' In other words, Arabic as it exists in present-day Spain is comparable to the situations of other minority languages of Spain that have been designated as 'established' or 'historical' communities. Unlike Arabic, these languages (e.g. Catalan, Basque, Galician) have official status and their speakers are granted certain linguistic rights. However, this reality puts into question the current status of Arabic as being viewed simply as an 'immigrant language', and why it continues to remain unrecognized as contributing to Spain's national heritage – a question that I return to at a later point in this book (see Chapter 9).

Conclusion

The primary aim of this chapter was to provide the sociohistorical context necessary to situate my study; namely, by looking at the present and past linguistic situations in Catalonia, how Spain's political history played a critical role in shaping language use in Spain, and how it has been particularly impactful in Catalonia. This was illustrated in the numerous language policies and plans implemented by the Catalan government, some of which relate to the Catalan population as a whole, while others specifically target immigrant populations who are non-Catalan-speaking (and in many cases, non-Spanish-speaking, though this aspect is notably absent in Catalan policy discourse). This chapter also provided an overview of the history of migration to Catalonia, and the presence of immigrant languages. Since Arabic, one of the most widely spoken languages among immigrants, is more frequently discussed in other contexts outside Catalonia, I drew on studies relating to Arabic maintenance and use among immigrant populations in other regions of Spain in order to highlight the significant presence that this language has among immigrant populations. While this was demonstrably linked to Arab immigrants – namely, Moroccan – some of these studies demonstrated that religious identity also has a part in ensuring the continued use of Arabic.

Still, while 'Muslim' and 'Moroccan' often go hand in hand in discussions about the use of Arabic, this constitutes an incomplete and inaccurate picture of Arabic use, because even if most Muslims associate with Arabic because of religious identity, it is not the native language of most Muslims, and this is certainly the case of many Muslim immigrants in Spain. Yet Arabic as a religious-heritage language for non-Arab Muslims – along with heritage languages tied to other non-Arab ethnicities – are not discussed. Additionally, as it was briefly mentioned in this chapter, gendered identities may also inform linguistic behavior, particularly that of heritage languages. As such, the relationship between language use and multifaceted identities is quite significant and complex and will be discussed at length in the next chapter; specifically, in terms of the construction of intersectional identities, as well as the negotiation of identities in an immigrant context through processes such as acculturation and linguistic investment.

Notes

(1) Although I use the term immigrant languages to refer to languages that are spoken among immigrant populations, it should be noted that some of these languages, most notably Arabic, have a more extensive presence in Spain. See Chapter 9.
(2) While there is a distinction between the Classical Arabic (used in the Qur'an and typically associated with religion), Modern Standard Arabic (used in current, written Arabic in formal contexts) and colloquial Arabic (spoken language with many dialectal varieties), the transcriptions from Moustaoui Srhir's (2016: 70) interviews indicate interviewees using the term الْعَرَبِيَّة (al-'arabiyyah) regardless of context, except in one case where an informant distinguishes between *darijah* (Moroccan Arabic) and *fus-ha* Modern Standard Arabic).

3 Acculturation and Negotiating Identity

Introduction

This chapter explores in greater detail some of the concepts introduced in Chapter 1; namely, theories relating to acculturation and identity negotiation, as well as how such processes relate to linguistic behavior. This chapter first looks at identity as a construct, and specifically draws on examples of gender and religion, both as individual and intersecting constructs. The latter discussion also involves a detailed examination of intersectionality as a theoretical framework for exploring identity. Here, I delineate theories on intersectionality and its applications in identity-related research. Because this study is also situated in an immigrant context, I also explore two related concepts that can help us understand how immigrants negotiate life in a new society: acculturation and investment. This section examines these two ideas in terms of their conceptualizations, applications in empirical research, and relevance to my study on first- and second-generation Muslim immigrant women. Finally, throughout this chapter, I offer both broader explanations of these various interrelated ideas, as well as specific contextualization in linguistic research.

Discursively Negotiating Gendered Identity

An individual's relationship with language use is one that is intertwined with identity, particularly when a language is tied to embracing or resisting acculturation in a new environment. Identity can consist of any number of elements: gender, religion, heritage, race, class and linguistic identities can all play a role in how language is used and perceived, and in fact have played an integral role in our understanding of linguistic behavior and ideologies of different speech communities. While the concept of identity began as a static factor influencing human behavior – including linguistic behavior – identity is now more widely understood as a dynamic, negotiable entity that is socially and contextually constructed (Bucholtz & Hall, 2005; Butler, 1993; Darvin & Norton, 2014; Inda, 2000; Kang, 2004). In the area of gendered identity and its connection to language use, a number of scholars laid the groundwork for this approach early on, questioning the naturalization and essentialization of gender. Lakoff's (1973) seminal work, 'Language and Woman's Place', describes how 'woman's language' – referring to how women use language and how language describes women – constructs gendered identity among women, in that the language used in discourse has contributed to naturalizing gender differences. Stating in her introduction that 'language uses us as much as we use language' (1973: 45), Lakoff argues that woman's language not only denies women the means of expressing themselves strongly, but also positions women in a role of subordination. Lakoff supports this claim by providing examples of specific vocabulary that has male and female counterparts, such as 'master' and 'mistress' – two words that were once equivalents in that they referred to one person's power over another. Lakoff indicates that 'master' is still used in a similar fashion: it can refer to someone who has power over someone or something, as well as mastery over something. 'Mistress' however, now has a sexual connotation, and furthermore is typically preceded by a possessive:

*She is a mistress.
She is his mistress.

'Widow' and 'widower' follow a similar pattern: A woman can be someone's widow, but a man is not described as someone's widower. Men, she points out, are defined independently, whereas women are defined by the men with whom they associate.

Judith Butler is another influential pioneer in the study of language and gender, whose works (1990, 1993) have laid the foundation for much of the current research in identity theory, which in turn has been applied across a number of disciplines including linguistics. Butler's conceptualization of performativity has especially impacted our understanding of the relationship between language and gender. Derived from John Austin's (1962) notion of performativity as the capacity for speech acts to not simply communicate but to also consummate an action or enact an identity, Butler uses this concept to reframe sex and gender as what one does rather than what one is, drawing on the notion of performativity as an act that constructs, naturalizes and enacts both sex and gender. They further describe performativity as an act that 'cannot be understood outside of a process of iterability, a regularized and constrained repetition of norms...this iterability implies that "performance" is not a singular "act" or event, but a ritualized production, a ritual reiterated under and through constraint, under and through the force of prohibition and taboo' (Butler, 1993: 60). Applying this process to gender and sexuality, Butler argues that it is through iterability of performativity that these categories can come to exist as 'natural'. In other words, normative gender and heterosexuality can be performed repeatedly over time, to the point that they appear as inherently fundamental categories of identity.

Butler's theory of performativity has been applied to various areas of identity theory, which not only demonstrates how different identities can be similarly constructed and manifested, but also suggests an interconnectedness of identities (see 'Intersectionality'). An illustration of this application is Inda's (2000) work in which he argues that while race may have biological foundations, as a meaningful category it is essentially the result of discourse. Furthermore, Inda argues that the racial body only becomes materialized and meaningful through historically specific discourses and supports his proposal by drawing on historical examples that have shaped Black identity as well Mexican identity. In one example, Inda shows the construction of Black as a naturalized racial difference by citing Stuart Hall's (1997) work that argues that racial ideologies tend to reduce the cultures of 'Black' people to Nature and to naturalize their differences, drawing on the example that during the 18th and 19th centuries, Blacks were commonly represented as subordinate due to their 'innate laziness' and 'innate primitivism' (1997: 244, as cited in Inda, 2000). By making these differences innate, natural characteristics of Blacks, such differences are permanent and fixed, and naturalization serves to keep these differences fixed forever, 'to secure discursive closure' (2000: 77). Likewise, Massey and Sánchez (2010) illustrate how immigrant identities are similarly brokered, in that they are formed through the categorical boundaries created and maintained by natives. As such, the authors argue that 'assimilation is very much a two-way street' (2010: 2) between immigrants and natives, one that immigrants may find difficult to cross with fixed boundaries.

The above works can also shed light on the relationship between gendered identity and language use, which – as illustrated above – Lakoff and Butler explore on a theoretical level. Much of individuals' linguistic behavior can be attributed to the gendered roles that are performed – often in accordance with social expectations. Freed (1996: 67) notes:

> language and gender studies conducted in natural settings may often find differences not similarities in women's and men's speech simply because women and men are frequently engaged in different activities and not because of any differences in women and men themselves. Since it is increasingly clear that speech patterns are products of the activities that people are engaged in and not inherent to the participants, we can conclude that communicative styles...are customs related to actions, activities and behaviors differentially encouraged for women and men.

These distinct gendered expectations are evident in various empirical studies, particularly with respect to the use of heritage languages among immigrant populations. For example, Zentella (1987) examines language and social identities among Puerto Rican women in East Harlem. In this investigation, Zentella found that female participants were not only expected to preserve Spanish-speaking traditions but were also expected to mediate between dominant and minority cultures. Additionally, they were found to have greater linguistic loyalty toward Spanish in comparison to their male counterparts. It was not surprising, then, that in an analysis of code-switching data, the most elaborate intrasentential code-switches in Zentella's study were produced by the most balanced bilinguals, who were usually women. Similar results can be found in other immigrant contexts, such as those of Holmes (1993) and Pauwels (1997), who look at immigrant language maintenance in New Zealand and Australia, and indicate a connection between gender and heritage language maintenance, where immigrant women typically maintained their heritage languages longer than men.

In another instance, Korteweg (2008) examines discourse about Muslim women's agency in Canadian newspaper articles covering a debate on the Islamic Institute of Civil Justice's decision to offer arbitration in accordance with Islamic legal principles. According to Korteweg, many interest groups questioned whether or not Muslim women's capacities were limited by Islamic ideologies and were therefore a vulnerable group under this form of arbitration. Korteweg indicates that while one perspective views Muslim women's agency as being embedded in religious contexts, the predominant perspective sees this group's agency as contingent upon their resistance to Islam, which, Korteweg argues, pulls Muslim women out of the very contexts that shape their agency and privileges it as being naturally associated with secularism, much in the way that Lakoff describes the naturalization of women's subordination and men's agency. This difference in agency and the use of language to naturalize women's subordination is evidently tied to religious identity as much as gendered identity, suggesting an inseparable connection between these two identities, thus raising the question of whether different aspects of identity can even be examined separately, as well as what approaches exist for studying interrelated identities.

Intersectionality: Gender and Religion

Examining single identities and the social contexts in which they are constructed has undoubtedly contributed to our understanding of how such identity interacts with language use; however, failing to acknowledge how other identities are borne out of the same social contexts inevitably gives us an incomplete picture that oversimplifies and distorts discussions of/about identity (Norton, 2000). In the context of migrant populations, sentiments of otherness – a common theme discussed in the field of migrant diaspora – may be attributed solely to ethnic, geographic and/or linguistic differences and thereby simplifying or homogenizing immigrants' experiences. As such, taking an intersectional approach to examining how multiple aspects of identity may collectively impact linguistic behavior is critical to linguistic research – particularly that which pertains to gender and language. Intersectionality, as originally proposed by Crenshaw

(1989), asserts that all aspects of social and political identity overlap – or 'intersect' – and are situated in power dynamics, thereby affecting those who are most marginalized in society. In the context of Black feminism, Crenshaw argues that the experience of being a Black woman cannot be understood through separate conceptualizations of being Black and being a woman, because these racial and gendered identities interact with and often reinforce each other. Acknowledging the inseparable nature of multiple identities is essential to the study of any social practice, since 'both our own, inner understandings of self and the kinds of access, opportunity and treatment we receive are the product of multiple and intersecting systems of social classification' (Levon, 2015: 297).

While intersectionality as a theory has provided a framework for better understanding how different identities may combine to create positions of marginalization or privilege, intersectionality as a research method is not clearly defined and is notably difficult to implement effectively (Rice *et al.*, 2019). However, this open-endedness also allows intersectionality theory the flexibility to be applied to research in different disciplines and therefore a variety of methodological approaches. One approach – which informs the present study – is using intersectionality to analyze macro-level structures (Crenshaw, 1989). This approach has been operationalized to a limited extent in sociolinguistic research. Norton (2000, 2013) and Menard-Warwick (2009), for example, rely on ethnography to examine the intersectionality of gendered, immigrant identity and how it shapes participants' involvement in language learning. In their respective studies, both authors connect participants' narratives about their gendered experiences as immigrant adults to their participation in language learning, such as the opportunities that are available to and pursued by them, as well as how their motivation to learn reflects an investment in their gendered identities. More recently, Levon and Mendes (2016: 12) produced a volume on language and sexuality from an intersectional approach, where each contributor examines how sexuality connects with 'other dimensions of lived experience' and thus informs language use.

Gender – as examined both alone and in conjunction with other facets of identity – plays a demonstrably important role in elucidating linguistic behavior. Within the scope of the present study, however, gender and religion present another point of intersection that is seldom discussed in sociolinguistic research, possibly owing to the reality that any given religion may not necessarily correspond to a single language or single culture. In the case of Islam, Arabic is frequently associated with religious traditions and thus so is Arab culture. However, Arabic is neither the native or second language for the majority of Muslims: currently, there are 50 Muslim-majority countries in the world (Pew Research Center, 2011), most of which are not Arabic-speaking. While Muslim populations do not offer the linguistic or cultural cohesion that many scholars seek when conducting social research, a number of studies look at gendered identity among Muslim immigrants, focusing on diverse populations in an effort to demonstrate that religion is a significant factor for Muslim immigrants regardless of cultural/ethnic background. For instance, Predelli (2004) and Furseth (2011) both look at Muslim immigrant women from diverse but predominantly Muslim countries. Predelli's (2004) study examines how Muslim women interpret and practice gender relations within a religious framework, specifically marital relations and participation in the labor market. Furseth (2011), on the other hand, focuses on the use of and discourse relating to the *hijab*, both among Muslim women who wear it and those who do not. Despite their distinct objectives, both studies examine how religion is an important medium through which gendered identity and gendered relations are negotiated irrespective of cultural background. Using a narrower geographic focus, Dwyer (2000) examines diasporic identities among South Asian Muslim women in London, arguing that among respondents is a 'supranational Muslim identity' that allows them to connect with other Muslims transnationally. She also argues that this identity is configured through gendered expectations, as evident from her respondents' interview answers that indicate an expectation that they – as Muslim women – have the responsibility of being the guardians of culture and religion and passing it on to subsequent generations. Despite this sense of responsibility, however, Dwyer points out that respondents indicate feeling excluded from sites of religious knowledge, such as activities at their local mosque – an exclusion that their male counterparts (such as their brothers) do not experience. These findings mirror Sadiqi's (2009) discussion about Moroccan women in a non-immigrant context, where she argues that because Moroccan Muslim women have been excluded for centuries from the public sphere – including the religious arena – they are distanced from publicly practicing Islam and are therefore also distanced from the use of Modern Standard Arabic – the medium of public expression in Morocco – which, Sadiqi argues, is far more accessible and significant for Moroccan Muslim men than for women. It is also worth noting that gendered religious identity is especially relevant for Muslim immigrant women in terms of their acculturation experiences, particularly for those who wear *hijab* and are visibly connected to their religious affiliation. For instance, in a study focusing on North African Muslim women in France, Killian (2003) looks at the *hijab* as an outward symbol of Islam that – for nearly a third of Killian's 41 participants – conflicts with social integration into the target language (TL) community; seven of these participants further suggest that immigrants who are not ready to socially adapt to the TL community (including, but not limited to the secularism that dominates French culture) should remain in or return to their countries of origin. Even now, *hijab* as a barrier to social integration remains a polarized topic. As will be demonstrated in subsequent chapters, wearing this head covering can limit social opportunities for Muslim women, particularly in the workforce, and thus prevent them from integrating into the professional domains of the TL community. This limited contact with the TL community can, in turn, impact the extent to which Muslim women may use the TLs of a given community. More recently (after the time of the study that I present in this book), the Court of Justice of the European Union ruled that prohibiting any visible form of expression of religious beliefs in the workplace (including but not limited to the *hijab*) 'may be justified by the employer's need to present a neutral image towards customers or to prevent social disputes' (Court of Justice of the European Union, 2021). This ruling thus gives greater power to employers to refuse to hire or to dismiss Muslim women who choose to wear a *hijab* and may indeed serve as a catalyst for further pushing Muslim women into social and linguistic isolation.

While gendered and religious identities are evidently intertwined and can be especially significant for Muslim women, the relationship between these identities and language use/attitudes among this population is almost entirely unexplored. Within the context of language learning, Rida and Milton (2001) argue that while migrant women from diverse backgrounds can experience numerous disadvantages accessing English language classes relating to gender and ethnic factors, Muslim women in particular may experience a third dimension of difficulty relating to religious barriers, such as feeling uncomfortable attending mixed-sex classes or in settings outside the Muslim community, or regarding the TL language (English) as more important for their husband and/or children for the purposes of work/school. These findings further support the notion of gender and religious identity being intertwined for Muslim women and shed some light on how this identity impacts language use. Given the lack of linguistic research focusing specifically on Muslim women, studies focusing on religious and gendered identity among other groups may also provide a framework for the present study. Fader (2001, 2006, 2007, 2009) has produced a significant body of work relating to Hasidic girls and women in New York City, and how religion interacts with gendered identity in the context of language socialization in Yiddish and English. Fader's (2001) study, for example, focuses on socialization in the educational sphere: Hasidic men have greater access to religious study, which consists of sacred texts that are read in Hebrew, but normally discussed in Yiddish. Meanwhile, Hasidic women's limited access to religious study results in limited proficiency in Hebrew and Yiddish (in comparison to their male counterparts), and instead are expected to be more dominant in English in order to navigate day-to-day life in Brooklyn. Fader (2007) argues that these linguistic boundaries are shaped by community boundaries – that is, religious beliefs about gender differences. As such, for Hasidic females, Yiddish is frequently associated with religious study and with males. This distinction shapes Hasidic female identity in that it is 'consistent with the rhetoric of continuity, which, in turn, is undergirded by Hasidic male authority and claims to religious continuity' (2007: 16).

Linguistic Identity Among Immigrants in Catalonia: Adopting Catalan and Spanish

In addition to gendered identity, linguistic identity and ideologies can also be linked to linguistic behavior. Specifically, language maintenance and/or shift are processes that can play a major role in the construction of these linguistic identities and ideologies. Given the complex linguistic situation in Catalonia (see Chapter 2), immigrant populations are in the unique situation of negotiating linguistic identities that involve both Spanish and Catalan, an experience that also extends to immigrants from Spanish-speaking countries who speak distinct varieties. Woolard (1989), for example, takes an in-depth look at identity among domestic Castilian immigrants in Catalonia, distinguishing between first- and second-generation immigrants in terms of not only their linguistic behavior but also the extent to which their identities are negotiable. One key feature of this distinction is that Woolard describes the first generation of immigrants as being forced to redefine their social identity upon arriving in Catalonia, but that this experience also means starting their lives in Catalonia with a blank slate: 'An individual who has severed basic ties in leaving the homeland has less at risk in exploring different identities symbolized by language use in Catalonia' (1989: 135). By contrast, second-generation Castilians born in Catalonia are not in the same position when it comes to adopting Catalan. 'Because they live in the social settings in which they were born and among the relationships that they formed from their earliest years they have more at risk in attempting to change their linguistic identity' (1989: 135). For Woolard, the negotiability of identity is rooted in one's social settings. Immigrants who have not yet integrated into the target community have greater freedom in recalibrating their identities than second-generation immigrants, who are typically more socially integrated than their predecessors and therefore face the issue of betraying their identity and social sphere should they choose to change the linguistic identity into which they were born.

In terms of attitudes and ideologies, immigrants from Spanish-speaking countries may offer differing experiences, depending on whether they come from Spain or Latin America. For instance, Trenchs-Parera and Newman (2009) examine identity and ideology among domestic and Latin American immigrants and found that domestic immigrants showed a wide variety of ideologies pertaining to language and identity, ranging from the 'parochial Catalan' who identified exclusively with Catalan to the 'parochial Spanish' who identified exclusively with Spanish, with several participants who identified themselves somewhere in between. One consistent thread in both groups was participants' connecting identity to ideology, with several participants taking the position that diversity, multilingualism and the maintenance of immigrants' cultures were important in Catalonia. From this, the authors argue that 'if the use of Catalan can be constructed as a symbol of inclusion and openness and not assimilation, there is a much greater chance that it will be attractive to ethnic minorities' (Trenchs-Parera & Newman, 2009: 522). Latin American immigrants interviewed contrasted with domestic immigrants in their language ideology by assigning political authority to Spanish (over Catalan) on account of its being more encompassing, both ethnically and linguistically, yet at the same time did not identify with peninsular culture. These diverging results mirror aspects of Schumann's (1978, 1986) Acculturation Model, which will be discussed at length subsequently; specifically, the idea of congruence between the cultures of the L2 group and the TL group being a factor that may increase the chance of social contact and facilitate L2 learning. Similarly, Huguet and Janés (2008) found in their study on Latin American students in Catalonia that young immigrants (aged 12–16) demonstrated the most favorable attitudes toward Spanish in comparison to their immigrant counterparts from other countries of origin while at the same time showing the least favorable attitudes toward Catalan (although they were generally not unfavorable).

While immigrants from non-Spanish-speaking countries have the added challenge of learning Spanish, this additional communication barrier does not necessarily suggest different attitudes toward Spanish and Catalan in comparison with their Spanish-speaking counterparts. Studying participants of both Latin American and African (North and Sub-Sahara) origins, Gore (2002) focuses on attitudes toward and use of Catalan among immigrants. While she does not specifically categorize her participants in terms of national origin, her findings indicate that the immigrant population holds mixed views about Catalan. Most participants recognized that the Catalan language was an important symbol of Catalonia, that it was advantageous for upward economic mobility and that speaking the language would assist in integrating socially and culturally in Catalonia. However, participants also indicated that they did not like being forced to learn it and that they saw Spanish as being the more practical language, particularly upon first arriving in Catalonia. This was indicated as much by an African immigrant (country of origin not specified) from Gore's study, who prioritized learning Spanish over Catalan as a new immigrant:

> Mourad: La primera cosa que haces es aprender castellano, ¿no? Es el idioma de la calle, para defenderse en la calle, ¿no?
>
> (Mourad: The first thing you do is learn Castilian, no? It's the language of the streets, for getting by on the streets, no?) (Gore, 2002: 98)

Additionally, several participants expressed frustration regarding their attempts to speak in Catalan with other Catalan speakers, only to be responded to in Spanish. Gore cites this as a means to deliberately exclude non-EU immigrants from Catalan society (2002: 101), which may in turn be a means of co-naturalizing language and race, such that Catalan is associated with whiteness and Spanish with non-whiteness (Khan & Balsà, 2021). Woolard (1989), however, identifies this as part of an accommodation norm, where native Catalan speakers assume that immigrants in Catalonia are likely to be more proficient in Spanish than Catalan and therefore switch to the former. Block and Corona (2019) point out that associating immigrants with Spanish may relate to many of them identifying as 'working class', which is typically connected more to Spanish than to Catalan. Pujolar (2010), on the other hand, argues that these experiences have more to do with the bilingual status of Catalonia and the mixed linguistic ideologies present on a political and societal level. Immigrants are left to interpret these ambivalent messages in terms of how these ideologies will facilitate in acquiring a legitimate bilingualism within their locality. These contradictions are evident in official discourse on language and identity and the linguistic practices of interlocutors in specific situations, specifically, the example of native Catalan speakers using Spanish with immigrants. Pujolar (2010) also cites Aracil's (1983) notion of 'interposition' – a way of characterizing asymmetry between minority and majority languages – as an explanation for the tendency for native Catalan speakers to use Spanish with immigrants. Some phenomena encountered in situations of interposition include the following: (1) all strangers are addressed in the majority language (Spanish), even if they do not speak it, or prefer to be addressed in the minority language (Catalan); (2) the majority language can be assumed to be universally valid for communication; (3) foreigners who know the minority language are supposed to know the majority language as well (Pujolar, 2010: 231). Using Aracil's idea of interposition, Pujolar argues that Catalan speakers are more inclined to use Spanish with anyone who they perceive as foreign, including immigrants, since the likelihood of their knowing and/or preferring Spanish is greater than that of Catalan. This motivation for switching from Catalan to Spanish is also widely known in Catalan as *la norma de convergència cap al castellà* (Vila i Moreno & Galindo Solé, 2012). Still, Pujolar concedes that this can result in social segregation for immigrants, particularly in more Catalan-dominant areas. This tendency may also be the reason that immigrants typically learn Spanish before Catalan (2010: 231).

This feeling of immigrant exclusion is echoed by informants in a study by Cortès-Colomé *et al.* (2016) that looks at changes in immigrants' language attitudes as a result of contact with Catalan. As a Senegalese informant described it, 'Even when you answer them in Catalan, they keep speaking Spanish...they don't realise it. Many of them are not even aware of it' (2016: 280). The authors point out that as a result, immigrants tend to accommodate to the language used by Catalan speakers, which in turn is 'experienced as discriminatory and exclusionary', which means 'failing to recognize the other...promoting rejection and the construction of opposing othernesses' (2016: 281). These sentiments are juxtaposed by informants' beliefs that being able to speak Catalan equates to membership in the Catalan community, as described by a Russian speaker and a Fula speaker, respectively: 'knowing the language gives you power' and 'you go to the greengrocer's and speak Catalan and he'll give you the best apples. It's like, I don't know, extra points' (Cortès-Colomé et al., 2016: 281).

However, one of the central themes of Cortès-Colomé et al.'s study is the 'mirror effect' that the exposure to Catalan has produced among immigrants. The authors argue that knowledge of the linguistic situation in Catalonia allows immigrants – particularly those who spoke a minority language in their homelands – to identify with Catalan as the minority language, and as a result they begin to mimic the language attitudes brought from their home countries, thus shifting their own ideologies. For example, one Moroccan informant commented:

> I discovered the resemblances between Catalan and Tamazight and that helped me to clearly understand the reality in Catalonia and that I must respect this reality and the attitude I should have towards my children and my environs...one thing reinforces the other. Discovering the differential features of Catalan reinforces my desire to fight for the uniqueness of Tamazight. (2016: 282)

These results also coincide with those of Estors Sastre (2014), where multilingual Pakistanis as well as Moroccan Tamazight speakers identified symbolically with Catalan. While many speakers of Spanish and Catalan hold distinct linguistic attitudes toward each of these languages, and each language plays a different role in the construction of identities among immigrants, these attitudes are naturally variant across individuals as well as ethnic groups. However, as demonstrated by findings from the above studies, the importance of integration is generally appreciated among immigrants – particularly by those from non-Spanish-speaking countries (Cortès-Colomé et al., 2016; Gore, 2002) – who understand that learning Catalan and/or Spanish is the direct route to achieve that goal.

Acculturation, Investment and Language Learning

While there are a multitude of diverse speech communities in Catalonia, Catalan and Spanish remain the dominant languages of everyday communication and thus the languages that immigrant populations may opt to learn in an effort to integrate into the TL community. Although measuring outcomes of second language (L2) learning is not in the purview of this study, second language acquisition (SLA) research focusing on the sociocultural factors that influence language learning can provide a better understanding of immigrants' experiences with negotiating life in a new society. One of the earliest models that deals with the social influences on L2 learning is Schumann's (1978, 1986) Acculturation

Model. The Acculturation Model proposes various factors influencing SLA by grouping together both affective variables and social variables into one cluster of variables. Schumann (1986) defines this joint cluster as acculturation, which ultimately entails the social and psychological integration of the learner with the TL group. With this model, learners can be placed on a continuum that ranges from social and psychological distance to social and psychological proximity with speakers of the TL. Schumann additionally argues that the learner will acquire the TL only to the degree that he or she acculturates (1986: 379). Among the various factors that may influence acculturation, this model accounts for social aspects, such as: (1) social dominance patterns, (2) integration strategies, (3) enclosure, (4) cohesiveness and size, (5) congruence, (6) attitude and (7) intended length of residence in the TL area. This model also takes into account affective variables, including: (1) language shock, (2) cultural shock, (3) motivation and (4) ego-permeability. Each of these are discussed in turn below.

As the first social aspect, *social dominance patterns* relate to how the learner and the TL community are positioned in relation to each other in terms of social, cultural and/or political dominance. For instance, in situations of language contact in colonial contexts, colonists may have had the opportunity to learn the widely spoken native languages of the original inhabitants but may choose to resist learning these languages because of their dominant social positions. Next, *integration strategies* on the part of the learner may include three strategies: assimilation, where the learner adopts the lifestyle of the TL group; preservation, where the learner maintains his or her own lifestyle and rejects that of the TL group; adaptation, which combines assimilation and preservation in that the learner only partially adopts the values and lifestyle of the TL group but still maintains some of his or her lifestyle and values. *Enclosure* refers to the extent to which the L2 learner/group and the TL group share social domains for interaction. In other words, this factor is an indicator of the extent of contact L2 learners may have with the TL, and thus the opportunities they may have to use the L2. *Cohesiveness and size* may also be indicators of the frequency with which L2 and TL speech communities are in contact. This factor describes not only how large an L2 group may be in comparison to the TL group, but also the extent of cohesion within the L2 group. The larger and closer-knit an L2 group is, the less contact it is likely to have with the TL group. *Congruence* refers to the cultural similarities shared by the L2 learner and the TL group. The more similar the cultures are, the more likely it is that social contact will occur between these groups. *Attitude* relates to both a learner's attitude toward the TL group as well as TL members' attitudes toward the learner's speech community, in that positive attitudes toward each other will more likely facilitate L2 learning than negative attitudes toward each other. *Intended length of residence in the TL area* indicates that the longer a learner (group) intends to stay in the TL area, the more likely it is that they will develop extensive contacts with the TL group and have more opportunities for learning.

Among the affective factors, *language shock* can be characterized as the fear or hesitation one may experience when speaking an L2, often a result of anticipating that the L2 speaker will communicate ineffectively or that their L2 usage will be received critically. *Cultural shock* also results in stress and anxiety, but instead stems from initial contact with a new and unfamiliar culture. Because of the disorientation experienced, this often diverts an individual's attention away from L2 learning. *Motivation* relates to the learner's reasons for acquiring an L2. Schumann cites Gardner and Lambert's (1972) distinctions between integrative motivation and instrumental motivation, where the former motivation stems from a desire to integrate into the TL group, while the latter draws on pragmatic reasons, such as learning the language as a job skill. Finally, *ego-permeability* draws on the notion that the various linguistic systems develop impermeable boundaries in a person's mind. Ego-permeability, then, refers to the learner's level of disinhibition and openness to TL input.

While Schumann's (1986) Acculturation Model served as a groundbreaking theoretical model that takes into account social factors in SLA, employing this model as a framework for empirical studies can be problematic. Geeslin and Long (2014), for example, point out that determining how to assess the affective factors in relation to the psychological distance between the learner and TL groups presents difficulties, and many of these factors may even lose their significance in a formal learning environment (Doughty & Long, 2003) and thus may only be applicable in a natural setting. Even in a natural setting, however, the Acculturation Model still presents a number of limitations and challenges in examining the language learning processes, particularly in the case of immigrants. Norton (2000) critiques the Acculturation Model, pointing out that it does not take into account (1) the bidirectionality of acculturation or (2) inequitable power relations. Norton challenges the assumption that if L2 learners give up their lifestyles and values in favor of those of the TL group, they will likely have more contact with the TL and enhance their SLA experience. She also challenges the assumption that positive attitudes between the TL group and L2 learners will positively contribute to SLA. Norton asserts that these two assumptions take for granted that members of the TL group are willing to accommodate attempts by L2 learners to assimilate and that they will reciprocate the positive attitudes of the L2 learners. In this sense, she takes issue with the Acculturation Model's insufficient account of the TL community's role in the acculturation process.

While Norton's (2000) argument may indeed reflect immigrant and TL groups' actual attitudes – ones that may not be reciprocated – Schumann's model is theoretical and is bidirectional insofar that it takes into account that positive attitudes on the part of both groups can facilitate L2 learning. Whether or not positive attitudes are being reciprocated in practice – and whether or not those attitudes affect language learning – may serve to support or invalidate this aspect of Schumann's model. Furthermore, Norton (2000) also critiques the above assumptions for neglecting to consider the possibility of inequitable power relations that may negatively affect L2 learners in terms of the quantity and quality of contact with TL speakers. Although the Acculturation Model does address power relations to a certain extent (social dominance patterns as a social variable), Norton calls for a more thorough examination of how power structures within society might push L2 learners into marginalized and unfavorable positions for L2 learning. Another problematic aspect of applying the Acculturation Model empirically is that it offers an insufficient framework for how personal identity plays a role in acculturation and subsequent L2 acquisition, a central focus of the present study. While the role of identity may emerge under the focus of social dominance patterns – given that identity is often shaped by power differentials in society – the Acculturation Model does not address the dynamic nature of identity and an individual's ability to perform various identities in order to adapt to different social contexts.

Despite its limitations, however, the Acculturation Model presents a number of factors that may be relevant to many immigrants' linguistic behavior and their connection to the TL community. Hammer (2017), for instance, looks at the relationship between the extent of integration and the extent of English proficiency among Polish immigrants in the UK and indicates a positive correlation between proficiency and acculturation. This correlation is also evident in Ansah's (2018) study which examines the role of acculturation in L2 acquisition among female migrants in Ghana. Specifically, factors such as the size of the immigrant group, the proximity of their residence to members of the TL community, and length of their residence all appeared to have an impact on L2 acquisition.

While the Acculturation Model offers a partial framework for understanding the role of language learning in the extent to which immigrants acculturate and negotiate life in a new society, another relevant concept that addresses the relationship between language learning and identity is the idea of 'investment', as proposed by Bonny Norton. First, one of the key ways in which Norton's conceptualization of the relationship between language learning and identity is a departure from previous models is how the notion of identity is operationalized. While a great deal of research in applied linguistics in the 70s and 80s – and indeed what may have also contextualized Schumann's model – viewed identity as static (and therefore learner motivation as static as well), identity is more widely accepted as being socially constructed and dynamic. This view informs Norton's construct of learner investment, where learner identity is equally complex, changeable and contingent on social interactions. With this view, Norton argues that inequitable power relations can shape language learning opportunities, as well as their 'investment' in L2 learning. Here, this concept – evoking economic principles – suggests that learners who choose to learn a language do so with the knowledge that they will increase the value of their cultural capital, or the wealth of knowledge and skills that an individual possesses which demonstrate both cultural competence and social status. This investment in language learning, then, also involves an expectation of 'returns' in the form of both symbolic and material resources (Norton, 2000). However, unlike the traditional views of learner motivation that often mirror individual personality traits (motivated vs. unmotivated, shy/anxious vs. confident, etc.), investment is socially situated and contextual. For instance, a female of color who is an otherwise 'motivated' learner may not necessarily be invested in her language learning experience if the classroom practices are racist and/or sexist. As such, the concept of investment as it relates to language learning attempts to demonstrate the social, historic and often inequitable elements that inform this relationship and therefore a learner's commitment to language learning.

Given that this conceptualization relies on the premise that identity is a dynamic entity in an ever-shifting social world, it is unsurprising that the idea of investment itself has undergone some revision to account for these shifts. More recently, Darvin and Norton (2015) have proposed a more extensive model of investment, arguing that – owing to many dramatic changes the world has seen in the past few decades, shifts in the global economic order, and the increasing reliance on technology for communication – systemic powers of control have become increasingly less visible, and for this reason, investment not only involves identity, but also intersects with macro power structures, such as ideology and capital, which, together, inform an individual's linguistic investment. They argue that an understanding of how these broader macro constructs operate not only shines light on power dynamics that take hold of individual social interactions and communicative events, but also on 'the structures of power that can prohibit the entry into specific spaces where these events occur' (2015: 43).

The concept of investment has been applied to many studies since its inception, including in some of the more current research in applied linguistics (Hajar, 2017; Mora *et al.*, 2016; Vasilopoulos, 2015), and more specifically in the area of gendered identity and language use in an immigrant context (Ali, 2020; Iikkanen, 2019; Kamada, 2010; Menard-Warwick, 2009; Norton, 2000; Skilton-Sylvester, 2002). One common thread that emerges from these works relates to how social contexts – and larger macro-structures in particular – may inform the language learning experiences and linguistic practices of migrant women. Many of these works, including those cited above, spring from the problematization of language learning among migrant women, where gendered practices and expectations within immigrant communities are commonly viewed as an impediment for women's successful integration in a new community. However, these works – along with the present study – demonstrate that for many of these women, individual linguistic practices and ideologies are far more complex, fluid and varied than what is often imposed or assumed by others, and much of this has to do with their investment in language learning as a means of social integration and acquiring the cultural capital that they regard as beneficial – or at times necessary – for navigating life in a new community.

Additionally, while the notion of investment is certainly applicable to any language speaker, native, HL and L2 speakers may invest differently in any given language, most notably because of their distinctive relationships with the language. In an immigrant context and from an acquisition perspective, a language associated with a culture that is not considered part of the TL community is a 'native' language to first-generation immigrants, but a 'heritage' language to second-generation immigrants. One key difference, then, that sets HL speakers apart from other groups is their relationship with the HL, which contrasts greatly from native and L2 speakers. Because of their personal connections with the language and culture (which are oftentimes somewhat removed or distant in comparison to the connection that native speakers may have), HL speakers have their own set of affective needs that need to be met when engaging in their HL, including – but not limited to – language classrooms. One necessity in particular is to recognize feelings of insecurities that many HL speakers may have toward their HLs as a result of criticism they may receive from native speakers for not demonstrating (oral) proficiency on a level that is comparable to a monolingual native speaker, or for having interference from their dominant language. This is a widely investigated experience, especially in the context of Spanish as an HL in the US (Goble, 2016; Park, 2011; Sánchez-Muñoz, 2016). In the context of HL speakers in Catalonia, some studies do focus on HL maintenance across generations (Fukuda, 2020; Lanz *et al.*, 2020); however, there is little research that specifically examines the experiences of second-generation heritage speakers in this region of Spain.

Acculturation and Immigrant Identity

In this section, I take some of the previously discussed notions to address intersectionality on another level: how gendered, religious identity interacts with immigrant identity throughout the process of acculturation, as well as some of the problematic perceptions that may be held with regard to immigrants and acculturation, particularly by members of TL communities. As briefly discussed in Chapter 1, acculturation can reflect different adaptation processes for immigrant populations, including integration and total assimilation. While the preservation of one's heritage identity and language(s) occurs with the former, they are abandoned in the latter. However, as noted above, all of these processes are informed by the efforts and behavior of immigrant individuals as well as members of the TL community, and even by the passage of time. As Deaux (2006: 4) notes, 'immigration is an experience that begins before people move away from their country of origin and that continues long after they arrive in a new country'. Given the considerable lapse of time and the multitude of people that immigrants may come into contact with as they acculturate, the very concepts of acculturation, integration and assimilation are often determined by members of the TL community. Given that TL communities have comparably more power than minoritized immigrant populations, research in migration studies has problematized the conceptualization of these processes. Specifically, discourse on integration often conceptualizes this process as a remedy, where immigrants are seen as problems that disrupt the social and economic order of the host society. Focusing on integration discourse relating to Muslim women, Korteweg (2017) argues that the notion of integration has in fact produced the opposite effect, that of gendered and racialized non-belonging for Muslim women, and that, owing to the sociocultural and economic distance between the two groups, non-immigrant communities may place social problems within immigrant communities. Korteweg also points out the intersectional nature of this gendered inequality, noting that Muslim women's gendered practices are often understood as racial or cultural, and therefore set them apart as outsiders. Not only that, such ideologies hold broader implications that can be connected to larger political events, such as the invasion of Afghanistan as an effort to 'save' Muslim women from Muslim men, as well as policies that ban Muslim women from wearing headscarves and/or face coverings (Korteweg, 2017), the latter of which is enacted on Muslim women's bodies (Killian & Johnson, 2006). This, Korteweg argues, 'relegates one group to outsider status even as it purports to build a bridge to insider status' (2017: 434).

Being assigned outsider status, however, is not lost on many immigrants, and some work to contest the identities that may be imposed on them by others. These efforts can be an especially arduous task for Muslim immigrant women, who have been historically othered through differences in nationality, race, religion and gender (Killian & Johnson, 2006). As Killian and Johnson (2006) note in their study focusing on Maghrebi Muslim women living in France, many respondents were reported to have rejected and reconfigured their identities by taking on a 'Not-Me' identity and essentially casting off and refusing to identify as immigrants. In some instances, a few women indicated being able to distance themselves from the immigrant label by simply having a lighter skin color and 'passing' for either French or an immigrant from a more socially accepted group. In other instances, efforts were made in the form of women managing their appearances so that they could conform to the expectations and standards of the TL community, a practice that undoubtedly reflects not only a desire to distance oneself from a low-status immigrant identity, but also a shift toward a French identity that reflects a higher socioeconomic status. Two points are particularly salient through these examples: first, identity negotiation for Muslim immigrant women can be deeply influenced by how members of the TL community treat them. As such, it must be reiterated that discussions on acculturation cannot exclude the role of the TL community. Second, beyond the acculturation process, it is also worth noting that TL communities have a hand in the construction of immigrant identity and thus they frequently create the dominant discourse surrounding immigration, and the conceptualization of the term 'immigrant'. Given that the notion of 'immigrant' is one that has met resistance by its own community members, we must interrogate the discourse that has played a dominant role in defining this identity.

Conclusion

In these first few chapters, I have delineated some of the key ideas and contexts that inform the present study. This includes detailing some of the broader concepts that are relevant to the present study, such as identity and intersectionality as it relates to gendered, religious and immigrant identity. As illustrated above, identities are imbricated and fluid; while individuals may certainly wield their own agency in constructing their identities or resisting labels, other individuals – such as members of TL communities – may exert influence on the construction of these identities as well. The collective participation of members of both the TL and immigrant communities plays a significant role in the process of acculturation and the extent to which immigrants may invest in language learning, and thus affect how they may negotiate identity.

While this chapter focused on identity construction on a micro level, Chapter 2 laid the foundation for understanding the macro-level structures that can shape identity, such as social, historical and cultural contexts. Specifically, Chapter 2 laid out a brief examination of political history in Catalonia and how it has shaped its present-day language ideologies, policies and planning, as well as the implications for migrant populations. Together, the background provided in these two chapters shapes the framework for the study that I present in the remainder of this book, and thus informs the main objectives that drive the present study; namely to: (1) continue the discussion on the linguistic behavior of immigrants in Catalonia by sharing the narratives of a triply overlooked population, namely, Muslim immigrant women; (2) use these narratives to demonstrate that acculturation is a transgenerational process reflected in linguistic behavior; (3) highlight the intersectionality of gendered and religious identity among Muslim immigrant women; and (4) illustrate how this identity is brokered through language use and attitudes in a multilingual context.

4 Research Design

Introduction

As I have highlighted in the previous two chapters, it is clear that language, migration and identity are overlapping practices for many individuals, particularly in the context of Spain, and more specifically Catalonia. Many of the previously cited studies have examined the linguistic behavior of individuals with a shared geographic background in order to provide a cultural constant. However, the relative absence of scholarship that explores other potentially significant aspects of identity – such as gendered and/or religious identity – leaves an incomplete picture of how immigrants' linguistic behavior and attitudes are shaped in a multilingual setting, attributing immigrant otherness solely to geographic and/or linguistic differences and thereby simplifying or homogenizing immigrants' experiences. As such, taking an intersectional approach as described in Chapter 3 in order to examine how multiple aspects of identity may collectively impact linguistic behavior is critical to sociolinguistic research. Specifically, religious and gendered identity can often be linked to marginalization, and – in the case of immigrants – negatively affect their experiences with the target language (TL) community. Without accounting for these intersectional identities, the nuanced experiences of groups such as Muslim women may be overlooked, resulting in an oversimplified understanding of this population's linguistic behavior. Muslim immigrant women in particular have remained relatively unaccounted for in linguistic research, which presents a critical research gap that I aim to address with this study. Given that they account for a significant portion of the population – especially in the context of immigrant populations in any part of Spain – it is critical to acknowledge and examine Muslim women's experiences in order to further our understanding of how immigrants negotiate life in a new society, as well as the role language plays in perpetuating marginalization.

The present study is driven by several aims. First, my goal is to continue the discussion on the linguistic behavior of immigrants in Catalonia by sharing the narratives of a triply overlooked population; namely, Muslim immigrant women. In the subsequent chapters, I will use these narratives to (1) demonstrate that acculturation is a transgenerational process reflected in linguistic behavior, (2) highlight the intersectionality of gendered and religious identity among Muslim immigrant women and (3) illustrate how this identity is brokered through language use and attitudes in a multilingual context. In this chapter, I delineate my research design; namely, the local setting for data collection, my role as the investigator and positioning in the Muslim immigrant community (which presented various limitations and advantages in data collection), basic background information of the informants who participated in this study, and the specific research tools I used for data collection: questionnaires and interviews.

Setting

I collected data for this study in 2017, focusing on the city of Barcelona and the nearby town of Mataró, both of which are situated in the province of Barcelona, located in the autonomous community of Catalonia. One of the main draws for localizing this study in the province of Barcelona was because there was already a large, long-established Muslim immigrant population, one that continues to grow even now. While data collection began within the city of Barcelona, Mataró later became a site for data collection as well because one of my initial contacts introduced me to an informant residing there, who in turn would also serve as a contact that would assist in introducing me to other potential informants living in the area. Mataró had also become my local residence for the last few weeks of my stay, making data collection in this city far more accessible, though I did continue to meet informants in Barcelona during this time. While Mataró became a data collection site out of necessity and convenience, this was, in fact, an advantageous site for meeting with Muslim informants, as its demographics are similar to those of Barcelona in terms of its immigrant presence. As of 2019, the foreign-born population accounted for 18% of the total population – 40% of which were of Moroccan origin and almost 3% of Malian origin (Ajuntament de Mataró, 2019) – the two representative ethnicities of my informants in Mataró. Additionally, much of this foreign-born population has demonstrated an interest in long-term residency: of the 268 foreign-born immigrants residing in Mataró that became Spanish citizens in 2015, 189 were of Moroccan descent (Ajuntament de Mataró, 2019). Finally, focusing on speech communities in Catalonia provides an additional layer of complexity to this study. Not only are Spanish and Catalan both official and socially dominant languages in this autonomous community, but language policies and ideologies have also been visible enough on a social level to impact linguistic attitudes (Newman & Trenchs-Parera, 2015).

Researcher Positionality and Informant Recruitment

One of the main motivations for conducting this study is an interest in addressing the minimal attention that Muslim immigrant women have received in sociolinguistic research, and prioritizing a population that previous scholarship has left unexamined thus far. However, as Pujolar (2007: 309) has noted, 'accessing immigrant women's perspectives is, I am convinced, a different type of project altogether'. Given the underrepresentation of minority women in sociolinguistic research – including those of immigrant backgrounds – it is unsurprising that a general lack of access to such communities can be a major contributing factor. Various elements can cause difficulty or even an inability to access immigrant women for research purposes: the researcher may be perceived as an outsider, or there may be significant cultural or linguistic barriers that prevent researchers from engaging with specific communities directly or extensively. Additionally, power differentials may be especially pronounced between immigrant women and researchers who do not identify as such, and these differentials may manifest themselves over the course of a research project, possibly impacting the quality of researcher-participant interactions.

Given the crucial role that researcher positionality can play in data collection, my own background as the investigator also bears mentioning as a factor that facilitated and influenced my interactions with informants. As a Muslim American woman and second-generation immigrant of Pakistani descent, having a shared gendered, religious identity – and heritage and linguistic identity in the case of South Asian informant – allowed for easier access to the Muslim community in Barcelona than a researcher from a different background may have been able to achieve. For instance, my initial contact upon arriving in Barcelona was a Pakistani Urdu speaker who knew a Muslim woman who was willing to host me for part of my stay. This woman, who also agreed to participate in this study as an informant and later introduced me to other potential informants, indicated that she had only agreed to host me because I too was a Muslim woman and that she would have otherwise not felt comfortable allowing a stranger into her home. Additionally, as a heritage speaker of Urdu and native speaker of English, I was able to use either or both of these languages when I met with informants who spoke little Spanish.

I began recruiting informants through two contacts that I already had upon arriving in Barcelona. Six of these initial informants also became contacts from whom I was able to recruit additional informants, and much of this recruitment occurred through socializing with my contacts and their family and friends over the course of my stay, typically at people's homes. Among the 34 informants, only seven informants were randomly solicited without prior introductions, and occurred in public spaces such as shops, restaurants and mosques. In this last case, my positionality as a Muslim woman is once again relevant. While non-Muslims are certainly not prohibited from entering mosques – and in many cases are welcomed for the purposes of tours or educational events such as classes on Islam or Arabic – Muslims are typically the only groups that are present for daily prayer congregations. Additionally, women and men are typically segregated at these gatherings, thereby limiting one's potential interlocutors. During my stay in Barcelona, I visited local mosques on Fridays, a sacred day of worship for Muslims that not only guaranteed larger congregations for the afternoon prayers but was also often the only time of the week I would encounter women in mosques.

Upon initial contact, I asked all informants to provide a meeting location and time that would be most convenient and comfortable to them, as I myself did not have a central workspace where I could invite informants. This resulted in collecting data in a variety of locations, including park benches, cafes and informants' homes. While this sometimes resulted in lower quality recordings (most notably in crowded, public spaces), accommodating informants in this way also proved to be advantageous in that it allowed for a greater likelihood of establishing an informal environment where I could solicit casual speech and more forthcoming responses.

Informants

This study uses data gathered from 34 women, all of whom were at least 18 years old, and of North African, West African or South Asian origin. This is a departure from previous works that rely on a certain degree of uniformity in terms of participants' countries of origin, the rationale for which is in part because they form a significant portion of the immigrant population in Barcelona (Generalitat de Catalunya, 2019a), but also because the vast majority of the populations from these regions are Muslim. Given the presence of Islamic culture embedded within the broader cultures of these different regions, such informants would likely provide a cultural constant to a certain degree vis-à-vis religious identity, which, as previous scholarship has suggested, is intertwined with gendered identity. This is especially the case for Muslim women who are from countries where Islam has a significant presence in the national culture. While gendered and religious identity are arguably shaped within sociocultural contexts and are thus variable across different geopolitical boundaries, many aspects of religious ideologies and practices – such as wearing a *hijab* – are invariant concepts across Muslim cultures. Moreover, gendered, religious practices such as the *hijab* may position Muslim women as a more visible minority in comparison to Muslim men and/or women of other faiths, and as a result may impact their experiences with the TL community. The choice of informants for this study, then, will thus help to demonstrate the intersectionality of religious and gendered identity among Muslim immigrant women and how this interwoven identity is reflected in linguistic attitudes and practices.

In determining the desired age range of informants, it was important to be able to discuss a number of complex and abstract themes such as one's experiences with language learning, acculturation and identity,

Table 4.1 Informant profile (self-reported) (Ali, 2021)

Pseudonym	Ethnicity	Country of birth	Generation	Age	Native language(s)	Other languages
Aisha	Moroccan	Morocco	1	47	Arabic	Spanish
Mona	Egyptian	Egypt	1	50	Arabic	Italian, English, Spanish, Catalan
Zainab	Moroccan	Morocco	1	48	Arabic	Spanish
Humaa	Pakistani/Spanish	Spain	2	25	Urdu, Punjabi, Spanish, Catalan	English, French
Jamila	Muslim (Moroccan)	Morocco	2	22	Arabic	Spanish, Catalan
Sarah	Pakistani	Pakistan	1	51	Urdu	Punjabi, Urdu, English, Spanish, Catalan, Arabic
Maria	Pakistani	Pakistan	1	35	Urdu	English, Urdu, Punjabi, Spanish
Sana	Pakistani	Pakistan	1	28	Urdu	English, Spanish
Asma	Pakistani	Pakistan	1	24	Urdu, Punjabi	English
Iman	Moroccan	Morroco	1	37	Arabic	Spanish
Yasmin	Pakistani	Pakistan	1	30	Urdu	English, Spanish
Sharifa	Moroccan	Spain	2	24	Catalan, Spanish, Darija	English
Laila	Moroccan	Morocco	2	24	Berber	Arabic, Spanish, German
Fatima	Moroccan	Morocco	1	34	Moroccan	Spanish, Catalan
Nadia	Moroccan	Morocco	1	29	Arabic	French, Spanish, Catalan, English
Mariam	Moroccan	Spain	2	23	Arabic	English, French, Catalan
Rehana	Pakistani	Spain	2	24	Spanish, Catalan, Urdu	English, German
Khadija	Moroccan	Morocco	1	40	Arabic	Spanish, French
Rabya	Algerian	Algeria	1	26	English, Arabic	Spanish, French, Dutch, Catalan
Shayma	Moroccan	Spain	2	21	Spanish	English, French, Arabic, Catalan
Dina	Moroccan	Spain	2	23	Moroccan, Spanish, Catalan	English, French
Zahida	Indian	Spain	2	25	Urdu	Spanish, Catalan, English, Arabic, Korean
Shabana	Indian	Spain	2	23	Urdu	Catalan, Spanish, English, Arabic, Korean, Hindi
Iram	Indian	India	1	57	Urdu	English, Arabic, Spanish, Catalan
Nasreen	Moroccan	Spain	2	20	Moroccan	Spanish, Catalan
Hana	Moroccan	Spain	2	25	Arabic	Spanish, Catalan
Salma	Moroccan	Spain	2	21	Spanish	Moroccan, English, Korean
Shereen	Moroccan	Morocco	2	20	Berber	Spanish, Catalan, Arabic, English
Sumaya	Moroccan	Morocco	1	51	Arabic	Spanish
Hawa	Malian	Mali	1	30	Mandinga	Spanish, French
Zahra	Malian	Mali	1	26	Bambara	Spanish, French
Aminata	Malian	Mali	1	30	Bambara	French, Spanish, Catalan
Aziza	Moroccan	Morocco	1	45	Arabic	Spanish, Catalan
Souhaila	Moroccan	Morocco	2	25	Moroccan	Spanish, Catalan, English, German

which would likely be best articulated by adult informants. I therefore set an age minimum, and only sought out informants who were at least 18 years old. Owing to this restriction as well as relying on my initial contacts for introductions to other potential informants, the age of informants ranged from 20 to 57 years old.

I also classified informants by generational differences in immigrant identity. While the difference between first- and second-generation immigrants is generally understood as a difference between having been born abroad versus being born in the target or host community, a simple application of this parameter is problematic. Among my informants, a few had moved to Spain either as infants or small children and would therefore be classified as generation 1.5. However, these informants indicated greater ease with Spanish and/or Catalan than with their native language, having learned those languages at a young age both in a natural setting and in an educational setting, much like their second-generation counterparts. Given the similarities shared with second-generation informants, generation 1.5 informants who moved to Spain at a young age (by the age of six) and indicated a linguistic skill set comparable to that of what would be expected of second-generation immigrants were classified as second-generation immigrants (four total).

Additionally, informants presented a wide range of linguistic competence in Spanish. While the majority were able to easily complete the tasks of the study in Spanish, a number of first-generation informants were unable to do so and as a result relied partially on Urdu and/or English to complete the tasks (these two languages were shared between myself and some of the informants, in addition to Spanish). The below table summarizes the self-reported ethnic and linguistic background of the 34 informants, each of whom were assigned a pseudonym for the purposes of this study:

As shown above, a wide variety of native languages are represented among the informants, including Urdu, Punjabi, Arabic,[1] Berber, Mandinga, Bambara, Catalan, Spanish and English. Only one informant, Asma, did not list Spanish as either a native or other language of use in her questionnaire responses.

Data Collection Tools

For this study, I used both questionnaires and interviews to learn more about informants' backgrounds and linguistic practices, including (1) the length of time that they had been residing in Spain, (2) any formal instruction in Spanish and/or Catalan they had received, (3) frequency of reported language use and (4) their attitudes toward Spanish, Catalan and their native/heritage language(s) and the associated cultures. Additionally, informants were interviewed for the purpose of elaborating on the themes covered in the questionnaire by eliciting narratives about their experiences living in Spain. The following sections detail the format of each of these tools.

Questionnaire

The structure of the questionnaire consisted of four parts: (1) basic background information consisting of 19 questions; (2) a series of 18 statements about language use and attitudes, where informants selected multiple choice answers using a five-point Likert scale to indicate to what extent they agreed with those statements (ranging from 'strongly disagree' to 'strongly agree'); (3) a list of 17 communicative activities (sending text messages, watching TV, listening to the radio, etc.) for which informants were asked to select which language(s) they most frequently used for each activity: Spanish, Catalan and/or their heritage language; and finally (4) loosely applying the idea that forms the basis of the matched-guise test (Lambert *et al.*, 1960) in which speakers of different languages are evaluated across specific traits – informants were asked to indicate which type of speaker they associated most with 18 adjectives (such as 'rich' or 'emotional') and were given the choice of either a theoretical speaker of their heritage language(s) or a theoretical bilingual speaker of Spanish and Catalan.[2] However, while the instructions included in this task asked informants to indicate which speaker they associated 'more' with the listed traits, suggesting that only one speaker should be selected, several informants opted to choose both speakers for some traits. Additionally, while this task in some ways adapts certain aspects of the matched-guise test, this task actually differs significantly from rating the spoken language of real speakers whose sex, gender, age and pronunciation may be apparent in actual speech and is also uniform for all informants. Contrary to the traditional matched-guise test, this particular task required informants to rate theoretical speakers, who may be represented differently in the minds of each informant.

One complication that was encountered with this method was that a number of informants indicated having more than one heritage language. While the diverse heritage languages represented in this study was the reason for not employing a true matched-guise test, it is not possible to determine from this task whether or not informants who identified with more than one heritage language imagined and rated theoretical speakers with the same heritage language repertoire as themselves. For instance, it is unclear whether Asma – who speaks Punjabi and Urdu – imagined a monolingual Urdu speaker, a monolingual Punjabi speaker or a bilingual Urdu-Punjabi speaker when she rated her theoretical heritage language speaker. Still, this technique circumvents some of the limitations of the matched-guise test, namely, those that result from relying on auditory stimuli. Listeners may recognize speakers as one and the same, while the use of different speakers makes it difficult for the researcher to control articulated differences between these speakers, such as pronunciation (Tsalikis *et al.*, 1991). Additionally, the feasibility of a matched-guise test relies on having few linguistic varieties for comparison; the present study, in contrast, draws on informants' diverse heritage and linguistic backgrounds that a matched-guise test could not easily accommodate. Ultimately, the goal of this task remains aligned with that of a matched-guise test: to determine attitudes toward different languages, namely, Catalan, Spanish, and – as a broader category – immigrants' heritage languages. It is also worth mentioning that because this study deals with both first- and second-generation informants, the term 'heritage language' was used loosely when addressing informants. For first-generation informants whose native languages were not Spanish or Catalan, the concept of a heritage language appeared clear. Many of the second-generation informants, on the other hand, required further clarification on what constituted a heritage language. Avoiding specific linguistic terminology, I verbally explained to all informants that their heritage language would be the language they spoke at home during their upbringing (all second-generation informants indicated speaking a second or third language at home, apart from Spanish and Catalan), that it would be a minority language in Barcelona (as opposed to Spanish or Catalan) and that it would be the language they would perhaps associate best with their ethnic identity/origin. While the majority of the informants used the Spanish version of the questionnaire, three informants requested the English version (two Algerian informants as well as one Pakistani informant, all of whom were first-generation immigrants). Both the Spanish and English versions of the questionnaire are included in Appendix A.

Interview

The interview consisted of a series of questions that intended to foster discussion on language use, self-reported linguistic competence, heritage language maintenance, gender and language attitudes. While the questions served as a script to guide the interviews, each question was kept broad in order to allow for follow-up questions and discussion when appropriate. All interviews were initiated in Spanish, and the majority were completed entirely in Spanish. However, because some of the informants that were first-generation immigrants had some difficulties interacting completely in Spanish, some informants relied on other languages to express themselves. In addition to being a Spanish speaker, my proficiency in English and Urdu allowed me to accommodate informants who also spoke these languages. As such, two interviews were done partially in English, and/or in the case of some Pakistani informants, two were done partially in Urdu. Ultimately, since neither measuring proficiency nor examining specific linguistic behavior/features was the objective of the interview, the variation in language choice during the interviews is not expected to impact the quality of the data. The goal of the interview was to learn about informants' language use and attitudes and to elicit candid responses, and allowing informants to use a lingua franca with which they were most comfortable and conversant (Spanish, English, Urdu) was an efficient way of facilitating that result. However, there were notably some first-generation informants who were more proficient and comfortable in their native languages/other languages that did not include Spanish, Urdu or English. Because I was unable to accommodate these informants due to my own limited or lack of proficiency in their dominant languages – such as Arabic and Mandinga – these informants relied entirely on Spanish in order to give their responses, which may not have been as developed or complex as the responses they may have been able to give in their dominant languages. Finally, all interviews were audio recorded with a digital recorder. While all informants consented to being recorded, the presence of such a device is also worth noting as a possible factor influencing the quality of responses. Both the Spanish and English versions of the interview questions are available in Appendix B.

Method of Analysis

As a study that centers on intersectional identity among what is essentially a small group of informants, the interview data will be the primary source for analysis, as narratives comprise a crucial component in how identities are constructed and expressed (De Fina, 2015). By drawing on narratives, this study can focus on the individual experiences of the informants, thereby demonstrating the complexity of Muslim women's experiences with negotiating multilingual and multicultural lives. Specifically, in this study, I employ narrative analysis (e.g. Park, 2011; Polkinghorne, 1995), whereby I will use the interviews to construct a story about these informants' experiences navigating life in Catalonia.

Using emerging themes that were identified in the interviews as a guide, the qualitative analysis will comprise thematic categories of discussion, including: identifying which languages they reportedly use and their attitudes toward these languages, narrating their experiences with integrating into Spanish/Catalan society, and sharing their beliefs about how they are perceived by members of the TL community. I also aim to show how these stories are shaped by various informant characteristics, such as gender, religion, whether they are first or second-generation immigrants, familial circumstances (such as marital status and whether or not they have children) and educational/professional background. This holistic approach is particularly advantageous for the scope of the present study, first, because the focus remains on informants' varied perspectives on their linguistic practices, relying on their own understanding of their experiences and actions. Additionally, narrative analysis allows for comparisons between different informants' experiences regarding specific themes and can also bring to the foreground any number of variables that may contribute to informants' perspectives, particularly where gendered and religious identity appear to be inseparable and mutually reinforcing elements that play a role in linguistic behavior and attitudes. Because I am interested in highlighting the generational differences of informants' experiences, Chapters 5 and 6 separately address the narratives of first- and second-generation informants, respectively.

In lending some degree of quantitative data to this primarily qualitative study, Chapter 7 focuses on an analysis of questionnaire data that examines reported language use and language attitudes, focusing specifically on Catalan, Spanish and informants' native/heritage languages. Because this study does not rely on a large sample size, the analysis of the questionnaire data will take on a more descriptive than inferential approach and will delineate informants' reported language use and attitudes across generations. While my initial analyses included an examination of other factors such as marital status (unmarried, married), parental status (with or without children), occupation status (student, employed, not employed) and educational background (up to secondary education, post-secondary education, postgraduate education), these factors will not be examined in great detail. These factors may certainly play an important role in informing the linguistic behavior of informants; however, interpreting such data in the context of this study was ultimately problematic, as a small sample size also resulted in a great deal of overlap between certain factors; for instance, younger informants who were students also tended to be second-generation informants, and informants with children were typically married. As such, analyses relating to these factors will be limited to brief comments.

I would also like to note here that, while using interviews and questionnaires to learn about informants' linguistic practices does not reflect direct experiences, this method of data collection can still be telling about informants' linguistic ideologies; specifically, their beliefs and feelings about their own language use. These ideologies, in turn, are notably impactful with regard to shaping actual language use (see Silverstein, 1979). Determining how to interpret such data, however, presents its own methodological challenges. For instance, interviews, like any speech act, may inherently impact what is produced during the interview itself. As Holstein and Gubrium (2003: 4) indicate, 'Treating interviewing as a social encounter in which knowledge is constructed means that the interview is more than a simple information-gathering operation; it's a site of, and occasion for, producing knowledge itself'. As such, both interviewer and interviewee are involved in creating meaning throughout the interview. Thus, the scope of the present study is not to focus on informants' direct sociolinguistic experiences, but rather their self-reported ones, and glean from this their beliefs and attitudes about language use.

Notations

Finally, I would like to briefly outline how data is organized and annotated in subsequent chapters, particularly that which relates to interview transcriptions. First, I have included informants' original comments, which were typically in Spanish, however, sometimes informants used English and/or Urdu, along with some insertions in Arabic. These transcriptions are followed by my own English translations in brackets. Instances of code-switching during the interviews are marked with italics. Where interview excerpts include Urdu or Arabic, I provide transliterations (along with translations) rather than using the scripts of either language. Each interview excerpt is also labeled with the informant's assigned pseudonym, as well as the heritage identity with which they self-identified. While this reflects the place of birth for many informants (first-generation and 1.5), for others (second-generation), this label reflects family identity that may still overlap with Spanish/Catalan identity. Lastly, while the interview transcriptions are generally limited to single turns on the part of informants rather than dialogue that includes myself, in instances where my own questions or comments are relevant to the context, I include these utterances in parenthesis on a separate line within the excerpt.

Notes

(1) Informants used a variety of terms to indicate Arabic as their native language, including 'Darija' and 'Moroccan'. Both of these terms refer more specifically to Moroccan Arabic, or the colloquial variety. However, since its formal counterpart, Modern Standard Arabic, is not a native language, 'Arabic' as listed by other informants will be interpreted as colloquial Arabic specific to their country of origin.
(2) A theoretical bilingual speaker of Spanish and Catalan was chosen instead of monolingual speakers of either language, as monolingual speakers of Catalan are virtually nonexistent.

5 Spaniard on Purpose: Narratives of First-Generation Informants

Introduction

Chapters 5 and 6 focus on the specific experiences of Muslim immigrant women residing in Barcelona, as shared in their interviews. This chapter in particular focuses on the experiences of first-generation informants who represent diverse backgrounds, ranging from new to longtime residents, minimally to highly educated, unemployed and employed. Throughout this chapter, I highlight the relationships that first-generation informants have with the target language (TL) communities, as well as with immigrant communities in which informants' native/heritage languages are spoken (hereafter referred to as HL communities). Here, it is worth reiterating that HL communities do not necessarily correspond with informants' nationalities, and often their HL communities may consist of members who share in other aspects of identity. For example, while some Moroccan informants may consider their HL community to be the local Moroccan community, others might consider it to be the Arab community and/or the Muslim community. Similarly, Pakistani informants may identify with other Pakistanis, more broadly with South Asians from other countries such as India, and/or the Muslim community at large.

The first part of this chapter focuses on informants' relationship with the TL community; specifically, through their use of Spanish and Catalan. Beyond this, I also examine how informants report on their sense of belonging to the TL community, as well as their positive attitudes toward language learning, not only for the purpose of acculturation, but also with regard to the prestige and instrumental advantages attached to Spanish, Catalan and – and as a language that many informants regard as globally relevant – English. Additionally, informants reflected on their own perceptions of the TL community's attitudes toward immigrant populations, many of which appeared to be positive. From here, I shift into a discussion on informants' distance from the TL community; namely, narratives reflecting indifference, resistance or difficulty with Spanish and/or Catalan, as well as how some informants may not feel a sense of belonging to the TL community, which is at times shaped by the idea that their cultural and religious values may not be compatible with those of the TL community. This discussion also includes reflections on some of their experiences with the TL community which reflect negative attitudes toward immigrant populations.

Finally, this chapter discusses informants' relationships with their respective HL communities. Here, informants illustrate how they still have connections with HL communities through language use and maintaining religious and/or cultural values and practices. Informants also discuss how their interactions vary between the TL and HL communities, and how gendered identity is strongly linked to heritage identity in the case of their interlocutors, and that this impacts the nature and boundaries of their interactions. In some cases, informants indicate a distancing from HL communities not only in terms of values and practices, but also in terms of how religious, gendered identity and expectations can clash with their Spanish/Catalan identities. Despite this distance, however, a number of informants also reflect on second-generation immigrants and their (limited) HL use and proficiency.

Connections to the TL Community: Navigating with Catalan, Spanish and Other Local Languages

For many first-generation immigrant individuals, successfully navigating life in a new society requires acquiring the TL of the host community. While both Spanish and Catalan have a strong presence in Catalonia, the former is often prioritized as the vehicular language among new immigrants, and as such, its acquisition is viewed as an initial and necessary step in socially integrating and functioning in Spanish/Catalan society, as indicated by two informants: Maria, a 35-year-old Pakistani shop assistant whom I had met through another Pakistani informant, and Iman, a 37-year-old Moroccan baker, who worked at a local bakery near my apartment:

> *We ourselves need to be better in Spanish* porque es muy importante nosotros sabes-sabemos castellano...pero poco- defes- dificultud--uh *difficulties*...en hospital, *when we went there and sometimes we need a translator*...ahora yo quiero...yo *prefer* español, porque tengo que practicar el mucho años, mi castellano, poco mal porque siempre yo hablo con mi hijo inglés, y ahora no quiero...él *parla català* muy, muy bien y castellano muy bien. Yo practicar castellano con mi hijo, con mi sobrino, con mi hermana. Yo prefería español todavía. Y después catalán también. (sic)

> [We ourselves need to be better in Spanish because it's very important that we know Spanish...but a little - difficulty - difficulties...in the hospital, when we went there and sometimes we need a translator...now I want...I prefer Spanish, because I have to practice it for years, my Spanish,

it's a little bad because I always speak with my son in English, and now I don't want...he speaks Catalan very, very well and Spanish very well. I practice Spanish with my son, with my nephew, with my sister. I prefer Spanish still. And then Catalan too.] -Maria, Pakistani

Es que cuando veni no sabía decir ni 'hola'. He vivido a trabajar...en un restaurante, en la cocina. Y con quien trabajaba, gente italianos, gente de Italia. Entonces esta gente, como..hola, vamos a salir con la mujer y...su marido...estaban...hablaba francés, italiano también, e inglés. Entonces me...me hablaban francés, inglés, y me enseñaban un poco, poco español. Yo vivido sin...saber nada de español...viviendo así...el primer año...era muy difícil...ahora no, ahora no tengo problema. Después de 11 años, 12 años ya..ya...te acostumbras. Te sientes una de aquí, está bien. Es la manera, siempre el acento y ya se nota que eres una extranjera, pero...lo que pasa que tú entiendes todo, contestas todo, lo que quieras, bueno, entiendes. (sic)

[When I came I didn't even know how to say 'hello.' I've lived here for work...in a restaurant, in the kitchen. And someone I worked with, Italian people, people from Italy. So these people, like...hello, we're going to go out with that woman and...her husband...they were...they spoke French, Italian too, and English. So...they spoke to me in French, English, and they taught me a little Spanish. I lived without...knowing any Spanish... living like that...the first year...it was very difficult...not now, now I don't have problems. After 11 years, 12 years now...you get accustomed to it. You feel like you're from here, it's fine. It's the way, always an accent and people notice that you're a foreigner, but...what happens is that you understand everything, you answer everything, what you want, well, you understand.] -Iman, Moroccan

At the time of the study, both informants had been living in Barcelona for some time: Maria had been living there for seven years, and Iman for 10–11 years, as noted in the above excerpt. Being native speakers of Urdu and Arabic, respectively, they both indicate struggling with their Spanish and not having any prior knowledge of it when they first moved to Spain. However, both note that – with efforts – they have gradually begun to acquire that knowledge, which in turn has provided some sense of belonging. Perhaps owing to her having spent less time in Spain, and possibly due to illness that required frequent hospital visits – as alluded to above – Maria offers a negative evaluation of her own Spanish, referring to it as '*poco mal*', citing the need for an interpreter at the hospital. While formal assessments of informants' language skills did not form part of this study, Maria's speech is particularly interesting with regard to how she navigates possible gaps in her knowledge of Spanish. Compared to Iman, who generally expresses herself in Spanish without hesitation, Maria frequently pauses and switches to English in moments where it appears she is having difficulties communicating in Spanish. Considering that her native language is Urdu – a lingua franca between interviewer and interviewee – her choice to turn to English might be a reflection of accommodation (with English being my native language), or possibly an instance of Maria reflexively applying a common linguistic practice of Urdu-English code-switching to her interaction in Spanish.

It is also worth noting Maria's mention of Catalan. While she prioritizes learning and practicing Spanish, she adds Catalan as a secondary priority and also comments on her son's advanced proficiency in Catalan, and in fact briefly switches to Catalan to describe his speaking abilities. This code-switch could be triggered by the topic itself – speaking Catalan – but may also be a reflection of demonstrating her own interest in and efforts with learning Catalan. Maria, in fact, is one of the few first-generation informants to indicate that both languages are a priority to learn. She reiterates this idea later in her interview:

> Actually, what I feel is I - I have to be too much better in Spanish and Catalan, I...I lacks a lot in Spanish because I'm living here and I...eh...I see my son's future here, so I have to be...uh...good in Spanish and I have to learn Catalan because I want to co- competate with them...so for the competency. (sic) -Maria, Pakistani

Similar to the previous excerpt from her interview, Maria connects language use and language learning to her son. In other words, since her son's life is in Catalonia and he functions in Catalan and Spanish, so must she. This sentiment is echoed by one of her friends, who had also been introduced to me at the same time as Maria had been:

> (Aap har zubaan ko us ke wakaar ke lahaaz se kese insaaf karte hai?)
>
> *Catalan, because we are living in Catalonia. So* ye log prefer carte hai, ke mathlab ke...catalan...bolna or catalan anee chaye. *Cause we are living here so it's important*...or muaziz bi...Spanish bi. *Spanish, overall, but.. Catalan because we are living in Catalonia.*
>
> (How would you evaluate each language here in terms of importance?)
>
> [Catalan, because we are living in Catalonia. So these people prefer it, I mean...Catalan....one needs to know how to speak Catalan. Cause we are living here so it's important...and it's prestigious. Spanish, too. Spanish overall, but Catalan because we are living in Catalonia.] -Sana, Pakistani

While Sana, a 28-year-old travel agent, did not speak Catalan, and in fact spoke very little Spanish (as illustrated above, the majority of this interview occurred in Urdu and English), Sana notes that it is important to learn Catalan if an individual is living in Catalonia, and in fact seems to prioritize it above Spanish, since the latter is added as an afterthought. Perhaps owing to her lack of proficiency in either language, however, Sana appears to set herself apart from the Spanish and Catalan-speaking TL community, referring to them as 'these people' ('*ye log*'), suggesting that she is not a member of this community.

Sana, however, was not alone in her sentiments. While several first-generation informants had been living in Barcelona for several years – even decades, in some cases – few indicated feeling any sense of belonging when asked if they felt a connection to life in Spain. Aisha, the first informant I had met in a chance encounter, was a 41-year-old emergency medical assistant who had been living in Barcelona for 16 years at the time of her interview and was in fact one of the few to express contentment with her life in Barcelona since moving from Morocco:

> Porque llevo muchos años aquí....entonces...yo sé que al principio costó mucho...por...la lengua...por la...costumbres de la gente..son diferentes.... pero....sí, luego yo me puse estudiar (castellano), me formé....y seguí aquí...viviendo...hasta...hoy, estoy contenta, estoy bien. (sic)
>
> [Because I've been here many years...*so*...I know that at the start it was really difficult...because of...the language...because of...the customs of the people...they're different...but...yes, later I started studying (Spanish), I educated myself...and I continued here... living ... until ... today, I'm happy, I'm fine.] -Aisha, Moroccan

Like other informants, Aisha attributes initial difficulties with adjusting to life in Barcelona to language barriers, as well as cultural differences. She also connects her eventual adjustment to her efforts to learn Spanish. This calls attention to the relationship between language education and social integration, a point that is also made salient in previous excerpts in which informants recognize the difficulties caused by language barriers and the need to learn Spanish, and Catalan. Beyond connecting language to integration, many first-generation informants instead connected language learning – and at times their own motivation to study a language – to prestige and its instrumental value. However, for several informants, English appeared to have more instrumental value than either Catalan or Spanish:

> ...el inglés es muy...ojalá que pueda hablar perfectamente el inglés porque me encanta hablar perfectamente...en el trabajo, si sabes inglés...es importante. Hay gente que no sabe decir ni hola en español, ni otra idioma y habla perfectamente inglés y trabaja. Y puede buscar...puede encontrar trabajo fácilmente. (sic)
>
> [...English is very...I hope I can speak English perfectly because I'd love to speak perfectly...at work, if you know English...it's important. There are people who don't even know how to say hello in Spanish, nor in any other language, and they speak English perfectly and it works. And they can find...they can find work easily.] -Iman, Moroccan

Lo que tiene poder, tiene peso. Entonces lo que tiene poder, como ve, que inglés tiene que ser el primer idioma, inglés tiene más prestigio, o catalán.

(Y otros-)

Todos otros son extras, ¿sabes?

[What has power, has weight. So what has power, as you can see, that English has to be the first language, English has more prestige, or Catalan.

(And other-)

They're all extras, you know?] -Sarah, Pakistani

I guess I would say English would be pretty high up there, because you can use it in..in so many different countries, so it has this...maybe.. implicit prestige tag...but I wouldn't say it's necessarily more prestigious than other languages...just depends, cause it's the language of business, that maybe it sounds more prestigious. -Rabya, Algerian American

As illustrated in these various excerpts, English is perceived as a prestigious language that supersedes both Catalan and Spanish. While Sarah – a 51-year-old business owner from Pakistan – simply associates English with power and thus as being a language with greater impact, Iman and Rabya point out that its utility and prestige relate to English being a widely spoken language. For Rabya, a 26-year-old Algerian American – who, like Sarah, is a business owner – English is an especially useful tool in the business sector. Additionally, Rabya has a second job as an instructor at an immersion-focused English institute and therefore is also tasked with motivating students to learn English. Iman, on the other hand, recognizes that many immigrants who may not know Spanish might speak English very well and thus rely on it more heavily than any other language. This may certainly be the case for many South Asian immigrants from Pakistan and India, where receiving some degree of English education is common, owing to the British colonization in this region, as well as the fact that English is a co-official language with Urdu and Hindi in Pakistan and India, respectively. In fact, two of the six first-generation South Asian informants – Maria and Yasmin – indicated having a master's degree in English.

Besides their own language use, first-generation informants' experiences with navigating a new life in Spain may also be eased by members of the TL community. Several informants commented on TL members' positive treatment, indicating that they perceived positive attitudes toward them individually, and toward immigrant groups more generally. For Maria, who works in a Pakistani clothing store, this positive treatment comes in the form of supporting immigrant-owned business:

I have all friends and uh..they like our culture as well. Many people really appreciate our..even races. You know, I'm working here (in a Pakistani clothing store) and many uh, Catalans came here and asked about our uh..dresses that they need to buy. (sic) -Maria, Pakistani

Here, she indicates that the presence of Catalan shoppers demonstrates an appreciation for Pakistani culture, and perhaps even an interest in adopting aspects of it, thus embracing some degree of reciprocity between HL and TL communities where social integration is concerned. Iman, on the other hand, reflects on the nonjudgmental attitudes that she perceives from Spaniards:

> Los españoles, la verdad es que son muy buena gente. ¿Vale? Que respeta. A mí, no he tenido problemas con nadie..de mi religión, o...al contrario. Siempre me han respetado, me han tratado bien hasta ahora...Son muy... te ayuda. Si preguntas en las calles y...son muy...muy amables...Siento más cómoda aquí por la gente. Vas tapada, vas desnuda, vas maquillada, vas como quieras, te respetan igual por la persona que es, no allí (Marruecos), te miran la ropa, cómo es, de dónde eres...¿sabes? Aquí, mira la persona. No miran la..físico (sic)
>
> [Spaniards, the truth is they're really nice people, right? They respect. For me, I haven't had any problems with anyone...not with my religion, or... on the contrary. They've always respected me, and have treated me well up until now....They're very...they help you. If you ask them on the streets and..they're really...really nice. I feel more comfortable here because of the people. You go covered, you go naked, you go with makeup, you go however you want, they respect you for the person that you are, not like there (Morocco), they look at your clothes, what you're like, where you're from...you know? Here, they see the person. They don't see the...physical.] -Iman, Moroccan

Iman denies any cultural clashing – particularly with regard to religion – and emphasizes the respect that Spaniards give her. Moreover, she goes further and elaborates on the openness she perceives in Spanish culture, indicating that there is less focus on outward appearances and that this has contributed positively to her experience living in Spain. She also juxtaposes this against her experiences of living in Morocco, pointing out that there is a greater tendency to judge individuals superficially compared to what she has experienced in Spain.

Such positive perceptions of the TL community can also be reflected in language attitudes, particularly in terms of how the TL community regards the heritage languages of immigrant communities, as Rabya indicates:

> (Do you think Catalan society values heritage languages?)
>
> I think so, I think so...because there are probably....they probably share this common thing where you have this heritage language that...you don't want it to disappear and you want more people to start speaking it...but... they have...they have a historical...this historical significance for them because they weren't allowed to speak the language for I don't know how many years or decades...a long time...so it's very important for them, and

they do value other heritage languages because of that. -Rabya, Algerian American

Rabya believes that heritage languages are valued in Catalan society, ascribing this to Spain's long history of linguistic suppression during Francisco Franco's regime. This narrative bears some resemblance to the 'mirror effect' as described by Cortès-Colomé et al. (2016) (see Chapter 3), which results in immigrants identifying with Catalan as a minority language if they themselves speak a minority language from their home countries. In Rabya's case, this mirror effect instead relates to the attitudes of the TL community, where she believes that they see both Catalan and heritage languages as minority languages, and that, given all the efforts made to normalize Catalan over the course of decades, heritage languages spoken by immigrants should be similarly valued and preserved.

Disconnect from the TL Community: The Role of Linguistic and Cultural Differences

As noted from all of the examples shown thus far, various factors can contribute positively to informants' experiences with socially integrating in Spanish/Catalan society, such as making efforts to learn Spanish and Catalan, as well as being received positively from members of the TL community. However, many informants also report on behaviors and attitudes that may distance them from the TL community. One area where this is salient relates to language learning, where informants report resistance to, disinterest in, or difficulties with learning Spanish. For example, while Maria cites the importance of learning Spanish and Catalan in a previous excerpt, she also indicates struggling with language learning:

> *Mi hijo siempre dice*, 'Mama, your accent is too bad in Spanish'. You have to change your accent in Spanish! But I always tell him that I need more practice. So vocabulary uh, as well. You know, in every language you have a lot of healthy and too much fast vocabulary, then you can speak good language, in any language. So I am learning - *estoy aprendiendo castellano y catalán, los dos idiomas porque yo quiero perfecto en idiomas…no me gusta siempre* when I don't uh…uh talk good Spanish and my accent is not too good, so I feel a bit, uh, I mean, uncomfortable, and it shakes my confidence as well. When you are here you have to learn the language. (sic)

> [My son always says, 'Mama, your accent is too bad in Spanish'. You have to change your accent in Spanish! But I always tell him that I need more practice. So vocabulary uh, as well. You know, in every language you have a lot of…too much vocabulary, then you can speak good language, in any language. So I am learning - I'm learning Spanish and Catalan, both languages because I want to be perfect in the languages…I don't always like it when I don't uh…uh talk good Spanish and my accent is not

too good, so I feel a bit, uh, I mean, uncomfortable, and it shakes my confidence as well. When you are here you have to learn the language.] -Maria, Pakistani

Maria evidently is making a conscientious effort to learn both Spanish and Catalan but reveals a number of struggles. She reflects on her own trouble areas, such as not having sufficient vocabulary in Spanish, as well as issues with her accent. Beyond this, Maria also elaborates on affective elements that may impact her language learning, such as criticisms from her son regarding her accent when speaking Spanish, and lacking confidence when she speaks, both of which can certainly be connected to linguistic insecurities and possibly impede her progress in developing proficiency. Still, she reiterates the importance of learning the language(s) of the TL community and expresses a desire to 'be perfect' in both Catalan and Spanish. Iram, a 57-year-old Indian homemaker with two daughters (who also participated in this study), similarly acknowledges the importance of learning languages of the TL community, though she expresses a general disinterest in learning them:

Yo no doy mucha importancia a otras idiomas (sic), entonces prefiero urdu..árabe...y...claro eso también es fundamental, ¿no? donde nos...estamos viviendo, tenemos que saber este idioma también.

[I don't place much importance on other languages, so I prefer Urdu.. Arabic...and...of course that's essential, isn't it? Where we...we're living, we have to know this language as well.] -Iram, Indian

Iram explicitly states a preference for her native language, Urdu, as well as Arabic, which she indicates in other moments of her interview that she connects with her Muslim identity. Unlike Maria, who expresses a personal interest in and motivation to learn Spanish, Iram connects learning these languages to necessity. It is also worth noting that despite her indifference toward the TLs, Iram was one of the few first-generation informants to conduct her interview entirely in Spanish, and did so with relative ease.

While few informants indicate difficulties with or indifference toward learning Spanish, all informants acknowledged the need to know Spanish. When comparing attitudes toward Catalan, however, several informants admitted that they did not speak Catalan, or were not motivated to learn it, owing to its limited utility outside of Catalonia:

El catalán, ¿para qué? Para...si sales de Cataluña, y...no lo utilizas, ¿sabes? Si vives por aquí, y yo..yo llevo aquí..12 años, trabajando sin catalán, y... no me...no me he sentido que me falta el catalán...si me hablan los catalanes...contesto en castellano, ni..no hay problemas, ¿sabes?...En vez de perder tiempo uh..aprendiendo catalán, puedo mejorar el inglés, el francés, otros idiomas, pero catalán...¿sabes?

[Catalan, for what? For...if you leave Catalonia, and...you don't use it, you know? If you live here, and I...I've been living here...12 years, working without Catalan, and...I don't...I don't feel that I'm missing Catalan... if Catalans speak to me...I answer in Spanish, nor...there's no problem, you know?...Instead of wasting time uh...learning Catalan, I can improve my English, French, other languages, but Catalan...you know?] -Iman, Moroccan

Iman points out that Catalan is only used in Catalonia, and therefore unhelpful if one were to move to any other part of Spain. She also indicates that she had survived and navigated life in Barcelona for a relatively long time without the use of Catalan and that she can use Spanish with any Catalan speaker. More than that, she suggests that other languages may be more valuable to learn, such as English and French. It is also worth noting here that while Iman did not include French or English as languages that she knew in her background questionnaire, she did mention in her interview that she used both from time to time, particularly with tourists and some of her co-workers at the bakery. As such, these languages do appear to serve an instrumental function in her work life. Still, other informants similarly indicate that they respond in Spanish when spoken to in Catalan, and doing so does not appear to create any problems or complications in their interactions, particularly since Catalan and Spanish are largely mutually intelligible:

...hay gentes, por ejemplo, el hospital, una visita, una enfermera o no sé que, una tienda, que una mujer que habla contigo catalán...no se importa que tu si me entiendes o no. Ella catalana, habla catalán. Pues estos gentes, uh..yo entiendo, pero puedo...respuesto para castellano. Para ella, no se, pero para mí, es mi respuesta, el castellano, entiendo pero mi respuesta...hay veces que si..si yo..si yo sabe...una palabra o una frase en catalán, digo, pero si no sabe, respuesta directamente en castellano. (sic)

[There are people, for example, the hospital, a visit, a nurse or I don't know, a store, a woman that speaks with you in Catalan...it's not important that you understand me or not. She's Catalan, she speaks Catalan. Well these people, uh...I understand, but I can...answer in Spanish. For her, I don't know, but for me, it's my answer, Spanish, I understand but my answer...there are times that if...if I...if I know...a word or a phrase in Catalan, I say it, but if I don't, I answer directly in Spanish.] -Nadia, Moroccan

(So you ever use Catalan?)

No. Very rarely. I understand it...I understand it completely, but I've never taken any official classes in Catalan, so I don't know the grammar, so I don't feel comfortable forming sentences myself...having conversations. But usually here, when someone speaks to you in Catalan my instinct is to reply in Spanish, because I understand what they say, but I don't register that it was Catalan, so I just reply in Spanish, and they immediately then switch to Spanish as well. And then later you think, oh wait, they spoke to me in Catalan. -Rabya, Algerian American

As noted previously (see Chapter 3), accommodation is a frequently cited speech practice among Catalan speakers. While it is more commonly described as an automatic and anticipatory switch that is not necessarily prompted by interlocutors using Spanish, in the examples above, Nadia (a 29-year-old teacher) and Rabya note that this accommodation occurs when they diverge from their interlocutors by initiating the switch to Spanish themselves, thus maneuvering the conversation to being entirely in Spanish. Additionally, they do not report having any experiences of Catalan-speaking interlocutors reacting negatively to this switch, which may serve to further validate their distanced relationship with Catalan.

Resistance to or difficulties with language learning can be tied to immigrants' lacking a sense of belonging to the TL community, or feeling any disconnect from it. This disconnect can be present across all or just some interactional domains, as Rabya notes:

(Do you feel that you fit in here? Why or why not?)

Um...yes...and no. Connected in terms of working...life..yes, I mean, I'm fully integrated in that way. I work like any Spaniard would, so...I feel perfectly integrated in that way, ...all of my friends are international, so I don't have...Spanish friends. So technically in that sense, I'm not fully integrated. -Rabya, Algerian American

Rabya's full-time job places her in frequent interactions with Spaniards, and, as noted above, she indicates that this brings her some sense of feeling integrated in Spanish society, or at least within the professional sphere. In contrast, she socializes with a diverse group of individuals, none of whom are Spanish, and identifies some degree of disconnect in this area. Both professional and social domains are significant ones for interactions and forming connections with other individuals, so Rabya's mixed 'yes and no' response certainly aligns not only with her simultaneous connections and disconnect with the TL community, but also with her reported and actual language use. Besides her indication that she did not use Catalan and typically relied on Spanish to communicate with Catalan speakers, it is also worth noting that – despite being proficient in Spanish – she conducted her interview entirely in English. While this may certainly be a reflection of a desire to use a lingua franca that was also our shared native language, this may also reflect her language use in social settings, where she often interacts in English among international friends whose lingua franca is English, thus maintaining her distance from the TL community, both through her interlocutors and language choice.

While Rabya connects her sense of belonging to different interactional domains and the backgrounds of her interlocutors, others indicate a more sweeping disconnect from the TL community, attributing this separation to cultural differences:

> No encajo bien...no todavía, falta mucho...Racismo. Racismo. Sí porque, claro...porque son tacaños. Pequeño corazón. Por un lado hablan de derechos mujeres, por otro lado solamente dejan trabajo de limpieza...a las mujeres, que merecen solamente eso. No comparten vida social.
>
> [I don't fit in well...not yet, it's a long way to go...Racism. Racism. Yes, because, of course...because they're stingy. Little heart. On the one hand they talk about women's rights, on the other hand they only leave cleaning jobs...to women, who only deserve that. They don't share a social life.] -Sarah, Pakistani

> ...la verdad es que no siento nada. A mi no me gustan estas culturas... aunque vivo aquí, pero no me gusta....las niñas saben...la cultura y todo... es que...somos diferente, alhumdulilah. (sic)
>
> [...the truth is I don't feel anything. I don't like these cultures...although I live here, but I don't like it...the girls know...the culture and everything... it's that...we're different, praise God.] -Iram, Indian

While Sarah criticizes members of the TL community for racism and hypocritical ideologies regarding women, and attributes her social distance to these shortcomings, Iram simply indicates that she does not like Spanish and Catalan cultures and points out that she and her family have different cultural values. These cultural values may also be embedded in differences in religious values, owing to her use of *alhumdulilah*, an Arabic phrase commonly used among Muslims to express gratitude toward God. Fatima, a 34-year-old travel agent from Morocco, similarly attributes religious differences – particularly visible religious symbols – to feeling disconnected:

> Lo que pasa que...la religión es diferente. O sea..cuando..no eres religiosa o no llevas hijab y todo es como normal. Sientes casi...100% conectada pero si llevas vestimenta islámica y tal es más complicado. Ya no te sientes tan...tan conectada, digamos.
>
> [What happens is that...the religion is different. That is...when...you aren't religious or you don't wear hijab and everything is like normal. You feel almost...100% connected but...if you wear Islamic clothing and such it's more complicated. You no longer feel as...as connected, let's say.] -Fatima, Moroccan

While she does not elaborate on how wearing Islamic clothing contributes to creating distance with the TL community, it is evident that to Fatima, a woman who wears a *hijab*, differences in religious identity are more salient when they are visible, such as for Muslims who wear a *hijab*. That said, as a gendered practice, this can especially position Muslim women as outsiders, an experience that is not limited to first-generation immigrants (see Chapter 6).

More than observing cultural or religious differences, distance from the TL community can also be exacerbated by negative treatment and/or negative attitudes that immigrants perceive from members of the TL community. Mona, a 50-year-old Egyptian shop owner who also hosted me for the first half of my stay in Barcelona, comments on stereotypes and derogatory language used among Spaniards:

> Hay mucha gente arabi aquí..sobre todo de Marruecos, entonces los de Marruecos vene aquí pedi ayuda del goberno...y los españoles pensa todo empezar hablar arabi, entonces todos moros. 'Moros' es...palabras feas. Eh...mi dijo de los egipcio...los arabe saudiya...de los marruecos todos moros. (sic)
>
> [There are a lot of Arab people here...above all from Morocco, so Moroccans come here and ask for government help...and the Spaniards think that everyone's starting to speak Arabic, so everyone's a Moor. 'Moors' are...ugly words...they say it about those from Egypt...Saudi Arabs...those from Morocco...everyone's a Moor.] -Mona, Egyptian

Mona criticizes the perpetuation of stereotypes and the derogatory use of the word *moro* for describing all Arabs, a term that frequently refers specifically to those of North African descent. However, Mona's point of critique appears to relate to generalizing all Arabs as being like Moroccans, whom she also seems to hold partially responsible for the negative stereotypes and xenophobia held toward Arabs more generally. As also noted in Mona's response, xenophobia toward Arabs can also be reflected in language use and attitudes toward Arabic and may function to create even further distance between immigrant and TL communities. Sumaya, a 51-year-old salesperson from Morocco, similarly notes negative attitudes toward Arabic, along with Berber:

> No tiene valor, ni beréber ni árabe, ni nada.
> (¿Hay actitudes negativas?)
> Si...cuando hablamos árabe, nos odian...no quieren esto.
> (¿tienes experiencias negativas con--)
> Sí, sí, sí. Y a veces en el trabajo. Cuando hablamos, por ejemplo, entre los marroquinas, o sea...'habláis en español, no habláis'--
> (¿Dicen eso?)
> Sí, muchas veces. Como no entienden, pues... (sic)
>
> [They don't have any value, neither Berber or Arabic, none of them.
> (Are there negative attitudes?)
> Yes, when we speak Arabic, they hate us...they don't want this.
> (Do you have negative experiences with--)
> Yes, yes, yes. Sometimes at work. When we speak, for example, among Moroccans, I mean...'you all speak in Spanish, you don't speak--'

(They say that?)
Yes, a lot of times. Since they don't understand, so...] -Sumaya, Moroccan

In this excerpt, Sumaya illustrates the divide between communities through both the negative attitudes she perceived from members of the TL community, as well as impositions relating to language use on the part of the TL community. In both instances, she indicates that Moroccan languages – namely, Arabic and Berber languages – are neither valued nor welcomed in Spain and that instead she has been met with an insistence on speaking Spanish, attributing this response to discomfort with not being able to understand. This type of reaction to multilingualism, of course, is not uncommon in perpetuating xenophobia, but it also suggests that retaining vestiges of one's heritage language/culture may not be accepted within the TL community and therefore does not have a place in the TL community identity, or rather, national/regional identity. This, in turn, raises the question of whether immigrant individuals are expected to integrate or assimilate into the TL community.

Connections to Immigrant Communities

As shown above, the relationship immigrants have with members of the TL community – as well as their attitudes toward each other – can have a profound impact not only on their sense of belonging, but also on their investment in learning the TL(s). Similarly, individuals' connections – or lack thereof – to the immigrant communities with which they identify can also play an important role in shaping their linguistic behavior. This is especially pertinent to many first-generation informants who identify very little with the TL community. In the previous section, for instance, Iram was noted for her disconnect from and indifference toward the TL community. Unsurprisingly, then, the bulk of her interactions reportedly involve other Urdu speakers:

(¿Sientes una conexión a la vida aquí? ¿Sientes que te encajas aquí?)
Sí, con las otras mujeres pakistaníes.
(Con las mujeres en particular...¿y con la comunidad española o catalana?)
No...La verdad es que siempre hablo urdu. [risa]. Es que mis amigas también entienden solamente urdu, entonces hablamos en urdu.

(Do you feel a connection to life here? Do you feel that you fit in here?)
[Yes, with other Pakistani women.]
(With women in particular...and with the Spanish or Catalan community?)
[No...the truth is I always speak Urdu. [laughter] Yes. It's that my friends also only understand Urdu, so we speak in Urdu.] -Iram, Indian

Despite the distance from the TL community that Iram previously indicated, she still feels a connection to life in Barcelona; however, she specifies that this connection is with Pakistani women.¹ Not only that, but her friends appear to be monolingual Urdu speakers (unlike herself), which might suggest that they are similarly distanced from the TL community. Additionally, Urdu is the vehicular language for members of this enclave of South Asian Muslim women. While it was evident from my conversations with Iram that she was proficient in Spanish, this social separation from the TL community may certainly reinforce her indifference toward Spanish and Catalan, and this may also be the case for her friends.

Another point of interest in Iram's comment above is her mention of socializing specifically with women. This gendered distinction, in fact, was a salient theme among informants, particularly those of the first generation. Here, religious and gendered identities become a relevant component in shaping their interactions, especially with members of Muslim immigrant communities, where distinct behavior expectations are upheld when interacting with different genders.² While Iram was one of the only informants to indicate (at multiple points during her interview) that she generally did not speak with men, several other informants reflected on specific differences they manifested, depending on the gender of their interlocutor:

> Jab hum *ladies* ke sath bath karthe ha...tho zara...um...(unintel) araamse...mathlab unse *friendly*, likin jab, mathlab...agar pakistani koi hai,gent, tho zara...mathlab apko...*reserve*...*reserve* ho ke bath karna...mathlab ye hai *difference*.
> (siraf pakistani admiyo ke sath..?)
> Ha mathlab Spanish logh ke sath, *normal*. Tik. Tik hai.
>
> [When we speak with ladies...it's a bit...um...calm...I mean friendlier with them. But then...if it's a Pakistani man, then it's a bit...reserved...you have to speak in a more reserved way...so that's the difference.
> (Just with Pakistani men?)
> Yes, I mean with Spanish people, it's normal. It's fine.] -Sana, Pakistani

In the above example, Sana differentiates between female and male interlocutors, but speaks of women more generally, but then specifies Pakistani men as being a point of difference for her in the way she speaks. This difference, namely that of formality and social distance, similarly characterizes the ways in which other informants report their linguistic behavior, where interactions with men are often described in more specific terms:

> Si hablo español con los españoles..pues, lo mismo...con los musulmanes - ya sabes - no puedes (unintel.) cerca de ellos...no puedes...con una mujer, podrías hablar lo que quieres, pero con un hombre, no. No puedes saludar ni nada...(risa).
>
> [If I speak Spanish with Spaniards...well, it's the same...with Muslims -you already know -you can't (unintel.) close to them...you can't...with a woman,

you could talk about what you want, but with a man, no. You can't say hello or anything (laughs).] -Sumaya, Moroccan

...puedes abrir directamente con otra mujer, pero la musulmana hombre no...con el...es mas,..bueno, un poco...más correcto, mucho...no es tu marido, no puedes...hay una conexión que no puedes hacerlo. (sic)

[...you can open up directly with another woman, but not with a Muslim man...with him...it's more...well, a bit...more correct, a lot...he's not your husband, you can't...there's a connection that you can't make.] -Hawa, Malian

First, it is worth highlighting Sumaya's interjection: 'you already know'. While my own (distinct) heritage background was known to her at the time of the interview, Sumaya seemed to draw on our shared religious identity in assuming that I would be able to understand or relate to her reported linguistic behavior. This supports the idea that religious identity plays an integral role in constructing the social space in which informants interact. Shifting to the other content of Sumaya and Hawa's responses, both separate Muslim men – regardless of ethnicity – as requiring greater social distance and more restrictions in their interactions. Moreover, they both characterize these distinctions with 'you can't' and 'you can', which perhaps suggests a sense of obligation to adhere to specific social rules for gendered interactions. In the case of Hawa, a 30-year-old homemaker, a further specification is offered, where she notes that a man who is not a woman's husband is off limits for more intimate interactions where 'a connection' can be made. Together, these comments may relate back to social structures in informants' countries of origin, where the predominant Islamic culture discourages mixed interactions between women and men. As seen in the examples above, informants appear to apply these rules to their new social surroundings in Spain, but perhaps only partially, in that they indicate applying them only to interlocutors who share their ethnic and/or religious identity, but disregard such expectations for interactions with others outside the Muslim immigrant community. This is further illustrated by Rabya:

I probably don't speak to them (Muslim men), because here the men don't...the ones that I've had experience with...you speak in a more distant manner...it's just about what needs...you don't socialize, basically. Whereas being a businesswoman here in Spain, if I were to have a meeting with a male or female, I wouldn't change the way I would speak...if they're speaking about a certain project or product that we're discussing...and...I wouldn't change the way I'd speak...so I guess it depends on my cultural surroundings, I would change based on that. -Rabya, Algerian American

Rabya similarly distinguishes the nature of her interactions with Muslims from those with Spaniards. She indicates more distant and transactional transactions with the former, while the gender of the interlocutor does not appear to matter to her when interacting with the latter group. While the examples above differentiate between the heritage or religious backgrounds of their interlocutors in the context of Spain, Iman situates these distinctions between interlocutors in Spain and in Morocco:

> Aquí en España, te sientes con...con más confianza de hablar con un hombre que hablar con la mujer allí...en Marruecos si quiero hablar con un hombre, es que te deja un poco incómoda, pero aquí era igual. Hombre, mujer, lo mismo...porque no...no sientes aquellos...los hombres como más...bueno, es hombre pero no es un hombre de Marruecos, no es hombres árabes...que son más cerrados, si estoy hablando...qué haces, qué dices, no tienes que comportar así, ¿sabes? Da igual...da respeta, tú comportas como...como quieres. Más abiertos, más...y dan igual. En Marruecos, no. Si hablas con hombre, tienes que...que buscar las palabras, cómo hablo, cómo comportar...te sientes incómoda. Aquí, de igual. (sic)
>
> [Here in Spain, you feel...more confidence speaking with a man than speaking with a woman there...in Morocco if I want to speak with a man, it leaves you a little uncomfortable, but here it was equal: man, woman, the same...because...you don't feel those...the men are more...well, it's a man but it's not a Moroccan man, they're not Arab men...that are more closed. If I'm speaking...what you do, what you say, you don't have to behave that way, you know? It makes no difference...you behave how... how you want. More open, more...and it makes no difference. In Morocco, no. If you speak with a man, you have to...have to search for the words, how I speak, how to behave...you feel uncomfortable. Here, it's all the same.] -Iman, Moroccan

While Iman's commentary echoes those of Sana, Sumaya, Hawa and Rabya, she now evokes two different spaces altogether – Spain and Morocco – and compares the different expectations encountered in each society. While it is not clear if Iman applies these gendered distinctions to her interactions with Moroccan and Spanish men in her local environment, her direct reference to differences in each country certainly lends further support to the idea that informants reflexively apply gendered interactional rules that are based on Spanish social structures and social structures from their countries of origin, depending on the background of their interlocutor.

The previous examples demonstrate how many informants maintain connections with local Muslim, immigrant communities, or how some of them may interact under differentiated social norms within such communities, particularly where the gender of the interlocutor is concerned. In some cases, however, informants also establish some degree of distance from these communities. Mona, for example, states directly that she does not socialize with Arabs, whom she had previously identified as being mostly Moroccan:

> Yo utiliza español aquí porque no conoces mucha gente de arabi...no tengo comunicado con muchos árabe aquí. Yo..la única comunicar...yo...mi familia...yo no queri comunicados más...yo no me gusta conocer muchos arabi...el mayoría de ellos...eh...les gusta mucho entra en la vida personal...yo...no me gusta la gente entrar de mi vida personal. (sic)
>
> [I use Spanish here because I do't know many Arab people...I don't communicate with many Arabs here. I...the only communication that...I...my family...I don't want to be in touch with anyone else...I don't like knowing many Arabs...the majority of them...eh...they really like to get into your personal life...I...I don't like people getting into my personal life.] -Mona, Egyptian

While discussing her linguistic practices, and more specifically, which languages she specifically uses in her day-to-day interactions, she indicates that she primarily relies on Spanish, since she not only knows very few Arabs, but also prefers not to speak with other Arabs, besides members of her own family. Much like in her previous comment regarding Moroccans taking advantage of government assistance and attributing this to Spanish racism, Mona once again shares a negative generalization, this time about Arabs more generally, and offers this as a reason for preferring not to interact with other Arabs.

However, Mona is not alone in her negative attitudes toward immigrant communities. Khadija, a 40-year-old Moroccan homemaker, similarly criticizes women in particular, though in her case, focuses more broadly on Muslims:

> Las mujeres...no me dicho *'salamu-alaikum'*...¿y por qué? Es muslim...¿por qué no...dice *salamu-alaikum*? Español, él me dicho, 'hola', 'gracias', 'adiós'...está bien, ¿no? No sé qué. (sic)
>
> [Women...they don't say 'peace be upon you'...and why? It's Muslim...why don't they...say 'peace be upon you'. A Spaniard, he says, 'hi,' 'thanks,' 'bye,'...it's alright, isn't it? I don't know what.] - Khadija, Moroccan

Here, Khadija complains that Muslim women do not acknowledge her with the traditional Islamic greeting, 'peace be upon you', which is frequently used among Muslims of all ethnicities, with friends and strangers alike, and in any variety of formal and informal interactions, including with momentary run-ins with Muslim passersby. She contrasts this distance with the interaction norms of Spaniards, indicating that they observe such courtesies. Khadija wonders why Muslims might not extend courtesies to one another, which suggests not only a belief that she views religious identity as a point of solidarity that transcends cultural or ethnic divides, but also a belief that this is a heritage practice that should be maintained among Muslim immigrants. Rabya similarly broaches this topic and points out that, perhaps for some Muslims, this is not the case, and that for some, one's heritage identity might precede religious identity:

> (and do you feel connected to the Muslim community here?)
>
> No...no, I don't. I tried to be...
>
> (What do you think stops -)
>
> I think the...the group of Muslims that are here are not necessarily um... diverse. So there are a lot of - mostly Moroccans, as I'm sure you've experienced, and they usually tend to come straight from Morocco, here. So they're still stuck in...well, I wouldn't say stuck, cause that sounds a little bit negative, but they're - they have their cultures and they only look at that...and...they don't really see Islam as...a world religion, but more... their thing, part of their culture. So if you as Muslim - but from a different culture yourself, try to integrate with them, it doesn't work because you clash in terms of culture. So...
>
> (Even among Arabs?)
>
> Yeah, definitely, yeah.
>
> (So they're kind of exclusive?)
>
> Exactly. Exclusive, close-minded...yeah.
>
> (Is it just the Moroccan Muslim community?)
>
> Honestly, I've only seen the Moroccan community, I haven't experienced other...countries here. I know there are a lot of Pakistanis here, but I haven't necessarily spoken to them. Just because the mosque I go to has mostly Moroccans there.
>
> (The one where we met?)
>
> I go there sometimes, but there's another one that's exclusively Moroccan...but it's a nice, big mosque, so I like to go there because it's spacious and...and...yeah, but I just don't feel...no not at all. -Rabya, Algerian American

Here, Rabya is critical – albeit hesitantly – of the local Moroccan community, pointing out that their status as the Muslim majority may result in their obfuscating Islamic identity and Moroccan identity and consequently excluding Muslims of other backgrounds who may have otherwise been able to identify with them. As a result of this, Rabya, an Algerian-American Muslim, reports that she has been unable to connect with the predominantly Moroccan Muslim community. This separation between Moroccans and non-Moroccans, however, is not an uncommon sentiment. Aisha, who herself is Moroccan, also differentiates herself from other Arabs, but only does so with regard to linguistic differences and needing to accommodate non-Moroccan Arabic speakers:

(...Y cuando hablas con árabes de otros países, y...¿Entonces hay que hablar en fus-ha? ¿Tienes dificultades con esto? ¿O ya te sientes cómoda?)

Sí...pero...no sé por qué Marruecos...por ejemplo, si me encuentro con una de Egipto, una chica de Egipto, ella me..no me va a entender...mi lengua. Pero yo lo entiendo de ella...porque la televisión allí...pasan películas, eso de origen Egipto más que..tiene más cine, todo de esto.. entonces...dominamos el el...dialecto de Egipto, por ejemplo..te doy un ejemplo. Entonces yo lo entiendo..ella me habla y yo lo entiendo perfectamente...ele poda hablar del..de...de su idioma, o sea..yo puedo - de su dialecto puedo contestar...pero...si yo hablo mio, ella no me ella no me... entenderá. (sic) -Aisha

(...and when you talk with Arabs from other countries...and...so do you speak in Standard Arabic? Do you have difficulties with this? Or do you feel comfortable?)

[Yes...but...I don't know why Morocco...for example, if I meet with someone from Egypt, a girl from Egypt, she...she won't understand me... my language. But I understand hers....because TV there...they make movies, of Egyptian origin more than...they have more cinema, all of that...so....we master the the...dialect of Egypt, for example...I'll give you an example. So I understand it...she speaks to me and I understand it perfectly...she can speak with...with her language, that is...I can..I can answer in her dialect...but...if I speak mine, she won't...understand me.] -Aisha, Moroccan

In this example, we come somewhat closer to seeing specific differences that may create distance between Moroccan and non-Moroccan Arabic speakers, which may also result in creating a general sense of disconnect with immigrant communities for some informants. Aisha describes the difficulties in communicating with speakers of non-Moroccan Arabic dialects, in that her dialect is less intelligible to Arabic speakers from other countries. However, since the reverse is not the case, this places the responsibility on Aisha – and similarly, other speakers of Moroccan Arabic – to accommodate Arabic speakers from other countries. Since she does not elaborate on her attitudes toward this tendency, this also raises the question as to whether or not such accommodation is done readily.

Additional Comments

In this chapter, I examined how the linguistic practices of first-generation immigrants' connect with their acculturation experiences, as well as the role of both TL and immigrant communities in shaping these experiences. Language learning, as in any society, plays a crucial role in the extent to which an immigrant may feel a part of the TL community. In the case here, informants typically emphasized learning Spanish as their main priority, while Catalan was either a secondary goal or not a priority at all. This may be a reflection of viewing language learning as serving instrumental purposes – where Spanish is viewed as more widely used in Spain and therefore of more utility than Catalan. This is further evidenced by some informants' reference to English as being a valuable language to learn, given its global purview. Indeed, English appears to play a significant role in the interactions of first-generation informants. For some informants, English was regarded as a useful language to know, especially in the context of a touristy and metropolitan hub like Barcelona. For others, particularly South Asian informants, English was already a part of their linguistic repertoire prior to moving to Spain and appeared to be an integral part of their linguistic practices, even in situations where other languages (i.e. Urdu) could be used exclusively.

While some informants indicated a disinterest in Catalan, very few expressed indifference or resistance to integration more broadly in Spanish society, and typically attributed this attitude toward cultural differences and, at times, the attitudes they perceived from members of the TL community. The latter is a particularly significant aspect of social processes such as integration, in that it highlights the bidirectional nature of this process. Specifically, informants frequently described their experiences in relation to how they have been treated or regarded by members of the TL community, in both positive and negative ways. While bidirectionality in integration is certainly recognized in scholarly research as well as in political discourse such as language policies and planning measures, the reality that is illustrated here is that members of the TL community do not always recognize the shared responsibility of assisting in the social integration of immigrant populations, an issue that merits further consideration by policymakers (see Chapter 9). As was demonstrated in this chapter, a number of informants have certainly had negative experiences with the TL community insofar as their heritage or religious practices – such as wearing a *hijab* or speaking Arabic in public – are seen as 'foreign' or as outside the realm of Spanish or Catalan culture. While this form of othering can be obscured by instances in which first-generation informants have not integrated (for example, not having a strong command of Catalan and/or Spanish, willfully or not), positioning immigrants as Others becomes more salient when it persists even among second-generation immigrants, as will be shown in Chapter 6.

Equally important to how informants negotiate their identities is the extent to which they identify with their respective immigrant communities, which can be characterized by both ethnic/heritage background, as well as religious identity. From this study, it is apparent that several informants employed distinct linguistic practices in the TL and immigrant communities. While language choice is certainly one parameter by which linguistic behavior may differ between communities – a tendency that is more pronounced in informants' questionnaire responses (see Chapter 7) – the informants' narratives highlighted another significant difference; namely, reporting distinct discursive practices when interacting with female and male interlocutors from their immigrant communities. For many women, interacting with Muslim men and/or men of their heritage background meant communicating with a greater degree of formality and distance than with female interlocutors of the same background. These gendered differences were reportedly absent from their interactions with members of the TL community. For others, such as Iram, male interlocutors appeared to be almost entirely absent from their social interactions, thus allowing these informants to position themselves in essentially female-only social circles. This is an especially noteworthy aspect of informants' linguistic behavior, as it illustrates not only how religious and gendered identities function collectively in informing discursive practices, but also how such intersectional identities are performed selectively in a diasporic context.

While various informants reported adapting their linguistic behavior, most reported some degree of connection to their respective immigrant communities, and very few expressed a desire to maintain distance or disconnect from them entirely. These few instances, however, appeared to reflect a clash of beliefs and attitudes regarding religious identity and how it should be manifested in a diasporic context. For example, the use of Islamic greetings – even between unacquainted Muslims – may be regarded as a practice that should be observed everywhere, regardless of whether or not the society is considered predominantly Muslim. Others, however, may prefer to dispense with this practice if it is not part of the socially dominant culture. Similarly, while some may view Islam as a global religion and an identity that cuts across geopolitical and cultural boundaries, others may see it as being bounded within their own culture. Along with linguistic barriers (such as communication barriers presented among speakers of different varieties of Arabic), these elements can all contribute to fragmentation among immigrant communities and thus result in a degree of disconnect for first-generation immigrants.

Notes

(1) While Iram describes her connections to other Pakistani women, she herself identifies as Indian. While these South Asian nationalities certainly have sociocultural, linguistic and – most notably – political distinctions, there is also a significant overlap in these areas. Additionally, her reference to the Pakistani community – rather than an Indian community – may also be attributed to the fact that the Pakistani immigrant community in Barcelona is significantly larger than that of the Indian immigrant community. As such, many Indian immigrants – particularly those who are Muslim – may identify more closely with the Pakistani community.
(2) See Ali (2021) for a more detailed account, where these analyses originally appear.

6 In Two Worlds: Narratives of Second-Generation Informants

Introduction

The previous chapter illustrates how first-generation informants' gendered, religious identity impacts their positionality in relation to the target language (TL) and immigrant communities with which they most closely associate, as well as how their interactions in these communities shape linguistic ideologies and practices. This chapter explores how these same relationships are regarded among second-generation informants. Where first-generation informants identify as L2 speakers of Spanish and Catalan, second-generation informants are typically native speakers of these languages (though, as shown in Table 4.1 in Chapter 4, not all second-generation informants identified these languages as such). Furthermore, most of the languages spoken by first-generation informants are now the heritage languages (HLs) of second-generation informants (primarily Arabic). This change in speaker type (heritage, native, L2) certainly has an impact on how they are positioned within the communities in which they interact, as well as how they use each of the languages in their linguistic repertoire. However, as I show in this chapter, their visible gendered and religious identity often positions many second-generation informants as outsiders, often being viewed as indistinguishable from their parents' generation in terms of the extent to which they are viewed as having acculturated, and thus the extent to which they 'belong' in the TL community. As in Chapter 5, I will use my interviews with second-generation informants to first illustrate their relationship with the immigrant community and the role of HLs, and second, their relationship with the TL community and the role of Catalan and Spanish. Through each of these discussions, I examine how informants' reported linguistic behavior and attitudes interact in relation to these communities, as well as the role of gender and religion in shaping these interactions.

Connections to Immigrant Communities: Heritage Language Use

For the second-generation informants in this study – and indeed what comprises a defining component of HL speakers' experiences – an individual's relationship with the HL and HL communities begins at home and specifically with their caregivers. Moreover, this is often the only exposure to the HL that many second-generation immigrants may have in their day-to-day lives. Sharifa, a 24-year-old salesperson of Moroccan descent, points to her upbringing as her connection to Moroccan culture:

> Bueno, es que la cultura (marroquí)...la aprendo en casa, ¿sabes? No es fuera...todo lo que...sé de las culturas de - o sea, de convivir - con gente marroquí, con mis padres, y también pues de haber ido a Marruecos y aprender eso.
>
> [Well, it's that the culture...I learn it at home, you know? Not outside... everything that...I know about the cultures...I mean, spending time with Moroccan people, with my parents, and also having been to Morocco and learning that.] -Sharifa, Moroccan

This is also the case for informants of other backgrounds. Humaa, a 25 year-old doctor of Pakistani descent, had invited me into her home to interview her and her sister. It was also there that I was able to observe some familial interactions and noted her siblings' and parents' comfortable conversations in Urdu. During her interview, she notes her parents' role in her Urdu usage:

> ...mi madre conoce a muchas uh..señoras pakistaníes, entonces sus hijos pues también eran pakistaníes, entonces he tenido relación con las dos culturas...si no nos hubieran seguido hablando en casa urdu, acabar no lo dominaríamos.
>
> [...my mom knows a lot of, uh...Pakistani women, so their kids, well, they also were Pakistani, so I had a relationship with the two cultures... if they (our parents) hadn't kept speaking to us at home in Urdu, we wouldn't be fluent in it.] -Humaa, Pakistani

In these examples, it is evident that upbringing plays an important role in the HL and cultural knowledge. While Humaa acknowledges that her proficiency in Urdu is a direct result of her parents choosing to socialize with other Pakistanis and maintain Urdu use at home, Sharifa focuses on culture rather than language, indicating that her heritage culture was learned at home and further specifies that other Moroccans – including her parents – exposed her to Moroccan culture, suggesting some degree of connection with the local Moroccan community. However, she also distinguishes these people, who form part of her environment 'at home', from those with whom she interacts 'outside'. This juxtaposition creates a distinct separation between two communities and two sets of speakers – those who are Moroccan and those who are not. This separation is not only an important component in constructing dual identities among many HL speakers but may also be a source of othering when interacting with the TL community (see 'Connections to TL Community'). Additionally, exposure to the HL at home is an experience that second-generation informants recognize as uniquely theirs and an important aspect of identity:

> Yo espero que no se pierda, porque es una pena, me gustaría que se conservara, es importante...yo creo que...al fin y al cabo, es parte de tu identidad, o sea...te hace un poco más diferente o tener algo especial...no sé... es importante, es bonito...al nivel cultural.
>
> [I hope it's not lost, because it's a shame, I'd like for it to be preserved, it's important...I think that...in the end, it's part of your identity, I mean, it makes you a little more different or have something special...I don't know...it's important, it's beautiful...at the cultural level.] -Humaa, Pakistani

While speaking about Urdu usage in her family, Humaa expresses a desire to see her HL maintained, identifying it as an important cultural component as well as a unique aspect of individual identity. Dina, a 23-year-old data analyst of Moroccan descent, echoes these sentiments, referencing her younger brother's generation as an example of a newfound pride in heritage and religious identity:

> La generación de mi hermano pequeño – tiene 18 años – y los más pequeños también...están como, muy orgullosos de su identidad marroquí...y la defienden pues...usando muchos elementos culturales marroquíes... tanto chicos como chicas. Y usando muchas palabras marroquíes en la conversación. Por ejemplo, escuchas esas chicas hablando de 15 años, y dicen '*habibti*, nos vemos luego,' eh, ¿sabes? 'Vale, *zwina*,' cosas que yo nunca usaba...y ahora sí que lo hacen y de hecho...creo yo que hay un aspecto religioso...decíamos 'si Dios quiere' o 'nos vemos' o 'voy a rezar,' 'voy a ayunar' y ahora...se usa mucho '*insha Allah*' '*salamu alaikum*' '*barak Allahu fi*' todas de estas cosas...sin usar la traducción. Y creo que también es...como, mostrar que eres musulmán árabe, a través del idioma.
>
> [My little brother's generation – he's 18 – and the younger ones too... they're like...very proud of their Moroccan identity...and they represent it...well, using a lot of Moroccan cultural elements....boys and girls alike. And using Moroccan words in conversation. For example, you hear those 15 year old girls talking, and they say 'honey, see you later,' you know? 'Ok, good,' things that I never used...and now they do it and in fact...I think there's a religious aspect...we used to say 'God willing' or 'see you later' or 'I'm going to pray' 'I'm going to fast' and now...they use a lot of

'God willing' 'peace be upon you' 'God bless you' all of these things, without using the translation. I also think it's...like, showing that you are an Arab Muslim...through language.] -Dina, Moroccan

Here, Dina – who is only a little older than her brother – illustrates how her brother's generation uses Arabic to reflect Moroccan and Arab identity, which includes vocabulary specific to Moroccan Arabic, such as *zwina*, vocabulary more widely used across Arabic dialects, such as *habibti*, and Arabic vocabulary with religious connotations that are familiar to many Muslims, regardless of linguistic or cultural background. As such, Dina points out that this practice is not only a display of heritage identity, but also religious identity. Interestingly, however, she describes this identity specifically as Arab Muslim, rather than simply Muslim, which echoes some of what Rabya had described (see Chapter 5) regarding Moroccan communities seeing Islam as a culturally specific practice, rather than a global one.

Second-generation informants generally conveyed an affinity for their HLs and cultures, as well as having interactions with the HL community through familial relationships. However, for some informants, identifying with the HL culture and language reflects more recently acquired attitudes. Sharifa, noted earlier for attributing her HL exposure to her parents, described how her attitude toward Arabic shifted in a more positive direction as she grew older:

De pequeña, sí que igual intentaba integrarme más, sentía más española, me daba vergüenza hablar en árabe, porque me quería sentir más...identificada...pero creo que, con el tiempo, en adolescencia, pues, cambias... te sientes más orgullosa de tus raíces, y de tu cultura, pues, de origen...o sea, dejes de renegar.

[As a kid, I certainly tried to integrate myself more, I felt more Spanish, I was ashamed of speaking in Arabic, because I wanted to feel more...identified...but I think that with time, in adolescence, well, you change...you feel prouder of your roots, of your culture, well, of your origin...that is, you stop rejecting it.] -Sharifa, Moroccan

While Dina described an attitudinal change that she identified as generational – that is, from one sibling to the next – Sharifa indicates an individual attitudinal shift that she experienced over the course of her upbringing, from childhood to adolescence. For Sharifa, her childhood sense of being Spanish was incompatible with her Arab identity and thus marked her knowledge of Arabic as a point of self-consciousness. As a young adult, however, she indicates a strong shift in how she identified with her heritage – from abject rejection of it to taking pride in it.

However, not all second-generation informants necessarily have strong connections with their respective HL communities. Rather, in many cases, the HL ties they have are with other second-generation peers who similarly have distanced themselves to a certain extent from the HL communities and instead have stronger connections with the TL communities.

> Tengo conexiones con la española...porque crearme aquí...mis amigos son mas españoles aunque tengo marroquíes, pero estamos como todos muy adaptados aquí..entonces.
> (¿Sientes que eres más española que marroquí?)
> Sí, sí.
>
> [I have Spanish connections...because being raised here...my friends are more Spanish, although I do have Moroccan (friends), but we're very adapted here.
> (do you feel that you're more Spanish than Moroccan?)
> Yes, yes.] -Souhaila, Moroccan

Souhaila, a 25-year-old nanny, attributes her connections to the Spanish-speaking community and to her upbringing in Spain, though without any reference to Catalan or the Catalan-speaking community, despite having grown up in Catalonia. While she concedes that she has Moroccan friends, she points out that, like herself, they have adapted to Spanish culture to the extent that she considers herself more Spanish than Moroccan.

While Souhaila was among the few second-generation informants to explicitly indicate a stronger identification with the Spanish-speaking community over the HL community, a number of informants questioned whether first-generation members of the HL community rely too much on their native languages or remain too attached to their heritage cultures at the expense of adapting to Spanish and/or Catalan culture:

> A veces...hacen exactamente lo mismo que una familia en Marruecos... no han - no han intentado a adaptarse aquí. No..no se han integrado, 100%. Es como si..han..han traído otro sitio de Marruecos aquí, y...no lo veo del todo correcto.
>
> [Sometimes, they do exactly the same thing as a family in Morocco...they haven't tried to adapt here. They haven't integrated 100%. It's as if...they have brought another Moroccan place here, and...I don't see it as altogether correct.] -Mariam, Moroccan

> Los que hemos venido desde joven, que sí, estamos muy adoptados, pero los que vinieron más de 5 años...o 10 años...como que..siguen con su cultura que no van a cambiar, porque se piensan que es algo malo.
>
> (¿Es problemático?)
>
> Claro...se piensan que es algo malo que van a perder su..sus valores y sus intereses por simplemente adaptarse aquí, y eso no es así. Tú puedes adaptar sin perder nada tu cultura ni tus valores ni tus intereses...y no se adaptan.

[Those of us who came here young, we're very adapted, but those that came here older than five years old...or 10 years old, they keep with their culture and they aren't going to change, because they think that it's something bad.

(is it problematic?)

Of course...they think that it's a bad thing that they're going to lose their...their values and interests simply by adapting here and it isn't like that. You can adapt without losing your culture, your values, or your interests....and they don't adapt.] -Souhaila, Moroccan

Both Mariam and Souhaila are critical of first-generation immigrants in their HL communities, citing that they have not integrated enough on account of their maintaining practices and behaviors that are normative in Morocco but not in Spain. Souhaila goes on to suggest that this may be due to an expectation that adapting to Spanish culture comes at the expense of one's heritage identity, which she denies. Humaa similarly assigns distinguishing characteristics of first- and second-generation immigrants relating to differences in beliefs and attitudes:

...ellos tienen otro punto, otra visión...somos más abiertos...nuestros padres tienen los valores, pero nosotros...un poco más abiertos.

[...they have another perspective, another vision...we're more open...our parents have values, but we're...a little more open.] -Humaa, Pakistani

While she does not overtly criticize first-generation immigrants for a lack of cultural or social adaptation in the way that Mariam and Souhaila do, Humaa does characterize her own generation more favorably in being more open, which may be interpreted as a tacit comment on the extent to which first-generation immigrants in her HL community have embraced Spanish/Catalan values. This was additionally echoed by Souhaila. While I was interviewing Aziza, a 45-year-old maid who is also Souhaila's mother and a first-generation Moroccan immigrant, Souhaila interrupted to question her mother's responses. This exchange – which focuses on acceptable styles of communication depending on one's interlocutors – highlights the generational differences between mother and daughter that are strongly informed by their respective affinities for heritage and Spanish cultures. To provide some additional context to this conversation, Aziza and Souhaila were my hosts during my stay in Mataró, and so over the course of a few weeks, I had been privy to numerous mother–daughter conversations, many of which involved disagreements about what they each considered acceptable social behavior, particularly around men. Souhaila's and Aziza's interviews occurred near the end of my sojourn, so our relative ease around each other may have been a contributing factor to lack of hesitation with which they allowed me to record this impromptu conversation. This dialogue is transcribed below.

> Aziza: Amigos, bueno, amigos no, amigas.
> [friends, well...male friends, no, female friends]
>
> Souhaila: Pues, esto es cerrado..esto no es abierto
> [well, this is close-minded...this isn't open-minded]
>
> Aziza: Por primer el religión no- (sic)
> [because of religion, no-]
>
> Souhaila: ¿No te permite hablar con gente?
> [It doesn't allow you to speak with people?]
>
> Aziza: Gente, no. Amigos..para ser un...un hombre amigo..vin a mi casa y- (sic)
> [People, no. Male friends....to be a...man friend...coming to my house and-]
>
> Souhaila: No, no hace falta que venga a tu casa, para ser tu amigo..no-
> [No, they don't need to come to your house, to be your friend...no-]
>
> Aziza: ¿y tomar un café con él?
> [and have coffee with him?]
>
> Souhaila: Pues, claro, estás tomando café, no te estás-
> [Well, of course, you're having coffee, you're not-]
>
> Aziza: Estás loca, que voy a tomar un café..no-
> [You're crazy, that I'm going to have coffee...no-]
>
> Souhaila: a ver, escúchame, escúchame-
> [Look, listen to me, listen to me-]
>
> Aziza: Escúchame tú.
> [You listen to me]
>
> Souhaila: Yo puedo...mi amigo, yo puedo ir con él a tomar un café, puedo ir a la playa, y no pasa nada, y no te falta que pase nada...vosotros...o sea...dices que no podemos tener amigos porque va a pasar algo...es porque -
> [I can...my male friend, I can go with him to have coffee, I can go to the beach, and nothing happens, and you don't need anything to happen... you all...I mean...you say we can't have male friends because something is going to happen...it's because-]
>
> Aziza: No, no va a pasar algo, porque el religión está prohibido una mujer con un hombre..está prohibido. (sic)
> [No, nothing is going to happen, because the religion prohibits a woman being with a man. It is prohibited.]
>
> Souhaila: Entonces...me voy a casar con él..Si -
> [So...I'm going to marry him...if-]

Aziza: No, casa (sic) con el porque estoy casada y además no puedo ir con -
[No, you don't marry him because I'm married and additionally I can't go with-]

Souhaila: Pero espérate...antes de - quiero entender - antes de casarme con él, ¿cómo voy a hablar con él? ¿Y cómo voy-
[But wait...before - I want to understand - before marrying him, how am I going to speak with him? And how am I going to-]

Aziza: Vas a hablar..pero tienes que estar con...al lado de la familia, o-
[You're going to speak...but you have to be with...the family's side, or-]

Souhaila: Pues, que miedo, ¿no? Viene el hombre...'Hola, ¿é tal? Ven con mi familia'
[Well, pretty scary, no? The man comes... 'hi, how are you? Come with my family.']

Aziza: La familia está siendo aquí, para que no pasa (sic) nada.
[The family is here so nothing happens.]

Souhaila: A ver, tú dices están más - españoles más cerrados. ¿Por qué? ¿Por qué los españoles están cerrados?
[Look, you say that they're more - Spaniards are more closed. Why? Why are Spanish more closed?]

Aziza: A ver, yo...lo que vi...yo tengo amigas marroquíes, más que españoles...y que-
[Look, I...what I saw...I have Moroccan friends, more than Spanish.... and-]

Souhaila: Y por eso puedes decir que son más -
[and because of that you can say they're more-]

Aziza: Un español va a decir, 'Hola, ¿qué tal?' Puedes hacer con - no..no voy a hablar con un español para ser mi amiga...
[A Spaniard is going to say 'Hi, how are you?' You can with- no, I'm not going to speak with a Spaniard so they'll be my (female) friend]

Souhaila: Pero, ¿por qué? Yo te estoy preguntando (unintel)...¿Por qué somos más cerrados?
[But why? I'm asking you...why are we more closed?]

Aziza: Porque ellos teni (sic) miedo de los árabes...no-
[Because they're afraid of Arabs...no-]

Souhaila: Pero esto no es cerrado..cerrado es..por ejemplo, em., que.... excluyen.....esto es racismo.
[But that isn't closed...closed is...for example, em...that...they exclude... this is racism.]

Aziza: Pero eso..lo que haces...(unintel)...mi religión ni nada.
[But that...what you do...(unintel)...my religion or anything.]

Souhaila: Pero eso es abierto, esto es mentalidad abierta..lo que yo hago... yo hablo con todo el mundo, tengo amigos de..como marroquíes, tengo-

[But that is open, this is open-mindedness...what I do...I talk with everyone, I have friends from...like Moroccans, I have-]

Aziza: no puedes hacer amigos, no-
[You can't make male friends, not-]

Souhaila: ¿Cómo? (unintel) me puede hacer amigos? (unintel) sola toda la vida-
[What? (unintel) make male friends? (unintel) alone entire life-]

Aziza: La vida no, se puede hacer-
[Life, no, you can make-]

Souhaila: Solo chicas.
[just girls.]

Aziza: No, todo el mundo...amigos, ami-
[no, everyone...male friends-]

Souhaila: ¿Amigos?
[male friends?]

Aziza: No.
[No.]

Souhaila: Mente abierta es esto.
[This is an open mind.]

Aziza: No.
[No.]

Souhaila: Eso es - mira, tú eres cerrada, yo soy abierta.
[That is - look, you're closed, I'm open.]

Aziza: No..perdóname..esto es lo que tú haces es loco.
[No, excuse me, what you do is crazy.]

Souhaila: Pues ahora esta es de locos.
[well now this is crazy.]

There are a number of interesting observations regarding this dialogue between mother and daughter. First, it is clear that Aziza and Souhaila have distinct views on acceptable manners of communication, and – more importantly – choice of interlocutors. Aziza indicates disapproval toward the idea of interacting with Spaniards – attributing her reluctance to xenophobia that she perceives from Spaniards. She also disagrees with her daughter regarding relationships with men, indicating that being alone with men and/or developing close relationships with them would be inappropriate and against her values as a Muslim. In strong disagreement, Souhaila calls her mother 'closed' for her attitudes toward Spaniards and men. She rejects these views, indicating that it would be uncomfortable and even impossible to marry a man if she were not allowed to be alone with him beforehand. Souhaila also questions the labels her mother uses, arguing that her mother was perhaps referring to experiences with racism from Spaniards, but that this was not the same as being 'closed', and in fact accuses her mother of being closed for not being more amenable to forming relationships with Spaniards. Souhaila also points to herself as an example of an open person who interacts with everyone. This, however, brings them back to the discussion of gender relations, where – for Aziza – 'everyone' should not include men.

In this exchange, we also see that Souhaila refers to herself as Spaniard, invoking 'nosotros' (we) and includes herself as part of the group that her mother is criticizing. Interestingly, Aziza does not mirror this in her response and refers to Spaniards as 'ellos' (they), excluding her daughter from that group as she accuses them of being xenophobic where Arabs are concerned.

While Souhaila strongly disagreed with her mother on all counts, other second-generation informants may conform more to Aziza's way of thinking, which may reflect how gendered identity is constructed through informants' religious and/or ethnic identity. This is evident in their self-reported language use through a pattern of interacting primarily with other female interlocutors, which was also seen frequently among first-generation informants in the previous chapter. For example, Mariam frequently uses feminine markers when referring to the friends with whom she interacts:

> Con mis amigas...que son de aquí también – árabes - pues, sí que alterno el español con el árabe...cuando estoy en Marruecos, pues, con mis amigas allí, alternamos el árabe con el francés...Yo no empezaría una conversación en catalán, no sé...nunca he hablado con mis amigas en catalán.
>
> [With my friends...that are from here as well – Arabs - well, I switch between Spanish and Arabic...when I am in Morocco, well, with my female friends there, we switch between Arabic and French...I would not start a conversation in Catalan, I don't know...I've never spoken with my friends in Catalan.] -Mariam, Moroccan

As shown above, the use of feminine markers in the context of generalizing her interactions suggests that for several of these informants, women are perhaps the default interlocutors with whom they interact. However, it must also be taken into consideration that in instances such as the above, informants spoke specifically about interactions involving their HL and other HL speakers who, like them, may also identify as Muslim. This factor bears some relevance, as one topic of discussion in the interview was stylistic variation in interactions with different genders, and how religious and/or ethnic identity plays a role in this variation.

Nasreen, a 20-year-old student of Moroccan descent, observed that her own speech was distinctive depending on the gender of her interlocutor, and further commented on how this tendency was not present in her speech as a child, but rather something she developed as she became older:

> Pues, con las mujeres te sientes, como...más tranquila, más en conexión...y con los hombres siempre hay esta' barrera de respeto para que no pueda sobrepasarse...siendo joven...no le das valor. Tratas a todo el mundo igual. Pero...creciendo...vas...con más conocimiento, y sabiendo de que entre el hombre y la mujer tiene que haber un cierto límite...si fueras un hombre...no estaría...con tanta fluidez, y hablando así...estaría un poco más contenida.
>
> [Well, with women you feel, like...calmer, more connected...and with men there is always this barrier of respect so that they can't pass...being young...you don't give it any value. You treat everybody equally. But...growing up...you go...with more knowledge, and knowing that between men and women there has to be a certain limit...if you were a man...I wouldn't be...with so much flow, and talking like this...I would be a bit more restrained.] -Nasreen, Moroccan

Here, Nasreen offers similar descriptors when characterizing her conversations with female and male interlocutors, and further points out that gendered distinctions in interactions come from maturation. Moreover, she suggests that these differences also reflect social mores or expectations that are learned and further exemplifies this by observing that her discursive practices during the interview itself were indeed informed by the fact that I as the interviewer also identified as a woman. Souhaila, in keeping with her attitudes illustrated in the conversation with her mother, was among the few second-generation informants to observe a shift in the opposite direction from Nasreen, where she distanced herself from the HL community as she became older:

> Antes mis preferencias eran los marroquíes y ahora mis preferencias son más...las de aquí. O sea es como...digamos...que antes era más cerrada...y me he ido adaptando poco a poco y he visto que por...salir con mis amigos, por tener amigos chicos, no dejo de ser musulmana, ni soy mala musulmana, ni nada de eso...simplemente me he adaptado.
>
> [Before my preferences were for Moroccans and now my preferences are more...for those here. That is, it's like...let's say...before I was more close-minded...and I've been adapting little by little, and I've seen that through...going out with my friends, through having male friends, I don't stop being Muslim, nor am I a bad Muslim, or anything like that...I've simply adapted.] -Souhaila, Moroccan

As in the earlier cited example of Nasreen, who indicated that varying her style of conversation according to gender was something that did not happen until she became older, Souhaila also indicates a shift from her youth. However, for Souhaila, rather than adopting the gendered distinctions of which Nasreen became increasingly more conscious, Souhaila instead indicates that she contested the social structures that governed her youth, attributing her previous attitudes as a reflection of close-mindedness. However, Souhaila also points out that the changes in her interactions – namely, interacting with more men – ultimately does not alter or take away from her Muslim identity or reflect negatively on her in any way.

Connections to the TL Community: The Role of Catalan

Most of the informants that I classified as second generation were born and raised in Catalonia, and those who were not and were generation 1.5 – having moved to Catalonia before school age – have all had significant exposure to Catalan and Spanish over the course of their upbringing. Still, many of these informants do not have the same experiences and relationship to the TL community as other members whose parents are not first-generation immigrants, which in itself is informed by a number of factors. Of course, for second-generation informants who have been raised and educated in Catalonia, it is unsurprising that they express strong connections with the TL community. This is perhaps most clearly seen through educational and other professional interactions, and more specifically through the use of Catalan. A number of second-generation informants assigned Catalan as an institutional language which they used frequently – given their university-level education – but not outside the educational sphere. Humaa, for instance, is a doctor who recently completed medical school and indicates the prevalence of Catalan in her professional (and to an extent, social) interactions:

> La mayoría de mis amigos habla catalán...hablamos en catalán...en catalán, me sale más natural, más rápido...pero porque...o sea, tengo más facilidad porque la mayoría de mis amigos en el instituto, en la universidad...hablan en catalán.
>
> [Most of my friends speak Catalan...we speak in Catalan...in Catalan, it comes out more naturally for me, more quickly...but because...that is, I have greater ease with it because the majority of my friends in the institute, in the university...they speak Catalan.] -Humaa, Pakistani

Here, Humaa identifies Catalan as the language which she is perhaps most comfortable using, describing it as coming naturally and most quickly to her, as well as the language that the majority of her friends use. It is also worth noting that since Humaa indicates that her friends are from the university, where Catalan is the official vehicular language, it is uncertain whether their use of Catalan comes from a preference independent of or as a result of using it in their day-to-day professional and educational interactions. Sharifa differs somewhat from Humaa, indicating that her use of Catalan is limited to her educational environment:

> Fuera de casa, pues, catalán y castellano indistintamente. No...quizá más castellano, pero bueno, catalán también sin problemas...pero en la escuela, la universidad, y eso...más catalán, pero en la calle en Barcelona,

se habla más castellano...En mi casa, hablo darija y español...60% español, 40% darija. Con mis hermanos quizá más castellano.

[Outside of the house, well, Catalan and Spanish equally. No...maybe more Spanish, but well, also Catalan without problems...but in school, in the university, and all that...more Catalan, but on the street in Barcelona, Spanish is spoken more...In my house, I speak Moroccan Arabic and Spanish...60% Spanish, 40% Moroccan Arabic. With my siblings maybe more Spanish.] -Sharifa, Moroccan

While she similarly indicates that she uses Catalan at her university, she begins by saying that she uses both Catalan and Spanish equally, but then clarifies that she uses Spanish outside of school ('on the streets') and Arabic at home, presumably with her parents since she reports using Spanish with her siblings. Mariam similarly indicates minimal use of Catalan, reserving it more for the educational sphere, but not a language in which she would initiate a conversation:

Yo trabajo...en un centro comercial donde...hay muchos turistas, entonces pues, hablo inglés y español. Con mis amigas...son de aquí también - eh, árabes, pues, sí que alterno el español con el árabe...yo no empezaría una conversación en catalán, no sé...nunca...nunca he hablado con mis amigas en catalán. Nunca. O sea, lo he utilizado en el...en el instituto, porque era el idioma obligatorio, principal...con el que nos enseñan...y ya está. Pero fuera del instituto hablamos el español.

[I work...in a mall where...there are a lot of tourists, and so, I speak English and Spanish. With my friends...they're from here too - eh, Arabs, well, I alternate with Spanish and Arabic...I wouldn't start a conversation in Catalan, I don't know...never...I've never spoken with my friends in Catalan. Never. That is, I've used in the...in the institute, because it was the obligatory, principal language...with which they teach us...and that's it. But outside the institute we speak in Spanish.] -Mariam, Moroccan

Here, Mariam explicitly states that her use of Catalan is not just limited to her interactions at her educational institution, but also that her use of Catalan is not a matter of choice and does not reflect her own personal preferences. She goes on to explain that Spanish is her preferred language, as well as the language that she uses at her place of work, which draws a great deal of tourists and requires languages that are more widely spoken than Catalan, such as Spanish and English.

From the above interview excerpts, it is evident that among second-generation informants, Catalan does have a clearly defined role as being the language for academic interactions and for interactions that stem from within this domain, such as friendships that are formed in school. It also appears limited to that particular domain of use, as second-generation informants opt to use Spanish and/or their heritage languages among friends. Not only is this telling of how informants reportedly use

Spanish and Catalan, the above comments also begin to shed some light on their relationship with the TL community, establishing that at the very minimum, informants have contact with the TL community – and more specifically, contact with Catalan – through their professional/educational lives and any friendships they may form in those spheres. Beyond these domains of use, however, few informants make any strong indications of more significant connections to the TL community. Shayma, a 21-year-old student, for instance, is among the few informants to indicate a stronger preference for the TL community over the HL community:

> Siempre...me suele llevar mejor con la gente de aquí. Pero no es por ninguna razón...simplemente...porque tenemos más cosas en común...o... nuestras formas de pensar son....se parecen más.
>
> [I always...I seem to get along better with people from here. But it's not for any reason...simply...because we have more in common...or...our ways of thinking are...more similar.] -Shayma, Moroccan

While she initially does not offer any reason for why she gets along more with people in the TL community, she later goes on to say she has more in common, attributing these commonalities to similar ways of thinking. This is perhaps a strong indicator of acculturation, in that 'ways of thinking' may describe a greater affinity for the TL community's customs and norms.

Heritage Languages and Racism: The Role of TL Community Attitudes

More often than not, however, the second-generation informants indicated a paradoxical sense of belonging to the TL community – given their common linguistic abilities, educational and socialization experiences – at the same time as being positioned as outsiders by other members of the TL community, which is often based on appearances. One second-generation informant, Dina, commented on the role of the TL community's attitudes toward immigrant languages and how this may relate to their status, observing that a person's accent can be perceived in different ways depending on one's nationality:

> El inglés, se valora muy bien...y el acento sudamericano se valora muy mal...y el marroquí también está mal valorado, el urdu también...se ríen de estas lenguas...y también del acento de las personas que hablan estas lenguas como lengua materna...cuando en español tiene acento, de su lengua materna...también se ríen de ellos. En cambio, no se ríen de un inglés hablando español con acento...o sea, tú por ejemplo tienes acento americano, nadie se ríe de ti...de tu español, pero otra persona que tenga acento pakistaní, se van a reír de él...si tiene acento marroquí, se van a

reír de él...un acento alemán? No. Entonces hay como un doble...bueno, un racismo de idiomas.

[English is highly valued...and the South American accent isn't valued... and Moroccan as well isn't valued, Urdu too...they make fun of these languages...and also the accent of the people who speak these languages as a native language...when they have an accent in Spanish, from their native language...they also make fun of them. However, they don't make fun of an English person speaking Spanish with an accent...that is, you for example have an American accent, no one laughs at you, but another person that has a Pakistani accent, they're going to make fun of him. If one has a Moroccan accent, they're going to make fun of him...a German accent? No. So there's a double...well, racism in languages.] -Dina

Here, Dina identifies which languages and accents are and are not valued by the TL community, pointing out that speaking Spanish with an accent from countries that are perceived as having predominantly White speakers (such as the US or Germany) is not stigmatized, while those who speak Spanish with an accent from countries that are perceived as predominantly non-White (such as Pakistan or any South American country) are frowned upon. As Dina observes, members of the TL community may use immigrants' linguistic 'deficits' to perpetuate racism. While second-generation immigrants are native speakers of Spanish and Catalan and are unlikely to speak with the accents described above, this treatment may still create a distance between themselves and the TL community, since their parents – all of whom are originally from non-White countries – may be the target of such disparagement.

Some informants disagree with this evaluation, such as Shabana, a 23-year-old student. Here, she indicates that the TL community in fact values HL speakers and their knowledge of other languages:

Yo sé leer árabe...y sé urdu, y te dicen, 'qué guay, qué chulo'...valoran... que sepas más idiomas...lo que no podrías decir es...por ejemplo, solamente saber urdu, ¿no? Es algo que...lo ven como negativo, que no sepas el catalán ni el castellano, y estás aquí, ¿no? ...para poder hablar con la comunidad, con los demás y tal, pues, deberías saber castellano, pero sí que valoran que tú sepas tu idioma de...herencia.

[I know how to read Arabic...and I know Urdu, and they say, 'how cool, how great'....they value...that you know more languages...what you couldn't say is...for example, only speaking Urdu, no? It's something that...they view it as negative, that you don't know how to speak Catalan or Spanish, and you're here, no? In order to speak with the community, with everyone else, well, you should know how to speak Spanish...but yes, they do value that you speak your heritage language.] -Shabana, Indian

While Shabana believes that many members of the TL community highly regard knowledge of HLs as a unique skill set, she also elaborates that this regard for HLs is only extended to speakers who have already integrated to some degree by speaking Spanish and Catalan, suggesting that HL knowledge may supplement or complement – but never replace – TL knowledge. With this distinctive set of valorations where TL knowledge is a requisite for integrating into the TL community and HL knowledge remains peripheral and even signals outsiderness, it becomes even clearer that language use plays an important role in how second-generation immigrants – as HL speakers – are positioned in the TL community.

Creating sentiments of othering not only stems from language use and attitudes, but also may result in acts of overt xenophobia and aggressions. Nasreen, for instance, shared an example of a time when she was targeted for harassment for wearing a *hijab*:

> Una vez una mujer intentó quitarme el velo…y pues, algún comentario feo que…pero bueno…si la contestas muy educadamente, mostrándole de que no eres una persona retrasada por llevar velo…que es lo que creen mucha gente, te puede pisar porque eres callada y sumisa, y no es así…las musulmanas no somos ni sumisas ni tontas…ni nada..entendemos y sabemos todo. Entonces es simplemente dar la cara y mostrarle de que soy una persona igual que tu…no tienes ningún derecho sobre mí.
>
> [Once a woman tried to take off my veil…and well, some ugly comment that…but well…if you answer very politely, showing them that you aren't a backwards person because you wear a veil…which is what a lot of people think, they can step on you because you're quiet and submissive, and it's not like that…we Muslim women are neither submissive nor stupid…or anything…we understand and know everything. So it's simply about facing them and showing them that I am a person equal to you…you don't have any rights over me.] -Nasreen, Moroccan

For Nasreen, these acts of aggression stem from a misunderstanding of Muslim women, where perpetrators may rely on stereotypes as a justification for harassing someone they perceive as different and thus inferior. However, she goes on to explain the need to respond with civility in order to challenge the negative attitudes she believed that members of the TL community may hold toward Muslim women. Wearing a *hijab*, as demonstrated above, can play a significant role in how members of the TL community position Muslim women as outsiders, even those who consider themselves members of the TL community, such as the second-generation informants of this study. Moreover, the beliefs held by some members of the TL community use religious differences not only to create distance with Muslim women like Nasreen, but also to perpetuate negative connotations with regard to Muslims. In a more subtle example than Nasreen's experience, Sharifa connected her outward Muslim appearance – wearing a *hijab* – to being positioned as an outsider among the TL community:

Hay gente...o sea...yo me considero española, pero digamos gente española no musulmana...te preguntan cosas de tu religión, y...tratan como... tú en tu país y tal...Pero en realidad yo no me considero de que sea de otro país, ¿sabes? o sea...hay veces...se consideran diferente...extranjera. Y hay otros temas que - por ejemplo - dices...'yo he nacido aquí,' y...'ah pues, no - eres española.' Pero a veces, dicen 'en tu país' Sin consciente, ¿no? porque se relacionan islam con extranjero. ¿Sabes? Y temas así, ¿no? Temas más... quizá...religiosos, o...como ves la vida, distinto...solo ven como extranjeros...Piensan que no entiendo cast- catalán...y me dicen 'oye, ¿quieres que mejor hablemos en castellano?' Porque dan por hecho que yo soy de afuera, solo por llevar hijab.

[There are people...that is...I consider myself Spanish, but let's say non-Muslim Spanish people...they ask you things about your religion, and... they treat you like...you in your country...but in reality I don't consider myself to be from another country, you know? Or like..there are times... it's considered different...foreign. And there are other matters that - for example - you say, eh...'I was born here,' and... 'ah, well, no - you're Spanish.' But sometimes, they say 'in your country' unconsciously, no? Because they relate Islam to foreignness. You know? And things like that, no? Things like...maybe...religious, or how you see life, differently...they only see (us) as foreign...they think that I don't understand -

Cast - Catalan...and they say to me, 'listen, would it be better if we spoke in Spanish?' Because they take for granted that I'm from outside, just because I wear a hijab.] -Sharifa, Moroccan

From this excerpt, it is evident that, for Sharifa, members of the TL community may consciously or unconsciously consider her an outsider because she wears a *hijab*, which she believes non-Muslim Spaniards to view not only as a symbol of Islam, but a symbol of foreignness because the values and worldviews associated with this religion are seen as different from those in Spain. This, in turn, calls into question the extent to which multiculturalism is truly a part of Spanish and/or Catalan society. Furthermore, being perceived as an outsider also results in others assuming that she does not speak Catalan, and perhaps only Spanish, since that is often the language that Catalan speech community uses by default when interacting with anyone whom they perceive to be an outsider.

Wearing a *hijab* can not only position an individual as an outsider among the TL community, but it can also limit the extent of one's contact with the TL community. Jamila, a 22-year-old secretary, expressed having difficulty in finding work because she wore a *hijab*:

Lo que es difícil aquí en España es trabajar con velo...lo que no me gusta de aquí...es trabajar con velo. Con pañuelo...es muy difícil que te acepten en cualquier tipo de empleo. Es muy difícil...tienes que quitártelo...y es muy difícil encontrar un empleo para poder trabajar con el velo. Tienes que quitártelo en cualquier sitio.

(¿Y has tenido dificultades con esto?)
Sí...los he tenido...me pidieron en muchos que ..lo tenía que quitar...y.. yo no accedí...y, intenté buscar, buscar, buscar..hasta encontré un sitio donde los de...de Marruecos, de mi..de mi ciudad, Tánger, me contrataron como secretaria. Para, para los inmigrantes.

[What's difficult here in Spain is working with a veil...what I don't like about here...is working with a veil. With a scarf...it's difficult for them to accept you in any type of work. It's very difficult...you have to take it off... and it's very difficult to find a job where you can wear a veil. You have to take it off everywhere.)
(And have you had difficulties with this?)
Yes...I've had them...they asked me in a lot of...I had to take it off...and...I didn't consent...and...I tried looking, looking, looking...until I found a place where those from...from Morocco, from my...from my city, Tangier, they hired me as a secretary. For...for immigrants.] -Jamila, Moroccan

Despite Jamila's qualifications as a college graduate, she indicates not being able to find a job that would allow her to wear a *hijab*, even if she were otherwise qualified. As she points out, this is not an uncommon problem for Muslim women seeking employment anywhere in Spain, which is a strong reflection not only of how assimilation – rather than integration – is the more operative practice across Spain, but also how this practice is operationalized to perpetuate discrimination. Muslim female job candidates who choose to wear a *hijab* are evaluated based on criteria other than their professional qualifications and experiences in a way that other candidates are not, and are thus deemed incompatible with the professional culture and norms of Spain. In Jamila's case, she was able to find alternative employment in a place where she would be allowed to wear a *hijab*: among the HL/Muslim community, at an agency specialized in assisting newly arrived Moroccan (and typically Muslim) immigrants settle in Barcelona. Thus, this association between visible religious identity and foreignness demonstrably pushes HL speakers away from their TL community, even if they speak both Spanish and Catalan and identify with the cultures. One notable result of this push away from one community and into another can certainly be seen in language use: while Jamila may have been qualified to work at a job that only required use of Spanish and/or Catalan, her experiences with discrimination instead thrusted her into a job that would rely on her knowledge of Arabic more than many of the available jobs in the TL community would have, thus resulting in a greater degree of enclosure in the HL community and a lesser ability to acculturate within the TL community.

Dina, however, suggested that the TL community's attitudes toward immigrant cultures are beginning to change. In the past, her heritage and religious practices such as wearing *henna* or a *hijab* were cause for ridicule, but more recently had become acceptable and even fashionable.

> Los adolescentes españoles de origen español también usan palabras en árabe ahora. Porque sus amigos se las enseñan...además hay un chico que hace...videos en YouTube que usa muchas palabras en árabe, también... están empezando a ver mucha apropiación cultural. Por ejemplo, cuando era pequeña, si llevabas henna se rían de ti....se llevabas hijab, se rían de ti....ahora...está de moda que pongan el henna...en Mango, venden babuchas - que las llevamos marroquíes toda la vida....y ahora las venden en Mango.
>
> [Spanish adolescents of Spanish origin also use Arabic words now. Because their friends teach them...there is also a boy who does...videos on YouTube that uses a lot of Arabic words, also...they're starting to see a lot of cultural appropriation. For example, when I was little, if you wore henna, they'd laugh at you...if you wore hijab, they'd laugh at you...now... it's fashionable to wear henna...in Mango, they sell slippers - that we Moroccans have been wearing all our lives...and now they sell them in Mango.] -Dina, Moroccan

In addition to adopting Moroccan fashions, Dina also points out that this change in attitudes is also reflected in language use via lexical borrowing from Arabic that has become popular among younger generations. While she does indicate that this change has occurred over time that suggests some degree of acceptance on the part of the TL community, Dina is also critical of this change:

> No me gusta la apropiación cultural...porque son cosas que...antes se reían de ti si hablabas marroquí, y ahora usan palabras en marroquí, o... como que intentan ser marroquíes, y eso no me gusta porque no saben lo que es..ser hijo de inmigrante. Eso no me gusta.
>
> [I don't like cultural appropriation...because they are things that...before they used to laugh at you if you spoke Moroccan, and now they use words in Moroccan, or...like they try to be Moroccan, and I don't like that because they don't know what it is...to be the child of an immigrant. I don't like that.] - Dina, Moroccan

For Dina, it appears that connections made on the part of the TL community come in the form of cultural appropriation, which she does not see as a legitimate way to connect with or integrate HL communities, as it fails to demonstrate any attempt to understand the actual experiences of immigrants. Dina made further observations on how language choice may play a significant role in how HL speakers are perceived by the TL community, and the extent to which they are accepted and deemed sufficiently integrated. For instance, she differentiates between the linguistic capital of Spanish and Catalan, as well as how immigrant populations may be perceived when using either of these languages:

Como el castellano está...siempre relacionado con un nivel socioeconómico más bajo, también los inmigrantes...los marroquíes, los pakistaníes...lógicamente, han aprendido castellano y muchos no saben hablar catalán....pero es normal.

[Since Spanish is...always associated with a lower socioeconomic level, also immigrants...Moroccans, Pakistanis....logically, they've learned Spanish and a lot of them do not know how to speak Catalan...but it's normal.] -Dina, Moroccan

Cuando hablas catalán, ya te perciben como una persona educada..que has recibido una educación aquí...que estás bien integrada, porque hablas los dos idiomas del país. Entonces cuando tengo que pedir un favor... pues, igual que..a veces en EE.UU. la gente negra dice que, 'cuando llamo por teléfono, pongo voz de blanca'...es lo mismo...hablo en catalán y.... pues, la gente es más amable.

[When you speak in Catalan, they perceive you as an educated person... that you received an education here...that you're well integrated, because you speak the two languages of the country. So when I have to ask for a favor...well, it's the same as...sometimes in the US. Black people say, 'when I talk on the phone, I use a White voice'...it's the same thing...I speak in Catalan and....well, people are nicer.] -Dina, Moroccan

From the above excerpts, Dina believes that – in the context of Catalonia – Spanish is viewed as a language associated with lower socioeconomic backgrounds, as well as with immigrants. As a result, she says, immigrants continue to uphold this linguistic expectation by focusing on learning Spanish instead of Catalan. Conversely, she observes that Catalan is more prestigious, associated with education and – in the case of immigrants – being socially integrated. For this reason, Dina indicates that she code-switches to Catalan when making requests because people are nicer to her. She likens this tendency to that of Black Americans code-switching from African American Vernacular English (AAVE) in order to be perceived as White or fit in with White interlocutors and therefore receive better treatment and/or be socially accepted in predominantly White environments (see Atkins, 1993; Billings, 2005; Craig, 2016; Doss & Gross, 1994, for further examination on this topic). From Dina's comments, it is evident that – for immigrant populations of any generation – Catalan is a tool for not only demonstrating one's successful social integration, but also for invoking membership in the TL community when their identity is questioned or looked upon negatively.

The TL community's perception of how integrated an individual is appears to be an important factor influencing linguistic behavior of second-generation informants. Jamila similarly indicates that immigrants often need to switch from their native/heritage languages to Spanish in front of members of the TL community, even if they are not directly involved in the conversation:

Bueno, si tú vas a un sitio, estás al lado de alguien español, mejor es hablar castellano para no ofenderle...para que él sepa que no estás insultando..que no estás hablando de él.

[Well, if you go to a place, you are next to someone Spanish, it's best to speak in Spanish so as to not offend them...so that they know that you are not insulting...you're not talking about them.] -Jamila, Moroccan

Like Dina, Jamila suggests that switching languages in the presence of TL interlocutors can be to the benefit of HL speakers; however, while Dina indicates switching for the purposes of better treatment, Jamila suggests switching for the purposes of avoiding insult. In both cases, however, language choice (i.e. using Catalan or Spanish instead of one's HL) appears to play an important role in how informants may position themselves within the TL community.

Multilingualism and Dual Identity

Ultimately, one of the most salient experiences that informants shared was a sense of dual identity that stems from being a second-generation immigrant. In some instances, this dual identity is described as a harmonious balance, such as in the case of Humaa and Rehana:

En realidad siempre cojo...yo siempre cojo lo bueno de cada una...porque nací aquí, tengo que seguir las de aquí...Yo creo que no hay una que diga esta es la que yo pertenezco, pienso solo como la de aquí...es más mezclar las dos...no acabo de encajar en una solo. Es muy raro.

[In reality, I always take...I always take the good from each one...because I was born here, I have to follow those from here...I believe that there isn't anyone who says that this is the one that I belong to, I think only like someone from here...it's more about mixing the two...I just can't fit into only one. It's very weird.] -Humaa, Pakistani

Como yo he nacido aquí, de muy pequeñita, entonces he vivido como entre las dos culturas...y...me ha nutrido entre las dos culturas...es como... que me siento de las dos

[Since I was born here, when I was very little, so I lived like between the two worlds...and..I was nurtured between two cultures...it's like...I feel like I'm from both.] -Rehana, Pakistani

Here, both Humaa and Rehana – who are sisters and live together in the same house – state that they identify as a mix of HL and TL cultures, rather than identifying with one group over the other. For other informants, such as Laila, a more negative sentiment was attached to this dual identity:

Siempre he sentido que tengo una doble identidad, entonces no acabo de encajar ni aquí y tampoco de donde vengo porque nunca he vivido allí.

[I've always felt that I have a double identity, so I don't fit neither here nor where I come from because I never lived there.] -Laila, Moroccan

Unlike Humaa and Rehana, Laila indicates that her double identity has left her feeling a lack of belonging to any community or culture neither with the TL community, nor with her heritage country, Morocco, not having ever lived there. It is also worth noting that Laila is one of only two Berber speakers among all of the Moroccan informants in this study, a fairly accurate reflection of the demographics of Moroccan immigrants in Spain, where the majority are Arab, not Berber. Identifying, then, with a relatively small HL speech community compared to her Arab-Moroccan peers may also contribute to an inability to identify with communities around her. Similarly, Jamila describes her dual identity as a balancing act, which is reflected in language use:

Cuando hablas mucho castellano, te olvidas de árabe. Y cuando hablas mucho árabe, te olvidas del castellano.

[When you speak a lot of Spanish, you forget Arabic. And when you speak a lot of Arabic, you forget Spanish.] -Jamila, Moroccan

Here, Jamila states that using one language comes at the expense of another, indicating that – for her – there is only room for one dominant language in an individual's linguistic repertoire. By extension, this begs the question of whether cultural identities are similarly at odds with one another for such individuals. In some cases, such as that of Dina noted below, multilingualism and multiculturalism may indeed exist harmoniously and construct multiple identities for individuals. However, as Dina points out, they may exist independently of one another and are compartmentalized with regard to their enactment:

Siento conexión con la cultura española porque he crecido aquí toda mi vida, entonces todos mis amigos son de origen español....entonces...siento una conexión por las fiestas de aquí, por la forma de hablar...la forma de interactuar con la gente, mi forma de interactuar con la gente es más española que marroquí. O sea...es abierta, pero quizás no tanto como una persona marroquí...con la cultura catalana también, en muchas cosas. Y luego con la cultura marroquí también con esto, claro. Pero más en el ámbito de casa...soy más marroquí, en casa. Pero en el ámbito social, soy más española.

[I feel a connection with Spanish culture because I was raised here my whole life, so all of my friends are of Spanish origin...so...I feel a connection to the holidays here, the manner of speaking...the manner of interacting with people, my manner of interacting with people is more Spanish than Moroccan. I mean...it's open, but perhaps not as much as a Moroccan person...with Catalan culture too, in many things. And then with Moroccan culture too, of course. But more in the home environment...I'm more Moroccan, at home. But in the social environment, I'm more Spanish.] -Dina, Moroccan

In this excerpt, Dina appears to strongly identify with Spanish and Catalan culture, citing that her interactional style is more Spanish than Moroccan. She describes herself as 'open', a commonly used term among informants for comparing and contrasting members of the TL and HL communities, as well as different generations. However, Dina adds that she is less open than Moroccans – presumably first-generation Moroccans. She then goes on to relate to Moroccan culture, but specifically designates the home environment as where she feels Moroccan, reserving her Spanish identity for social environments. Like other informants, Dina appears to have dual identities. However, rather than being at odds with one another, Dina specifies where each identity tends to emerge more strongly and does not make any indication of having difficulties with this. Regardless of how informants conceptualize dual identities, it is apparent that heritage culture and all that it entails is not viewed as part of the TL culture. As mentioned earlier, this goes against a great deal of political discourse in Spain – including language policy Catalonia – which highlights the importance of multiculturalism (see Chapter 2). Rather, much of what informants shared in their interviews suggests that heritage culture may exist alongside Spanish and Catalan culture, but are not a part of it.

Additional Comments

This chapter has highlighted second-generation informants' experiences with and connections to both TL and HL communities, as well as how gendered and religious identity often work as inseparable and mutually reinforcing elements that may play a role in linguistic behavior and attitudes. As shown through informants' interviews, visible religious identity as a Muslim woman can impact the way informants interact with the TL community. This can take various forms, such as limited job opportunities available to women who wear a *hijab* and being limited to working in their HL community where displaying religious identity would be accepted but where they would consequently have less contact with and less connection to the TL community. This is also illustrated in second-generation informants often being considered 'foreign' despite being raised in Catalonia and being native speakers of Spanish and Catalan. Through instances such as these, it is evident that linguistic behavior is often connected to a sense of otherness that members of the TL community may consciously or unconsciously assign to informants. Furthermore, this is not necessarily generation-specific, but rather a reflection of their outward appearance as Muslim women. However, this experience of othering can certainly be more pronounced for second-generation immigrants, who have typically integrated into the TL community to a far greater degree than their parents, yet have still not received reciprocated acceptance from the TL community.

Looking at informants' connections to the HL community, there is some degree of pushback against first-generation values and practices, though many second-generation informants simultaneously acknowledge the value of their HLs, and deeply identify with them. Taking these two speech communities together, many second-generation informants evidently live in two worlds, each of which comes with their own set of sociolinguistic structures and norms through which they must navigate. While they at times seem to *distance* themselves from the HL community and the values they associate with the first-generation, they are often *distanced* by the TL community, who do not always see second-generation immigrants as true members of their community. This contributes to the broader discussion of identity negotiation in that it is apparent that an individual can have the agency to enact certain identity – such as using Catalan to prove to other TL speakers that they are educated and integrated – while at other times lose some degree of agency when it is imposed by others – such as when TL speakers assume that second-generation immigrants are not TL speakers themselves and offer to use Spanish as a form of accommodation. These impositions, however, are not individual, isolated instances, but rather the product of larger social structures that control and at times constrain how immigrants of any generation navigate society. These social structures often position members of the TL community with the power to implicitly or explicitly label immigrants as 'the other', or as 'foreign'. This, in turn, often puts even native-speaker, second-generation immigrants at a social disadvantage because not only are there specific linguistic expectations of immigrants regarding social integration (such as knowledge of Catalan), but second-generation immigrants who do know Catalan are often assumed to not know it and are thus not spoken to in Catalan. Consequently, their membership in the TL community either goes unacknowledged, or otherwise they are shouldered with the responsibility of initiating conversations in Catalan so as to signal TL community membership.

While multicultural coexistence is certainly a reality across Catalonia and more widely in Spain, informants' narratives suggest that different cultures coexist at a distance from one another and that perhaps there is a general failing to acknowledge different heritages as being a part of Spanish and/or Catalan culture, rather than separate entities that occasionally interact with it. Furthermore, this cultural separation is reflected in language use, as well as perceived TL attitudes toward heritage and religious identities as 'foreign'. Under such a system, it can be argued that perhaps no immigrant can truly be considered integrated by a TL community's standards unless they embrace total assimilation at the expense of their heritage identities. While this ideology clashes with discourse in Catalan language policy that encourages multiculturalism and identifies it as a vital component of Catalan society, it simultaneously upholds other discourse in language policy regarding the importance of social cohesion in Catalonia. As it will be discussed further in Chapter 9 ('Implications for Language and Immigrant-targeted Policies'), such disharmony should be addressed in such a way that heritage cultures and languages are not merely acknowledged as being *in* Catalonia, but also *part of* Catalan culture. In the same way a multilingual person is not a combination of multiple monolinguals, a society cannot be truly multicultural if cultures are treated as separate, isolated entities.

7 Catalan, Spanish and Heritage Languages: Reported Language Use and Attitudes

Introduction

Chapters 5 and 6 examined informants' self-reported language use and attitudes, how Muslim women position themselves within Spanish/Catalan society, as well as how gendered and religious identity plays a role in interactions with the heritage language (HL) and target language (TL) communities. This chapter continues this discussion, shifting now from informants' narratives to their questionnaire responses. While qualitative data is an invaluable resource for the study of linguistic behavior in a social world, qualitative analyses also present their own challenges and limitations, such as the possibility of various observation biases. Because of this, I was interested in including questionnaire data in this study in order to see if a quantitative analysis at a descriptive level would lend further support to my observations about informants' narratives. The questionnaire covered themes that were similarly discussed in the interviews; specifically, it included the following sections:

(1) Background information.
(2) A series of various communicative domains (such as 'social media' or 'at the grocery store') for which informants indicated which language(s) they used.
(3) A series of Likert-scale statements relating to informants' attitudes toward Spanish, Catalan and their HLs.
(4) A series of speaker traits (such as 'educated' and 'friendly') that informants assigned to either a theoretical bilingual speaker of Catalan and Spanish, or a theoretical speaker of their HLs.

This chapter examines first-generation and second-generation informants' questionnaire responses relating to their self-reported language use and attitudes and also briefly discusses the significance of other informant variables that I examined, such as marital status, parental status, employment status and educational background.

Reported Language Use

I included this section of the questionnaire in my study in order to move beyond simply identifying which languages informants used, and gauge the frequency with which each of these languages were being used in their day-to-day lives, as well as gain an understanding of the social contexts in which informants used specific languages.[1] In this portion of the questionnaire, I provided informants with a list of communicative domains in which informants may speak, write, listen or read. Informants were to select the language that they most used in each of the domains and were offered Spanish, Catalan and HLs as their options. However, there were a number of unanticipated responses to this particular section of the questionnaire. First, while the intent was to elicit single responses for each domain, 25 of the 34 informants marked more than one language for some domains. As a result, responses that indicated more than one language are included in a separate column in the below tables, marked 'combination', for which a further breakdown of different language combinations is provided. Additionally, some informants also indicated using other languages – namely English and French – in the questionnaire instead of or in addition to the languages that I had provided. These languages are denoted in the 'other' column, although they also appear in combination with other languages. First- and second-generation responses are recorded in separate tables below.

Table 7.1 Domains of use: First-generation (19 informants)

Code:	S: Spanish	C: Catalan	H: Heritage	F: French	E: English
Domain	Spanish	Catalan	Heritage	Combination	Other
TV/movies	7	0	9	SCH (3)	0
Radio/music	4	0	9	SCH (3) SH (3)	0
Reading	6	1	8	SC (1) SH (1)	E (1) F (1)
Social media	5	0	8	HF (1) SF (1) SH (4)	0
Professional life	8	2	5	SC (1) SH (3)	0
Daily life	6	2	8	SCH (1) SH (2)	0

Domain	Spanish	Catalan	Heritage	Combination	Other
Emails	8	0	4	SC (2) SF (1) SH (1)	E (1) F (1)
Family/friends	1	0	11	SCH (1) SE (1) SH (5)	0
Texting	7	0	6	SC (1) SE (1) SH (1) SHF (1)	E (1) F (1)
Strangers	14	0	1	HE (1) SCH (1) SH (2)	0
Restaurants	16	1	0	SC (1) SH (1)	0
Doctor's office	13	2	0	SC (1) SH (1)	0
Grocery store	18	0	1	0	0

Table 7.2 Domains of use: Second-generation (15 informants)

Domain	Spanish	Catalan	Heritage	Combination	Other
TV/movies	9	1	1	SH (3)	E (2)
Radio/music	7	0	2	SC (1) SH (2)	E (3)
Reading	5	3	1	SC (3) SE (1) SH (1)	E (1)
Social media	12	0	0	SH (1)	E (2)
Professional life	9	1	0	SC (2) SH (1)	E (2)
Daily life	12	0	0	SH (3)	0
Emails	11	2	0	SC (3) SE (1)	0
Family/friends	2	0	4	SCH (1) SH (8)	0
Texting	13	1	0	SH (1)	0
Strangers	10	2	0	SH (3)	0
Restaurants	13	1	0	SH (1)	0
Doctor's office	10	4	0	SH (1)	0
Grocery store	14	0	0	SH (1)	0

A cursory review of these tables shows that Spanish is clearly the most frequently used language among informants, closely followed by HLs, particularly among first-generation informants. In comparing first- and second-generation informants, there are several domains where there is little difference between the responses. In the domain of professional life, both groups primarily indicated using Spanish either alone or in combination with another language, with a few informants among each generation who used Catalan either alone or in combination with another language. Eight first-generation informants, however, also indicated that they used the HL in this domain, three of whom used it in combination with Spanish. Likewise, in transactional domains – such as with strangers, restaurants, the doctor's office and the grocery store – both groups mostly indicated using Spanish, with few choosing the HL in combination with other languages. Catalan, while infrequently selected in these domains, was primarily chosen among the second-generation informants, with nearly a third of them indicating that they used Catalan when going to the doctor's office. Finally, among family and friends, most informants among both generations selected either their HL or a combination of Spanish and their HL, with only four informants choosing options that did not include the HL.

There are, however, a number of salient differences between each generation's reported language use. In entertainment domains (movies/TV, radio/music, reading), second-generation informants indicated a stronger preference for Spanish as well as Catalan, particularly for reading. In the domain of daily life, first-generation informants appeared to rely more on the HL than second-generation informants. Finally, in the domains of written communication (emails, texting, social media), first-generation informants' responses were split between Spanish and the HL, while second-generation informants generally chose Spanish, with only one second-generation informant indicating that she used the HL in combination with Spanish.

From these noted differences, Catalan appears to have a stronger presence among second-generation informants in written media such as reading and emails, though this is not the case in less formal written media, such as texting and social media. This is likely owing to the fact that these informants indicated receiving a minimum of 15 years of education in Catalan.[2] As highlighted in the previous chapter, a number of second-generation informants positioned Catalan as a more institutional language which they used frequently – given their university-level education – but not outside the educational sphere.

While Catalan evidently has a stronger presence among second-generation speakers than first-generation speakers – particularly through their interactions in the educational domain – it is important to consider the functions that such a domain serves. One of the main purposes of interaction in the educational sphere is to foster learning and professional development; however, it is important to acknowledge that personal relationships and friendships are also formed through interactions in such settings.

Given that these relationships develop through interactions in Catalan, such practices point to a greater degree of assimilation to the TL community not necessarily present among first-generation informants. This is also the case for Spanish among second-generation informants; their general tendency to choose Spanish for written communication where first-generation informants were split between Spanish and the HL again suggests a greater degree of assimilation than first-generation informants. However, there is still a widespread use of HLs in several other domains for both generations that demonstrates HL maintenance. Additionally, across generations and in every domain, there are cases where multiple languages are used. The majority of informants, in fact, indicated using more than one language in one or more domains in their questionnaire responses. From these findings, it can be surmised that at the social level, informants interact in speech communities that are multilingual and do not necessarily assign a single language to different domains of use.

While this study focuses primarily on generational differences as the most significant factor influencing the linguistic behavior of Muslim immigrant women, I also examined other potentially significant factors that merit some discussion. For instance, two family-related factors that I examined include marital status and parental status, both of which produced similar results because of the significant overlap in informants when categorized as 'with children'/'without children' and 'married'/'unmarried'. Informants with children (most of whom were also married) showed a greater tendency to use both their HLs and Spanish in several domains. In contrast, childless informants (most of whom were also unmarried) frequently reportedly used more Spanish in those same domains. These results are perhaps indicative of how familial roles may influence language use for some of the informants and also corresponds to a number of informants' interview responses in which they emphasized the importance of transmitting HLs to their children as part of a parental responsibility – or possibly in a more gendered role as a mother.

The role of family – and perhaps the gendered role of being a mother or a wife – may also be relevant when examining employment as a factor. Those who reported not having an occupation responded similarly to those who were parents and/or had children and also reportedly used their HLs more than those who were employed or were students. While no additional data regarding family life was collected, it could be surmised that those who were not employed perhaps spent more time interacting in a personal/informal rather than professional/formal capacity, maintaining their familial roles throughout their daily activities instead of transitioning to professional roles, as their employed counterparts would be doing. In contrast, employed and student informants reported using their HLs less and relied on Catalan more. This is also reflected in some of the interview excerpts shared in previous chapters in which informants recognized Catalan as being instrumental insofar as it was a language that marked 'belonging' to the Catalan community and would result in better treatment. Employed/student informants' knowledge of Catalan and their reported ability to navigate certain domains using Catalan could perhaps be explained by the likelihood that – in their professional roles – they are more likely to have interactions with the TL community and therefore have a greater awareness of the status of Catalan.

Similarly, educational background may play an important role in shaping informants' linguistic behavior, particularly in terms of Catalan use. While the number of informants in each educational category was not balanced and therefore limits the soundness of subsequent observations, the results presented in this chapter suggest a direct relationship between informants' level of education and their reported Catalan use, likely owing at least in part to the continued exposure to Catalan with continued education. In other words, the higher the level of education, the greater frequency with which Catalan was reportedly used. Conversely, informants' level of education appears to have an inverse relationship with reported HL use. Here, as educational levels increased, reported HL use decreased and appeared to be displaced by both Spanish and Catalan.

In terms of how reported language use may intersect with informants' acculturation experiences and/or different aspects of their identity, such as religion, heritage culture and/or gender, a number of social factors can play a role in one's opportunities for learning and using different languages when residing in the TL community. Specifically, as indicated in previous chapters, several first-generation immigrants (and one second-generation immigrant) indicated that they had jobs that placed them among other Muslim immigrants – particularly those from the same country of origin as them – which was partially due to not being able to find more desirable work in the TL community. This increased social isolation from the TL community may result in not only less exposure to the TL, but it may also limit informants' motivation and/or opportunities to learn Spanish and/or Catalan. Additionally, acculturation in the context of Catalonia must take into account societal bilingualism, and whether or not immigrants acquire one or both languages. Informants' reported language use would suggest that acculturation – particularly among first-generation immigrants – would be limited to Spanish. Two explanations that arise from the presented data are, first, Spanish was evidently the predominant or only language of use in nearly all domains for most informants; second, informants' interview responses shared in Chapter 5 indicated a lack of investment in learning Catalan because they did not consider it to be a pragmatic language, given that it is generally not spoken outside of Catalonia, and as a result they prioritized learning Spanish. However, another possible explanation for immigrants' tendency toward Spanish over Catalan is that many immigrant populations are positioned as being lower in social status, and so they are pushed toward the language that is less socially prestigious, Spanish.

Language Attitudes: Likert-Scale Statements

While the previous section described informants' self-reported language use, the remaining sections in this chapter focus on the language attitudes that may be extrapolated from the questionnaire responses. In the Likert-scale portion of the questionnaire, I provided three different statements regarding language attitudes, each of which had three versions to reflect the heritage language/culture, Spanish and Catalan. These statements are translated from Spanish below:

(1) I like (Spanish/Catalan/my heritage) traditions and customs.
(2) I am satisfied with my language abilities in (Spanish/Catalan/my HL).
(3) If I have children, it is important that they know (Spanish/Catalan/my HL).

For each of these statements, informants indicated the extent to which they agreed, selecting from a range of options: 'totally disagree', 'disagree', 'neither agree nor disagree', 'agree' and 'totally agree'. Beginning with Statement (1), first- and second-generation informants' responses are recorded below:

Table 7.3 First-generation: 'I like the traditions and customs of....

Degree of agreement	...my heritage culture'	...Catalan culture'	...Spanish culture'
Totally agree	6	4	3
Agree	10	3	9
Neither agree nor disagree	2	7	6
Disagree	1	2	1
Totally disagree	0	3	0
Total	19	19	19

Table 7.4 Second-generation: 'I like the traditions and customs of....

Degree of agreement	...my heritage culture'	...Catalan culture'	...Spanish culture'
Totally agree	8	6	1
Agree	5	4	8
Neither agree nor disagree	1	5	6
Disagree	1	0	0
Totally disagree	0	0	0
Total	15	15	15

For this statement, first- and second-generation informants generally appear to hold favorable attitudes toward heritage and Spanish cultures; however, the corresponding statement relating to Catalan culture provides distinct responses. Here, fewer than half of the first-generation informants chose agreement for this statement, while the majority indicated either disagreement or indifference ('neither agree nor disagree'). These responses contrast with those of second-generation informants, two-thirds of whom indicated agreement, while the remaining third's responses suggest indifference.

While Statement (1) focused on attitudes toward culture, statements (2) and (3) look specifically at language. In the absence of any systematic attempt at measuring informants' linguistic proficiency in multiple languages, Statement (2) gauges informants' satisfaction with their linguistic abilities. The below tables summarize first- and second-generation informants' responses:

Table 7.5 First-generation: 'I am satisfied with my language abilities in…

Degree of agreement	…my heritage language'	…Catalan'	…Spanish'
Totally agree	8	1	7
Agree	11	7	8
Neither agree nor disagree	0	6	3
Disagree	0	5	1
Totally disagree	0	0	0
Total	19	19	19

Table 7.6 Second-generation: 'I am satisfied with my language abilities in…

Degree of agreement	…my heritage language'	…Catalan'	…Spanish'
Totally agree	4	11	13
Agree	9	1	1
Neither agree nor disagree	1	2	1
Disagree	1	0	0
Totally disagree	0	1	0
Total	15	15	15

Unsurprisingly, all first-generation informants agreed that they were satisfied with their abilities in their HLs – where 'heritage' in this case refers to their native languages. Most first-generation informants indicated similarly for Spanish, with only one informant indicating that she was not yet satisfied with her abilities. Nearly half of these informants also indicated being satisfied with their abilities in Catalan, while the remaining first-generation selected 'neither agree nor disagree' or 'disagree'. While it was expected that second-generation informants may provide reversed responses and indicate a lack of satisfaction with their abilities (and possibly suggesting a lack of proficiency) in their HLs, the majority of these informants indicated agreement with this statement. However, it is worth

112 Multilingualism and Gendered Immigrant Identity

noting that most of these responses corresponded to 'agree', while the majority of these informants selected 'totally agree' for Catalan and Spanish. This would suggest that – regardless of actual linguistic proficiency – their confidence in their abilities in their HLs is perhaps not as strong as compared to their abilities in Catalan and Spanish.

Statement (3) in the Likert-scale section focuses on language maintenance, and which languages informants view as being vital for the next generation.

Table 7.7 First-generation: 'If I have children, it is important that they know…

Degree of agreement	…my heritage language'	…Catalan'	…Spanish'
Totally agree	12	10	11
Agree	6	5	6
Neither agree nor disagree	0	1	1
Disagree	1	1	0
Totally disagree	0	2	1
Total	19	19	19

Table 7.8 Second-generation: 'If I have children, it is important that they know…

Degree of agreement	…my heritage language'	…Catalan'	…Spanish'
Totally agree	15	10	13
Agree	0	3	2
Neither agree nor disagree	0	2	0
Disagree	0	0	0
Totally disagree	0	0	0
Total	15	15	15

Here, both first- and second-generation informants almost unanimously agree that subsequent generations should know their HLs – with only one informant among the first-generation informants who disagreed. The majority of informants similarly agreed that subsequent generations should know Spanish and Catalan; however, the extent of agreement diminishes slightly. This is particularly evident among first-generation informants, one-fifth of whom disagreed or were neutral with regard to Catalan.

In addition to the variations of the three statements discussed above, I also included a series of statements in this section of the questionnaire that relate specifically to HLs and cultures in order to further ascertain informants' attitudes toward their heritage and its role in their daily lives and the extent to which they view it as part of their identities. The English translations of these statements are as follows:

(1) My native/heritage culture can survive without the native/heritage language(s).
(2) Maintaining my heritage/native language is important to me.
(3) My native/heritage language(s) is/are an important part of my identity.
(4) My ethnicity/heritage plays an important role in my personal life.

Table 7.9 First-generation: Attitudes toward heritage language and culture

Degree of agreement	Statement (1)	Statement (2)	Statement (3)	Statement (4)
Totally agree	2	12	11	10
Agree	9	6	8	6
Neither agree nor disagree	0	1	0	2
Disagree	4	0	0	1
Totally disagree	4	0	0	0
Total	19	19	19	19

Table 7.10 Second-generation: Attitudes toward heritage language and culture

Degree of agreement	Statement (1)	Statement (2)	Statement (3)	Statement (4)
Totally agree	2	14	15	7
Agree	2	1	0	7
Neither agree nor disagree	2	0	0	1
Disagree	6	0	0	0
Totally disagree	3	0	0	0
Total	15	15	15	15

With regard to HL/culture maintenance, a narrow majority of first-generation informants agreed with Statement (1), suggesting that they do not view HLs as playing a crucial role in culture maintenance. Still, almost all first-generation informants agreed that HL maintenance was important to them (Statement (2)), and important in their personal life (4), while all agreed that it was important to their identities (3). Second-generation informants differ only slightly in their responses. Statement (1) produced mixed results, though in this case a narrow majority disagreed, connecting HL to culture maintenance. With the remaining statements, however, second-generation informants were similarly almost entirely unanimous in their agreement and connected their HLs to their identities.

One final set of questions that I included in the Likert-scale portion of the questionnaire related to informants' preferences regarding the ethnicities of the people with whom they socialize. While these statements do not explicitly mention language use or choice, informants' responses to these statements may still reflect their preferences for socializing with other individuals who may or may not know their HLs, if not their actual linguistic preferences.

(1) 'I like to be with people who are of different ethnicities than me'.
(2) 'I like to be with people who are of the same ethnicity as me'.

Table 7.11 First-generation: Socialization preferences

Degree of agreement	Statement (1)	Statement (2)
Totally agree	8	5
Agree	9	9
Neither agree nor disagree	1	4
Disagree	1	1
Totally disagree	0	0
Total	19	19

Table 7.12 Second-generation: Socialization preferences

Degree of agreement	Statement (1)	Statement (2)
Totally agree	14	5
Agree	0	1
Neither agree nor disagree	1	6
Disagree	0	2
Totally disagree	0	1
Total	15	15

Looking at first-generation informants, there is little difference between their responses to each statement, with only a slight shift toward indifference ('neither agree nor disagree') regarding socializing with others who are of the same ethnicity as them. Given that there is almost no disagreement with either statement, first-generation informants generally appear to be open to socializing with individuals within and outside their HL communities. By comparison, second-generation informants provide somewhat different responses. Second-generation informants are similarly in agreement with Statement (1), though – with 14 out of 15 marking 'totally agree', this group appears to feel more strongly about socializing with others who are perhaps not members of their HL communities. Their responses to Statement (2), however, are more varied. In comparison to their responses to Statement (1), second-generation informants are in less agreement about their willingness to socialize with others of the same ethnicity, where almost half of them express indifference, and a few of them even disagree altogether. These responses suggest a greater degree of distance from their HL communities among the second-generation, which in turn suggests more infrequent use of their HLs, a possibility that is certainly confirmed by second-generation informants' responses regarding domains of use.

Language Attitudes: Speaker Traits

While the Likert-scale statements relied on mostly direct statements relating to language attitudes and required informants to reflect on their personal valoration of Spanish, Catalan and their HLs, this final section of the questionnaire takes an indirect approach to gauging language attitudes among informants. This lists speaker traits that can be associated either with a hypothetical bilingual[3] Spanish/Catalan speaker or with a hypothetical monolingual speaker of the informant's HL. Adapting criteria used in matched guise tests by Bentahila (1983) and Chakrani (2011), I divided these traits into two categories in terms of what they index for speakers: status and solidarity. As demonstrated in the aforementioned research, in situations of diglossia, status has demonstrably been associated with the 'high' official variety, while solidarity has been associated with the 'low' or vernacular variety. Within the scope of this study, I predicted status to be more strongly associated with a Catalan/Spanish bilingual, while solidarity would be more strongly associated with the HL speaker. The speaker traits included in the questionnaire are listed as follows:

Status:

(1) Moderno/Modern
(2) Mentalidad abierta/Open-minded
(3) Culto/Educated
(4) Rico/Rich
(5) Alfabetizado/Literate
(6) Internacional/International
(7) Prestigioso/Prestigious
(8) Poderoso/Powerful
(9) Formal/Formal
(10) Autoritario/Authoritative

Solidarity:

(1) Sociable/Sociable
(2) Simpático/Friendly
(3) Informal/Informal
(4) Emocional/Emotional
(5) Religioso/Religious
(6) Puro/Pure
(7) Bello/Beautiful
(8) Práctico/Practical

Informants selected the hypothetical speaker they associated the most with the above traits, with the option of choosing a Catalan/Spanish bilingual, a monolingual speaker of their HL, or both.

Solidarity traits

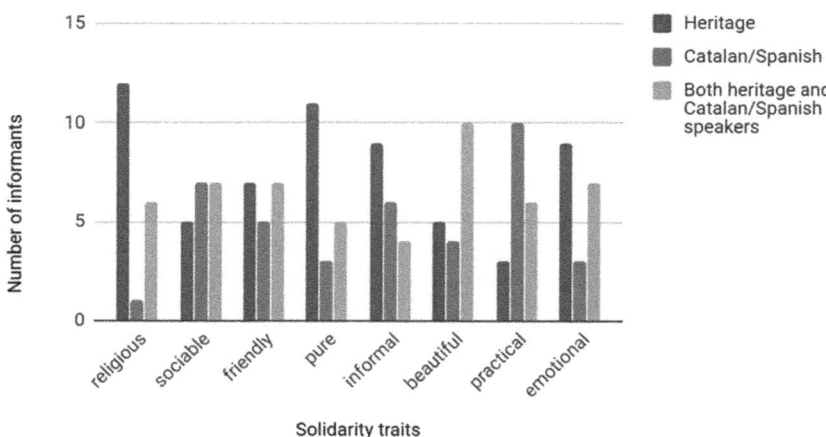

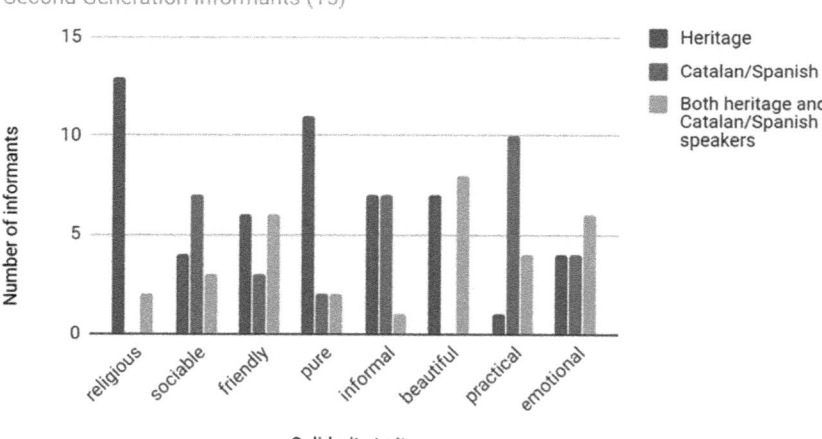

Figure 7.1 Linguistic attitudes: Solidarity traits

Looking across all solidarity traits among first-generation informants, the HL speaker is evidently the predominant choice for several traits, including 'religious', 'pure', 'informal' and 'emotional'. This creates a significant contrast with the responses of second-generation informants, where the HL speaker as the predominant choice is limited to 'religious' and 'pure'. Additionally, while first-generation responses were otherwise mixed and fairly evenly split among the different available options – often choosing both speakers for various traits – second-generation informants' responses were less varied. Apart from having a diminished association between solidarity traits and the HL speaker, this group also selected both speakers with far less frequency and, in some cases, selected the Catalan/Spanish speaker more ('sociable' and 'practical'.) This association with the Catalan/Spanish speaker – albeit to a limited degree – contrasts with that of first-generation informants, where 'practical' was the only trait that was predominantly associated with the Spanish/Catalan speaker, and only by a little over half of the informants.

Status traits

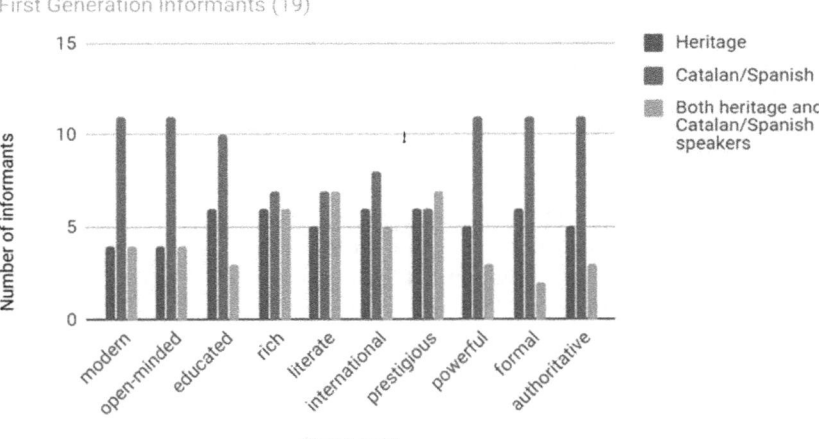

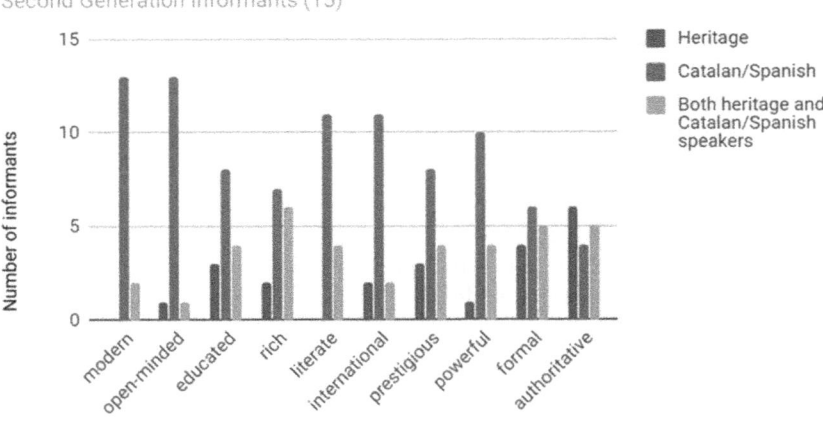

Figure 7.2 Linguistic attitudes: Status traits

One of the most evident shifts seen between solidarity and status traits is that the latter appears to generally have a stronger association with the Catalan/Spanish speaker. Second-generation informants generally selected this speaker with greater frequency compared to first-generation informants, who, in contrast, selected the Catalan/Spanish speaker and the HL speaker in equal measure, specifically for the traits 'rich', 'literate' and 'prestigious'. Associating status traits with the HL speaker was, in fact, scarce among second-generation informants. For example, fewer than one-third of second-generation informants selected the HL speaker for the traits 'open-minded', 'educated', 'rich', 'international,' 'powerful' and 'formal', and for traits such as 'modern' and 'literate', selections for just the HL speaker are entirely absent. Finally, it is noteworthy that selections for both speakers – while present among all traits and by both generations – second-generation informants tended to select a single speaker rather than both with far greater frequency than first-generation informants.

Together, the Likert-scale statements and trait assignment task help to illustrate Muslim immigrant women's attitudes toward Spanish, Catalan and their HLs, and how these attitudes vary across two generations. While factors such as marital status, parental status, occupation status and educational background may play a role in how language attitudes are shaped, it is difficult to draw concrete conclusions based on the data presented, given the limitations I noted earlier regarding the small sample size for this study, as well as the overlap in variables (e.g. married informants and informants with children). Given this overlap, the focus of this discussion remains on generational differences, since this variable seemed to be the most significant indicator of distinct language attitudes among informants.

Looking at how parental status (and in the case of all but one informant, marital status) may impact language attitudes, those without children answered more uniformly by frequently associating the HL speaker with solidarity traits and the Catalan/Spanish speaker with status traits, essentially assigning these traits in the manner that conforms to both Bentahila's (1983) and Chakrani's (2011) studies. Those with children followed a similar pattern, but to a lesser degree, and often chose other options – particularly both speakers – among solidarity and status traits. This could be attributed to parents with children being motivated to value all languages: the HL represents their child's connection to the heritage identity and culture, while Catalan and Spanish are their child's connection to the TL community, as demonstrated in Chapter 5 by informants' narratives that positioned language use in relation to their children.

Occupation status and educational background are other potentially important factors that may impact language attitudes. However, given the unequal and small numbers of informants in specific categories (particularly in the categories of 'student', 'without occupation', 'has up to secondary education' and 'has postgraduate education'), it is not possible to draw concrete conclusions about these variables from this study, only speculative observations relating to their impact. Student and employed informants – both groups who likely have greater contact with the TL community – had more distinct patterns in the trait assignment task – associating the HL speaker with solidarity traits more so than informants without an occupation. The opposite occurs with status traits: while all groups tended to associate these traits with the Catalan/Spanish speaker, student and employed informants also frequently chose both speakers in several instances, which was not the case for informants without an occupation. One possible reason for this can be that – given that student and employed informants might have greater exposure to the TL community, particularly in a professional context – they may value multilingualism differently, such as seeing it as a marketable and/or useful skill in the workforce. These results, however, differ somewhat from those that examined educational background as a variable; status traits in particular appeared to become increasingly associated with the Catalan/Spanish speaker as educational levels increased among informants. These findings, then, raise the question of whether the type of employment informants had and the level of education required of their positions could account for more highly educated informants not necessarily selecting both speakers, particularly since all informants with postgraduate education were either employed (7 total) or a student (1 total).

Shifting the focus of this discussion to generational differences, results from the Likert-scale portion of the questionnaire suggest that first-generation informants generally held more favorable attitudes toward Spanish in comparison to Catalan, a finding that conforms to the observations of Pujolar (2010) on immigrants' greater degree of exposure to Spanish instead of Catalan even among Catalan speakers. This contrasts with the second-generation, which appears to value both languages equally. While the second-generation does value both languages of Catalonia, the HL and culture also seem to have a distinct space among this group, more so among them than among the first-generation, who placed less importance on HL and cultural maintenance. Still, language maintenance appears to be an important goal for the vast majority of informants, one that extends beyond conversational skills at home and among family. For these informants, developing and maintaining a high level of proficiency in both oral and written skill sets in the HL evidently remains a priority across generations.

Taking into consideration informants' responses to the trait assignment portion of the questionnaire, the selection of just one speaker versus both speakers offers further insight into how Spanish, Catalan and HLs are regarded by informants. Both speakers – the bilingual Catalan/Spanish speaker and the monolingual HL speaker – were selected across all traits, however, this occurred with greater frequency for the solidarity traits. In contrast, status traits were more heavily associated with only the Catalan/Spanish speaker. One possible conclusion that can be drawn from these results is that Catalan and Spanish are entering a domain which – based on the findings of Bentahila (1983) and Chakrani's (2011) studies – have been associated with the HL. It is also worth noting that this shift is unidirectional in that the reverse did not occur for status traits, which remained heavily associated with the Catalan/Spanish speaker. This is especially the case among second-generation informants, which is indicative of a transgenerational shift in attitudes, one that creates a greater distinction between the solidarity language and the status language.

Another observation that requires further elaboration is how informants' language attitudes may be impacted by the TL community's attitudes toward immigrant communities, or rather, how these attitudes are perceived by informants. Although the methodology of this study did not account for an examination of such external factors, several first- and second-generation informants reflected on how they believed members of the TL community to perceive them as members of the immigrant community, as illustrated in Chapters 5 and 6. While the individual anecdotes shared in previous chapters cannot sufficiently support the conjecture that the TL community's perceived attitudes had an impact on the results relating to linguistic attitudes toward specific languages, such narratives do suggest informants' cognizance of the TL community's attitudes toward gendered, religious identity. Given the bidirectional nature of the acculturation process (see Chapter 2), it follows that the TL community's attitudes – or at least how immigrant populations perceive them – may shape immigrants' experiences with language learning and language use as much as their own attitudes do. Further examination of this possible connection could serve to gain an even greater understanding of the different components that collectively inform immigrant language use.

Connecting Reported Language Use to Attitudes

Taking together the observations presented in the last three chapters, a number of observations can be made about the role of Spanish, Catalan and HLs for Muslim women in Catalonia. First, there are several parallels between reported language use and attitudes that can shed light on how each language is used and valued by the informants in this study. Catalan – while seldom used in comparison to Spanish and informants' HLs – was reportedly used most frequently and was viewed most favorably by second-generation informants. Furthermore, results from the trait assignment task indicated that second-generation informants had more distinct attitudinal categories for the languages, in that Spanish and Catalan were heavily associated with status traits while HLs were associated more with solidarity traits. First-generation informants, however, while following a similar pattern, did not categorize the languages as uniformly and did not appear to have as clear of an association between specific languages and traits. Additionally, first-generation informants – as indicated by responses to the Likert statements and interview questions – did not necessarily have negative attitudes toward Catalan; however, they viewed it less favorably than Spanish and their HLs and did not see it as a practical language in comparison to Spanish. This was also reflected in their responses relating to domains of use, where Spanish was frequently selected across almost all domains with almost as much frequency as second-generation informants, while Catalan was absent in nearly all domains. However, as seen in the trait assignment task, Catalan and Spanish were still heavily associated with status traits.

These findings mirror previous work (Cortès-Colomé et al., 2016; Gore, 2002; Huguet & Janés, 2008; Marshall, 2007; Trenchs-Parera & Newman, 2009) that looks either at Spanish-speaking Latin American immigrants or immigrants from non-Spanish-speaking countries, and thus support the notion of Catalan as an in-group language to which immigrant populations – particularly first-generation – do not always have access, either because Spanish is seen as a more widely used and practical language to prioritize in learning, or – as some of the second-generation informants in this study indicated – members of the TL community simply do not expect them to know Catalan if they appear to be immigrants, and will opt to use Spanish instead (see Pujolar, 2010). This is further supported by informants' perceptions of the TL community's attitudes toward them, which were explored in informants' narratives in Chapters 5 and 6. Much like in the investigations cited above, several second-generation informants in the present study had indicated that many members of the TL community assumed that they were first-generation immigrants due to their appearances (such as wearing a *hijab*) – and thus also assumed that they did not know Catalan. Such attitudes can perpetuate the otherness of immigrants and the exclusivity of Catalan, and – in the context of this study – may account for the minimal usage of Catalan in most domains. Yet the present study and previous studies (Cortès-Colomé et al., 2016; Gore, 2002) indicate that foreign-born immigrants often regard Catalan as a status language, one that marks belonging to Catalan society, and – as at least one informant in this study indicated – using Catalan in public domains sometimes results in better treatment from their Catalan interlocutor. Collectively, these findings suggest that, despite Catalonia's language policies and successful efforts to make Catalan the dominant language in public space, it remains a language associated more with exclusiveness than inclusiveness, which may be a contributing reason for its scarce usage among immigrant populations.

With regard to HLs in Catalonia, this study has shown that HLs clearly have a role in informants' daily lives. Not only did all informants report using their HLs in at least one domain, but they unanimously expressed positive attitudes toward their HLs, as seen in the results from the Likert-scale statements, where informants' indicated valuing and liking their HLs/cultures as much as – and sometimes more than – Spanish (and significantly more than Catalan), and also agreed or strongly agreed with statements that placed importance on the HL/culture or connecting it to heritage identity.

However, there is some variance in HL use and attitudes among informants. First-generation (and similarly, married and parent) informants generally reported using their HLs more than their second-generation, unmarried and childless counterparts, specifically in written domains, such as emails and texts. Additionally, despite the presence of HLs in all domains, fewer than half of the informants reported using these languages exclusively in any given domain, and often reported using them in combination with other languages. Interview responses help to explain this consistent yet limited use of the HLs among informants and also connect it to language attitudes, in that, despite having favorable attitudes toward their HLs, informants also heavily associated their HLs specifically with home and familial use, and often discussed the importance of their HLs within the context of family and the home environment, such as expressing a parental responsibility to transmit the HL to their children.

Results from the trait assignment task also suggest a limited scope for HLs. As already pointed out, HLs were associated more with solidarity traits than with status traits, though among informants in any category of variables, this association was not as strong as that between status traits and Catalan/Spanish. However, one solidarity trait that stands out as being almost unanimously associated with the HL speaker was 'religious'. This particular outlier suggests that HLs – for these informants – are associated with religious identity, and – taken with the Likert-scale results – also point to an overlap between religious and heritage identity, an intersection that is also seen among Muslim immigrants in other metropolises in Spain (see Moustaoui Srhir, 2016).

One unanticipated result from this study, seen both in reported language use and language attitudes, was the frequent selection of multiple languages across different domains of use, as well as the selection of both Catalan/Spanish and HL speakers in the trait assignment task. At first, this tendency suggests a situation of multilingualism where different languages are used in the same domains and informants value the languages in question similarly. However, the data shows that even in these instances of shared domains (both in terms of reported use and attitudes), it is evident that the multilingualism among these informants is not entirely balanced. While informants indicated using a combination of languages in every domain of use, these language combinations included Spanish with Catalan and/or the HL, and in some instances, in combination with French or English. However, a combination that consists solely of Catalan and the HL is entirely absent from questionnaire responses. Additionally, the HL was rarely chosen exclusively; only in three domains (TV/movies, radio/music, family/friends) did at least a third of informants choose the HL alone. This pattern corresponds to that of the trait assignment task: although the HL speaker was most associated with solidarity traits, only two traits ('religious' and 'pure') were associated with the HL speaker by more than two-thirds of the informants, while the other traits were frequently assigned to either the Catalan/Spanish speaker or – more commonly – both speakers. This uneven selection of multiple languages/speakers in both tasks indicate that although the various languages spoken by informants are either used interchangeably in many domains and/or are viewed similarly in terms of assigning traits, HLs have neither their own, exclusive domains of use nor a distinctive association with solidarity traits because they are shared with Spanish, and sometimes Catalan. However, the reverse does not apply: Spanish was exclusively used in several domains for many informants, and the Spanish/Catalan speaker had a clear association with status traits. Together, these findings suggest that while informants certainly participate in Catalonia's societal multilingualism (and indeed contribute further to this linguistic situation through the use of their HLs), Spanish appears to have its distinct domains and – along with Catalan – distinct social categorization (status), while HLs do not, and instead share that space with Spanish and Catalan. One notable exception previously mentioned was in the area of religion, which was almost unanimously associated with the HL speaker. This further supports the idea that HLs are connected to Muslim identity for the informants in this study.

The evident connection between HLs and religious identity has been delineated to some extent in this chapter. However, gendered identity also plays an important role in the reported linguistic behavior of these informants. In terms of how informants' language use and attitudes are informed at least in part by gendered identity, we saw that a number of informants often discussed HL maintenance in terms of their gendered role as mothers or future mothers that had the responsibility of teaching the next generation. Furthermore, results from this study offer further evidence to the notion that identity – be it gendered, racial or immigrant – is performative and brokered through reiterative discourse created and maintained by others (Butler, 1993; Inda, 2000; Massey & Sánchez, 2010). In the context of this study, informants' perceptions of the TL community's attitudes toward them are often rooted in the identities created for and imposed on them: foreigners who are unlikely to know Catalan and should thus be spoken to in Spanish. This attitude is often rooted in informants' visibility as Muslim women, often through wearing a *hijab*. These perceptions can be manifested through language use, such as choosing to use Spanish instead of Catalan with informants. Furthermore, informants who shared these experiences discussed them not as specific, singular acts, but rather as repetitive ones, which – as Butler (1993) argues – is a necessary component of naturalizing identity over time.

Notes

(1) For a further discussion on informants' reported language use as it relates to code-switching, see Ali (in press).
(2) Education in Catalonia is mandatory until the age of 16. Under Article 35 of the Catalonia Statute of autonomy of 2006, 'Each individual has the right to receive an education in Catalan, as established in this Estatut. Catalan shall be used as the teaching and learning language for university and non-university education' (Parliament of Catalonia, 2006).
(3) Spanish and Catalan were grouped together because of the prevalent bilingualism found in Catalonia, and the general absence of monolingual Catalan speakers.

8 Implications for Sociolinguistic Research

Introduction

The findings that I have presented in the last few chapters have focused on a relatively small cross-section of the immigrant community in Barcelona and have highlighted some key aspects of the linguistic behavior of Muslim women, as well as how gendered, Muslim identity is produced through language choice and other discursive practices. In this chapter, I summarize some of the key findings presented throughout this book, piecing together questionnaire and interview data and evaluating them jointly here. Additionally, there are a number of broader implications for sociolinguistic research that can be taken from this small-scale study, which I also discuss in this chapter. Specifically, I highlight the significance of better understanding immigrants' experiences in acquiring societal bi-/multilingualism, as well as the importance of acknowledging the intersectionality of identity in linguistic research in terms of how multiple, overlapping characteristics can collectively contribute to experiences of otherness and marginalization. Finally, in this chapter, I will also lay out directions for future research, such as examining the bidirectional nature of acculturation and a need for further investigation of target language (TL) community members' attitudes toward immigrant communities, as they may also serve to provide a clearer picture of the setting in which immigrants are attempting to acculturate, and/or if members of the TL community have distinctive attitudes toward different immigrant communities and languages.

Immigrants' Experiences with Societal Multilingualism

The data presented in previous chapters has shed some light on the acculturation process for Muslim women in a multilingual society and can thus provide some insight on how this experience may be different from those of migrant populations in otherwise monolingual societies. For informants in this study, acculturation involves acquiring societal multilingualism and being able to navigate life in both Spanish and

Catalan. However, it is evident from both questionnaire responses and interviews that – while Catalan and Spanish are regarded as comparatively higher status than heritage languages(HLs) – first and second-generation informants have distinct relationships with Spanish and Catalan. As demonstrated in Chapter 7, Catalan is more widely used among second-generation informants than first-generation informants. This may be in part due to the central role that Catalan has in public and institutionalized domains such as education, thus giving most second-generation informants extensive exposure to Catalan in a domain that many first-generation informants only had access to in their countries of origin. It should also be noted that while the main function of educational institutions is to foster learning and professional development, the reality is that this domain is also a significant and often primary source of socialization for young individuals. As such, many of their personal relationships and friendships develop in this domain. Since these interactions are often in (but certainly not limited to) Catalan, constructing a Catalan identity may be easier for second-generation immigrants in a way that is not possible for their first-generation counterparts. This is made even clearer by first-generation informants' questionnaire responses, where Catalan was almost entirely absent from every domain of use.

In contrast, first-generation informants generally show a greater investment in Spanish than in Catalan, a preference that contrasts somewhat with second-generation informants. One of the reasons that many first-generation immigrants are not invested in learning Catalan is because it is regarded as less practical than Spanish since it is generally not spoken outside of Catalonia. Additionally, it may also be that first-generation immigrants are even pushed toward Spanish, in the sense that they are often automatically positioned as having a lower socioeconomic status than natives, and are thus assumed or expected to use the less socially prestigious language of Catalonia. This association between Spanish and economic class, however, appears to be treated as an essentialized trait, and thus preserves the separation and distance between immigrant and TL communities and can certainly prevent immigrants from feeling integrated into the latter.

This push toward Spanish is further supported by the TL community's attitudes that informants have reported, where not only first- and second-generation immigrants are not expected to know Catalan, but second-generation immigrants are sometimes assumed to be first-generation immigrants because of their appearances and outward display of heritage and/or religious identity. Such attitudes can perpetuate the otherness of immigrants and may account for the minimal usage of Catalan in most domains in the context of this study that is present even among the second-generation informants, even if it is comparably more frequent than that of first-generation informants. Since the present study and previous studies (Cortès-Colomé *et al.*, 2016; Gore, 2002) indicate that foreign-born immigrants often regard Catalan as a status language that also marks belonging to Catalan society, this reported tendency to associate Spanish with immigrant populations further solidifies Catalan's position as a language of exclusivity. While such attitudes do not appear to prevent second-generation informants from identifying with both Spanish and Catalan – even if others may not recognize these identities – it may impact their connections to their heritage and religious identities, as these distinctions can at times seem incompatible with their linguistic identities and may set them apart as outsiders. Still, it is evident that several informants have chosen to integrate in such a way that they have adapted partially while avoiding total assimilation into Catalan/Spanish society. This can be seen in informants' tendency to designate specific domains for preserving their heritage cultures and languages, most notably at home and among family, a practice that is not uncommon among second-generation immigrants.

Informants' attitudes toward their own heritage communities and languages are also impactful in how individuals forge new identities and connections to the TL community. On the one hand, Chapter 7 showed that all informants reportedly use their HLs in at least one domain, unanimously expressed positive attitudes toward their HLs, and also agreed or strongly agreed with statements placing importance on the HL/culture or connecting it to heritage identity. On the other hand, fewer than half of the informants reported using their HLs exclusively in any given domain and often reported using it in combination with other languages. Furthermore, HLs were associated more with solidarity traits than with status traits in questionnaire responses, though this association was not as strong as that between status traits and Catalan/Spanish (with the exception of 'religious' being associated almost unanimously with HLs, which is further discussed in the next section). Additionally, as illustrated in Chapters 5 and 6, several informants from both generations expressed negative attitudes toward immigrant communities because they believed that many of its members were failing to adapt to the TL community and that this was often attributed to a lack of effort on the part of first-generation immigrants. The results from this study do not necessarily support these claims, as neither interview nor questionnaire responses from first-generation informants indicated a significant detachment from the TL cultures or languages, apart from some informants who had not been living in Catalonia for very long. One notable exception, however, was Iram, who was a longtime resident of Barcelona and had raised all of her daughters there. However, despite her disinterest in socially integrating and participating in Catalan/Spanish culture, she was one of the few first-generation informants to conduct her interview entirely in Spanish, and with relative ease. Still, such negative attitudes toward HL community members – as well as Iram's demonstrable proficiency in Spanish – would suggest that both generations are generally invested in acquiring and integrating the

TL cultures and languages in their lives to some degree, and perhaps view this acquisition as paramount to successfully navigating life in Catalonia.

While these findings relate to a very specific population, there are certainly a number of broader implications for more general discussions of immigrants' experiences with acculturation and linguistic assimilation. First, while many discussions on this topic focus on or assume that immigrant populations are faced with learning only one language upon arriving in another country (e.g. learning English in the US or the UK), there are certainly many instances where immigrants enter into officially bi- or multilingual societies and may feel obligated to learn more than one language in order to gain membership in the TL community and a sense of belonging. In such contexts, the acculturation process may be significantly different for immigrants. While monolingual societies often pressure immigrants to make choices between their HL(s) and a single TL, the multiple languages present in a bi-/multilingual society create a more complex hierarchy for immigrant populations to decipher. In the latter case, and as seen in Catalonia, each language may have a different status or set of ideologies attached to it, and oftentimes these language ideologies are connected to political ones. Immigrants are thus obligated to interpret a linguistic pecking order while simultaneously attempting to make decisions about language learning and practices that can best assist in their social integration, both on a practical level and also in terms of how they want to reconstruct their identities or position themselves within the TL communities (or at a distance from TL communities, if they are not integrated yet and do not feel a sense of belonging). Furthermore, competing language ideologies within a society can send mixed messages to immigrant populations, which can present additional challenges to them as they attempt to negotiate life in a new society and thus delay or impede the integration process for them.

More broadly speaking, informants' narratives that reflect on how they are positioned relative to the TL community call attention to the very conceptualization of integration and what this process entails for immigrant populations. While language policies recognize integration as being bidirectional and a shared responsibility of the host society and immigrant individuals (see Chapter 2), it is clear from this and previous studies that this is not reflected in many immigrants' experiences and that in many instances, immigrants are typically the ones to shoulder the burden of their own social integration. The one-sidedness of this process can also be tied to the very language used to describe integration: it is often expressed as a process in the passive voice, in which a newcomer is incorporated or accepted into a community. Alternatively, it is described in a way that places the unintegrated individual as the active agent: a newcomer joins or becomes part of a community. Seldom do descriptions of integration spotlight the role of the host society, for instance, 'a host society accepts a newcomer'. The very definition of acceptance requires participation from two parties: the acceptor and the accepted. Similarly, the concept of integration also requires mutual participation of two parties; yet integration is rarely operationalized as such, but must be if it is to actually begin to reflect a bidirectional process.

Intersectional Identities in Sociolinguistic Research

One of the central goals of this study was to examine gendered and religious identities and how they may shape or be shaped by linguistic behavior. Informants in this study demonstrated that their language use and attitudes were informed at least in part by these identities. As noted in Chapter 5, a pattern among first-generation informants was to employ distinct discursive practices that depended on the gender of their interlocutor. This was practiced specifically with interlocutors from their heritage communities, where many women maintained a degree of formality and distance when speaking with Muslim men or with men of the same heritage background. For most women, this distinction was not present in their interactions with members of the TL community, and for a few women, male interlocutors were almost entirely absent from their day-to-day communications outside the home environment. These interactions show how religious and gendered identities function together – and selectively – to shape informants' discursive practices, as well as the social circles in which they interact.

While such tendencies are also present among second-generation informants, Chapter 6 highlighted another aspect of how gender, religion and language use intersect: specifically, how informants' visibility as Muslim women has impacted their interactions, particularly with members of the TL community, with whom many of these informants actually identify. From limiting informants' job opportunities to simply being assigned to a monolithic 'foreigner' identity, many second-generation informants who wear a *hijab* are often viewed as outsiders and are thus kept at a distance from other members of the TL community and have less contact with Spanish and Catalan than their non-*hijab*-wearing or non-Muslim counterparts. In the case of Catalan, accommodation norms that focus on the use of Spanish are already a common practice among White, native Catalan speakers, and are frequently imposed on a number of informants, particularly those who appear to be 'foreign'. While this may not be a generation-specific phenomenon, it can be a particularly exclusionary experience for second-generation Muslims, who have been educated and socialized in Catalan to the same extent as non-Muslim Catalan speakers but are nonetheless regarded as outsiders, thus reinforcing the sense of otherness that many immigrants feel, regardless of generation.

These attitudes that stem from the TL community also offer further evidence to the notion that identity – be it gendered, racial or immigrant – is performative and brokered through reiterative discourse created and maintained by others (Butler, 1993; Inda, 2000; Massey & Sánchez, 2010). In the present context, several informants – particularly second-generation – report on TL community members' attitudes that appear to reflect imposed identities: foreigners who are unlikely to know Catalan and should thus be spoken to in Spanish. While this attitude is often rooted in informants' visibility as Muslim women, often through wearing *hijab*, gendered and religious identities may also be naturalized within the Muslim community through expectations of other members, oftentimes parents and/or first-generation members, as seen in the mother–daughter dialogue between Aziza and Souhaila in Chapter 6. In all cases, informants who shared these experiences of imposed identities discussed them not as specific, singular acts, but rather as repetitive ones, which – as Butler (1993) argues – is necessary to naturalize identity over time. However, at times informants contest such impositions, not by rejecting or distancing themselves from Muslim identity, but rather, transforming what it means to be Muslim.

Looking at the broader implications of these findings, the present results lend support to the idea that the performativity of identity can be shaped by any aspect of social interaction, including the identity of one's interlocutor. Interlocutors of different social groups can prompt individuals to reflexively enact specific identities and, as a result, specific linguistic practices. This further supports our understanding of identity as fluid and susceptible to change, and religious identity is no exception. It is neither monolithic nor static, and its manifestation can vary across an individual's interactions, much like any other identity. While religious identity is certainly not crucial or even a part of many individuals, those who do identify religiously may find that it is tightly intertwined with other aspects of their identities. As such, sociolinguistic research focusing on identity needs to consider how these intersections may vary when examining specific sociocultural contexts. For instance, gendered, White identity is not the same as gendered identity for a person of color; there are different nuances for a woman who is Black, and still others for Asian women or Latinx women. Similarly, a Jewish woman or a Muslim woman also experiences gender differently. These distinctions, then, can play a crucial role in how each of these individuals discursively negotiate their respective identities.

Additionally, the results of the present study – particularly those that highlight the sense of otherness that many immigrants experience regardless of whether they are first/second-generation or beyond – also bring into question how the term *immigrant* is used, and the connotations that are associated with it. As demonstrated throughout this book, it is often synonymous with words such as *other*, *outsider* and *foreigner*. In many instances (including the present study), these connotations are gendered and carry additionally negative connotations, such as in the case of Muslim women, who – as shown in Chapter 6 – may be regarded as submissive or unintelligent. Together, these negative connotations may be associated with even more hostile ones, such as *threat*. Ultimately, the word itself and its referents are both associated with distance and separation from TL communities, which is especially problematic in some cases. For instance, the specific language and cultural practices that are associated with an immigrant group will often become naturalized as immigrant languages and cultures, which, in some contexts, seriously diminish the profundity of their presence because they are removed from the non-immigrant contexts in which they exist. This is certainly relevant in the case of Muslim women in this study, where many of the informants were Arabic speakers, a language that has a long history in Spain and a permanent presence in the Spanish language. Despite the profound impact Arabic has had on the Spanish language and culture, it is still widely regarded as an immigrant language in Spain that plays no role in the construction of modern Spanish heritage, thus erasing its historical contribution and casting Arabic speakers (and indeed Muslims of other backgrounds who are often assumed to be Arab) as being *foreign*. For this reason, it is necessary to critically examine how the term *immigrant* is operationalized and connoted in social discourse in Catalonia, both among individuals and in mass communication. This is especially relevant in the social context of Catalonia, where secularism plays an important role in progressive politics and nationalist ideologies. While the Catalan government has certainly provided provisions for accommodating religious diversity (Astor, 2020), the intersection of nationalism, secularism and the Catalan language can position individuals with religious convictions as outsiders within Catalonia, whose beliefs and social practices may be regarded as incompatible with those of the TL community. This, in turn, may also reinforce the notions of Catalan as an exclusive language, and languages associated with religion (e.g. Arabic) as foreign.

Future Directions

There are a number of factors in this study that should be acknowledged not only as limitations that impact the scope of the findings presented, but also as touchstones for moving forward in this field of investigation. First, this study relied entirely on data from female informants from diverse geographic and linguistic backgrounds. While my goal was to specifically highlight the experiences of female informants and demonstrate how religious identity in this context is shared among varied ethnic identities, a different approach to selecting informants could offer a more comprehensive understanding of the relationship between gendered identity and reported language use and attitudes. For example, including other genders as well as having equal numbers of informants from different geographic backgrounds could allow for moving beyond an examination of the generational differences that I examined in this study, and carrying out a comparative analysis of gendered and ethnic differences. By the same token, my own identity positioned me advantageously for working within the narrow focus of Muslim women. Yet, as an American with limited proficiency in Catalan, my findings are presented from an outsider's perspective. Similar research conducted by academics who identify more closely with Muslim women in this context (i.e. Muslim women from Catalonia, and living in Catalonia) may provide even richer data and more telling insights.

The scope of this study may also be extended in other ways: having focused on informants residing in the province of Barcelona, a large metropolis with a diverse international and multilingual presence, this particular setting presents a unique linguistic situation in comparison to the rest of Catalonia. Still, as I noted in Chapter 2, foreign-born immigrants account for a comparable percentage of the total population in each of Catalonia's *vegueries*. For this reason, looking at other parts of Catalonia where Catalan has a stronger presence than Spanish might yield different results from what was presented in this study. Furthermore, given the linguistic situation in Catalonia, this study – while contributing to a better understanding of immigrants and acquiring societal bilingualism – is not necessarily a representative of broader experiences of immigrants who migrate to other parts of Spain that are not officially bilingual. This work, however, does provide insight on the process of acculturation in the context of linguistic conflict, where immigrant populations' decisions regarding language learning often revolve around practicality, which may be at odds with popular language ideologies.

Furthermore, the methodology that I employed for this study allowed me to examine the linguistic behavior and attitudes of immigrants by looking at reported language use rather than actual language use. Data collected in this manner has its merits: in taking an emic approach to this investigation, the data of this study relied on informants' own views and interpretations of their behavior rather than the researcher extrapolating from observations as an outsider. This method thus provided a window into informants' linguistic ideologies; specifically, their beliefs and feelings about their own language use, which can also be impactful on actual language use. Still, examining informants' actual language use in a natural setting would not only mitigate partiality that perhaps might have stemmed from informants with regard to their linguistic practices but would also provide a more concrete evidence of how language attitudes are reflected in language use. In terms of the specific languages examined, this investigation maintained a fairly extensive purview, focusing on Spanish, Catalan and HLs. Additionally, in grouping HLs together in this study, no comparison was made between different HLs and if/how these languages may have been an influencing factor in the results. As such, an analysis of reported language use and attitudes that includes a comparative analysis of different HLs could be useful to understanding how acculturation experiences in Catalonia may vary according to different immigrant groups.

One additional language that emerged as an important one for many informants and certainly merits further exploration is the role of English for immigrants. While this study's design did not account for this language as a potentially significant one in this particular setting, English nonetheless played an important role in the daily lives of several of the informants, as evidenced by the use of English during interviews – most notably among several Urdu-speaking informants who code-switched between English and either Urdu or Spanish. This prompts the question of what role English might have as a prestigious international language in terms of impacting immigrants' investment in other languages such as Spanish and Catalan, particularly if English is more highly valued among immigrants and/or if they already have a strong command of English. While results from this study do point to English having an important role as a frequently used, high-status language for several informants, this study did not methodically examine English alongside Spanish, Catalan and HLs, and so little can be said for informants who indicated knowing English but did not rely on it as an option for the questionnaire tasks or for their interviews. Therefore, the present study cannot offer sufficient observations relating to the role of English among these informants as a collective, but rather serves as a benchmark for further investigation.

Additionally, as I have pointed out throughout this study, acculturation is arguably a bidirectional process that is influenced by members of the TL community as much as it is by TL learners. The narratives of this study's informants certainly suggest as much; therefore, an examination of TL community members' linguistic practices and attitudes toward immigrant communities may also serve to provide a clearer picture of the setting in which immigrants are attempting to acculturate and whether or not members of the TL community have distinctive attitudes toward different immigrant communities and languages. The results of my study suggest the affirmative, which calls attention to the need to acknowledge specific sociocultural contexts when discussing immigrant populations, and recognize that such discussions are not one-size-fits-all. In other words, some immigrant groups may be more readily accepted into the TL community than others and critical to examine why such disparate treatment occurs. Additionally, focusing on members of the TL community may shed light on how their linguistic behavior interacts with and positions members of immigrant communities. This is an especially critical component to not only understanding acculturation, but also taking actionable steps to ensure that this transition goes smoothly for immigrant populations. Frequently, immigrants are expected to shoulder in its entirety the responsibility of integration, when in fact the responsibility of meeting such expectations should be actively shared by members of the TL community as well.

Conclusion

Ultimately, the central goal of this study was to gain a better understanding of language attitudes and language use among Muslim women in Barcelona. While this population has been extensively investigated in scholarly research – owing to an interest in how their gendered, religious identity informs their life experiences – such studies are scarce in the field of sociolinguistics. As such, this study aimed to call attention to this significant gap in our understanding of how language functions as a social practice by focusing on this relatively unexplored intersection of identity from a linguistic perspective. Given the increasing attention given to examining immigrant populations' experiences with multilingualism in Catalonia, this study has demonstrated that Muslim women are a distinctive and significant population in this linguistic setting, in that many of them are uniquely positioned as outsiders in a way that other immigrant groups are not, owing to visible signs of their religious, gendered identities. Adding this population, then, to the existing body of linguistic research relating to immigrants in Catalonia not only offers a more thorough understanding of multilingualism in Catalonia as experienced by immigrant populations, but also highlights the role of religious and gendered identity in linguistic behavior and attitudes – specifically those which may impact language acquisition or loss in a multilingual setting.

Given that some of the most salient themes discussed in this book involve the exclusion and minoritization of immigrant populations – and in the case of my study, Muslim women – as well as the imbalance in the responsibilities that TL and immigrant communities should but do not share with regard to the integration process, one last point of discussion that is critical to any study on marginalized populations is a reflection on actionable steps that can enact positive change. The final chapter of this book returns to a discussion on language policy and planning in Catalonia, and how changes at the institutional level can better serve immigrant populations in the integration process.

9 Implications for Language and Immigrant-Targeted Policies

Introduction

This book has explored the linguistic behavior of Muslim immigrant woman in Catalonia through their narratives and self-reports. The findings that I discussed in previous chapters demonstrate not only that acculturation is a transgenerational process, but that – among Muslim women – gendered, religious identity plays an important role in their language use and attitudes. This research sheds additional light on our understanding of immigrants' experiences in acquiring societal bilingualism, as well as the importance of acknowledging the intersectionality of identity in linguistic research in terms of how multiple, overlapping characteristics can collectively contribute to otherness and marginalization. However, given that the use of Catalan and Spanish in Catalonia is very much historically and politically situated, it is worth reflecting on how these findings relate back to language and immigrant-targeted policies that have been implemented in Catalonia (as discussed in Chapter 2). Specifically, how do some of the previously discussed policies achieve and/or fall short in their goals? How might future iterations of these policies be constructed to mutually and better benefit immigrant populations along with the larger Catalan society as a whole? In this final chapter, I reflect on how ideologies from language policies may be manifested and/or challenged by informants' language self-reported language practices. In an effort to problematize language policy and planning in Catalonia, I also discuss how these policies may at times appear to be incompatible with the realities lived by immigrant populations. Finally, I offer suggestions for future policy iterations (both immigrant-targeted and those for the Catalan population as a whole) that address not only the use of Spanish and Catalan, but also the status of and discourse on other widely used languages in Catalonia, particularly those spoken by immigrant populations.

Language Policy in Practice: Informants' Perspectives

While the informants of this study did not engage explicitly in discussions about language policy in Catalonia, much of what they reported on their own language practices can still tell us a great deal about the extent to which language policy is put into practice. At times, we can see how linguistic ideologies from these policies are manifested in individual linguistic behavior; for instance, looking first to some of the patterns found in questionnaire responses, it is apparent that discourse in language policies that promote Catalan as the vehicular language does not entirely align with informants' self-reports. While informants often indicated using Catalan in different domains of language use, this was mostly limited to second-generation informants and was often paired with Spanish as a co-vehicular language. This balance between Spanish and Catalan may have mixed implications for the Catalan population: for some, this may be seen as a sign of harmonious coexistence between two languages, whose speakers do not view as being at odds with each other. For others, this may signal an incomplete revitalization of Catalan. Still, informants' questionnaire responses also showed that they valued the use and maintenance of Catalan alongside Spanish and their heritage languages (HLs). That said, the relative importance that informants gave to using and maintaining HLs and the general absence of such languages from policy discourse shows further misalignment between policy and reality. This can be further supported by the fact that in assigning solidarity and status traits to HL speakers and Spanish/Catalan speakers, the latter were more strongly associated with status traits than the former, suggesting that – although they may be valorized insofar as they are associated with cultural heritage and identity – HLs do not carry the same linguistic capital as Catalan or Spanish.

Ideologies shaped by policy discourse are also manifested, though more frequently challenged, by informants' narratives. For instance, the political and historical context that has shaped so much of current language policy in Catalonia is known even among first-generation informants, who were not raised or educated in Catalonia. As noted by Rabya in Chapter 5, the preservation of Catalan is historically significant, and in fact, the years of linguistic prohibition under Francisco Franco certainly had a hand in informing the multilingual framework that has shaped Catalan language policy. Still, one of the central tenets of language policy is the normalization of Catalan and its use as the 'vehicular' language of Catalonia. However, this was evidently not the case among the informants in this study. While Catalan is certainly used by several informants and in different contexts, its use was limited, and in fact its value was often challenged because of its perceived lack of practicality in comparison to Spanish, as noted by both first- and second-generation informants, such as Iman in Chapter 5, who indicated that Catalan was not useful outside of Catalonia, or Sharifa and Mariam in Chapter 6, who pointed out that they preferred to use Spanish and Arabic in the streets over Catalan, and that Catalan was really only the dominant language in the educational sphere. While this may appear to demonstrate the limited reach of Catalan, its presence in educational institutions may in fact be significantly impactful: as noted in Chapter 7, questionnaire data suggested that higher levels of education among informants signaled a greater affinity for Catalan, though simultaneously a decreased use of HLs. Still, given that the Catalan government's reach extends to public sectors such as educational institutions, it comes as no surprise that language planning has had limited success outside of such domains. In the case of first-generation informants, it is also worth reiterating that a number of them connected their language learning priorities to practicality, and therefore prioritized Spanish as being more instrumental to their adjustment to life in Catalonia, thus reassigning Spanish as the more 'vehicular' language. Considering that the practicality of Catalan does not come into question among second-generation informants suggests that these distinctive attitudes of each generation may relate back to their respective training in Catalan. While second-generation informants received their full-time, obligatory education in Catalan from a young age, first-generation informants are, at best, able to complete basic training as adults. Given the limited resources that are provided to first-generation immigrants for learning Catalan, as noted in Chapter 2, viewing Spanish as the more practical language may be more of a reflection of insufficient training in Catalan to confidently navigate their day-to-day lives than a lack of Catalan-speaking interlocutors available to speak with them.

Additionally, while language policies of Catalonia set forth goals of establishing Catalan as a de-ethnicized, public language that is inclusive to all of Catalonia's population, this does not appear to be the experiences of some of the informants, which is especially salient among the second-generation, as shown in Chapter 6: Sharifa, who associated the Catalan language with Catalan identity, and pointed out that others distanced her from the language, having assumed that she was an outsider who did not know the language (despite having received an education in Catalan). Similarly, Dina also highlighted the exclusivity of Catalan in her remark about receiving better treatment from others if she used Catalan, marking it as an exclusive, higher status language. However, there may be other explanations for informants' distance from Catalan that have nothing to do with personal or social factors. Because language ideologies and practices are often tied to political ideologies or ideas about national identity, one element that is often overlooked by policymakers in multilingual societies is the typological relationship between languages and how that may play a role in people's linguistic behavior. Rabya had noted in Chapter 5 that she understood Catalan but often did not register that she was hearing Catalan and would automatically respond in Spanish. As typologically similar languages, there is a degree of mutual intelligibility between Catalan and Spanish, and so this close relationship may hinder individuals from being motivated to learn both languages, particularly if one is capable of making do with one language (Catalan) while being proficient in the more socially dominant language (Spanish).

As noted in Chapter 2, language policies certainly acknowledge the presence and value of languages besides Catalan, most notably through an emphasis on linguistic pluralism as a critical component of Catalan identity and culture. While specific languages are not mentioned beyond Catalan, Aranese and Catalan Sign Language, policies do recognize the linguistic diversity that comprises Catalan society, particularly that which comes from its migrant populations. However, a number of comments from informants indicate a sense of separation between HL and target language (TL) cultures, where the former is either not tolerated by members of the TL community, or at best a component of Catalan society that is more additive than constitutive. Much of this stems from informants' perceptions of TL members' attitudes, which they often viewed as negative. For example, Mona had claimed that Spaniards viewed all Arabs as *moros*, which can be a comment on both the pejorative and homogenizing use of the term. While most second-generation informants expressed pride in their HLs and valued their maintenance, none of them connected this to Spanish or Catalan identity, which perhaps is indicative of separation between heritage and Spanish/Catalan identities. While it is difficult to designate a correlation between these attitudes and language policy discourse, it is still worth noting that there is a general absence of any explicit instructions or programming that aim to protect the linguistic vitality of HLs. Not only that, but – where immigrant-target policies are concerned – immigrants themselves are the only participants involved in these texts, disinvolving members of the TL community from the responsibility of linguistic pluralism and language maintenance. Bearing that in mind, that pluralism (as realized by immigrant populations) does not appear to form a significant part of Catalan identity may very well be connected to the way responsibilities are discursively set forth in language policies.

Problematizing Language Policy and Planning

While much of the intentional policy work that has been done since the 1980s has seen success in terms of revitalizing Catalan and reshaping the collective linguistic identity of Catalonia, the data from this study has illustrated that language policy and planning in Catalonia still appears to fall short of some of its goals, particularly where immigrant populations are concerned. As shown throughout this book, some of the fundamental goals and ideologies that are set forth and reiterated across different policies do not always reflect the linguistic reality of many individuals living in Catalonia, which would suggest a need to not only reevaluate the implementation of such policies, but also reexamine the relevance of present ideologies and whether or not they are compatible with the linguistic behaviors and ideologies of the modern Catalan population. One key limitation that I identified above is that – despite the efforts to construct Catalan as the vehicular and common language of Catalonia – language planning thus far has resulted in Catalan (language and identity) to be associated with exclusivity and prestige rather than inclusivity. Because of its rather overt prestige, Catalan is often inaccessible to marginalized populations, particularly those of lower socioeconomic status and/or immigrant background. These groups account for a large portion of the Catalan population, and as such, the long-standing goal of linguistic normalization may remain unfulfilled for some time. This obstacle can be addressed in a number of ways, the foremost being policy and planning in Catalonia's education system. As noted in Chapter 2, there is a good deal of segregation in schools between immigrant and Catalan students (from which linguistic segregation follows), where welcome classrooms for the former may be in isolated parts of a school, or even the latter avoiding altogether the schools with significant immigrant populations (Trenchs-Parera & Newman, 2015). A number of adjustments to language in education policies can be made in order to foster inclusivity in the use of Catalan. First, while there is no doubt that providing immigrant students with some degree of differentiated instruction and separate space from other students may be helpful to their learning experiences, schools and educators should make efforts to ensure that immigrant students are not experiencing social isolation from their peers. This can be achieved through curricular design that provides differentiated instruction within classrooms that caters to the linguistic, social and affective needs of all students. Such instruction should not treat immigrant students as exceptional cases against the 'normal' Catalan student; nor should it treat immigrant students' identities as merely tolerated entities, but rather as integral members of their school communities. Such practices would not only place immigrant students in a better position to be active participants in Catalan classrooms, but also take some of the burden off of them in their efforts to socially integrate. More generally, accessibility in language education is key, and it is paramount that policymakers focus on identifying equity gaps, both for child and adult learners from diverse backgrounds. In the case of the population examined here, Muslim women may have limited access to language education if they are uncomfortable attending mixed-sex classes and/or interacting outside the Muslim community (Rida & Milton, 2001). Still, even for Muslim women who may not feel discomfort with such settings, EU policies have targeted Muslim women – among other religious groups – in condoning bans on visible displays of religious identity. Such policies can certainly trickle down and across the EU, and as such, policymakers in Catalonia may need to consider the implications of such rulings, particularly in the way that Muslim women may be barred from certain sectors of the TL community and thus have limited or no access to TLs like Catalan.

A second area that merits reevaluation in language policy is discourse relating to social integration as a two-way process. As noted in Chapter 2, policy and planning discourse, such as that found in the *Citizenship and Migration Plan, 2017–2020* [*Pla de ciutadania i de les migracions, 2017–2020*] (Generalitat de Catalunya, 2017a) that pertain specifically to immigrant populations, do indeed note that social cohesion, intercultural education, and therefore the social integration of immigrants are a collective responsibility of all Catalan residents. However, while the above document offers guidance regarding resources for immigrant populations (such as welcome classrooms) that require their initiative in order to move forward with the integration process, language policy generally sidesteps discourse relating to the role of the TL community in social integration. Once again, the burden is placed on immigrants. This is further evidenced by the narratives of the informants from this study, such as seeing informants' HLs (as well as heritage identities and cultural practices) existing separately from the TL community, rather than being an integral part of it. In order to move toward an integration process that is truly bidirectional, it would be beneficial for future iterations of language policy to be more explicitly inclusive of immigrant populations. This would be particularly useful in policies that are aimed more generally at the Catalan population, rather than solely those that focus specifically on immigrant populations, since the former often describe the diversity of the Catalan population in broad terms without specifying what comprises that diverse population. Additionally, all language policy and planning discourse should emphasize the bidirectionality of integration more; specifically, such discourse needs to clearly operationalize this concept. For instance, what does it mean for integration to be bidirectional? What are the responsibilities of immigrants? What are the responsibilities of members of the TL community? What actionable measures are available to guide both groups in terms of fulfilling this civic duty? If language education is part of this bidirectional integration process, what is the role of HLs? Without engaging in such questions, the responsibility of social integration will remain largely on the shoulders of immigrants, which not only places an unfair burden on this group, but also serves as a hindrance to achieving a truly multicultural society in which HLs and cultures are not only tolerated, but welcomed and accepted in the mainstream, TL culture.

Finally, policymakers may reevaluate the way in which multilingualism is operationalized in language policy. While language ideologies are frequently attached to a 'multilingual framework', and policies emphasize the right to use and duty to learn 'both languages', such discourse is often ambiguous about which languages are being referenced in these contexts. While it may easily be assumed that 'both languages' refers to Catalan and

Spanish, much of the existing policy discourse only makes explicit mention of Catalan, and rarely mentions Spanish. Effectively, such discourse simultaneously acknowledges and disregards Spanish as one of the official and dominant languages in Catalonia. As discussed previously in Chapter 2, this discursive erasure of Spanish is rooted in historically situated political ideologies, as well as in one of the central goals of language policy in Catalonia: revitalizing Catalan and undoing decades of linguistic suppression that was largely manifested by the implementation of Spanish-only language planning.

The trajectory of Catalan revitalization and the resulting absence of Spanish from policy discourse has fairly transparent historical and political foundations, and policy discourse that centers Catalan in favor of Spanish may indeed reflect popular ideologies and attitudes. However, such discourse does not reflect the linguistic reality of Catalonia in which Spanish is still a widely used language, particularly in large, international hubs such as Barcelona. Moreover, as demonstrated throughout this book, the misalignment between policy discourse and reality can be especially troublesome for immigrant populations, as it sends mixed messages to them, thereby further complicating their transition in a new and multilingual society. This is further problematic when also taking into consideration the discourse on the 'multilingual framework' that shapes Catalan society, as noted in *Language and Social Cohesion Plan* [*Pla per a la llengua i la cohesió social* (Generalitat de Catalunya, 2004)], a framework that is described as being critical to social cohesion in Catalonia.

Considering the ongoing tension between the two languages, particularly in the context of public spheres where the Catalan government maintains some degree of jurisdiction in terms of putting language policy into practice, policymakers may also need to review discourse that pertains to multilingualism, and more specifically Spanish and Catalan. Because Spanish is indeed a significant language in any part of Catalonia, it may be beneficial to explicitly acknowledge it by name in policy discourse. Additionally, future policy iterations may be more beneficial if there were more explicit, clear discourse that focuses on the desired role of Spanish and Catalan. Should these two languages exist in a diglossic situation, where they are used in distinct domains, and would such diglossic practices further perpetuate high-low status distinctions between the two languages? Should they coexist across all domains? Should Catalan supplant Spanish altogether? Such questions should be addressed clearly in language policies, eliminating ideological ambiguities that may be the source of some of the tensions and conflicts that arise in everyday language use. Moreover, intentionally overlooking Spanish in favor of Catalan may actually fuel negative attitudes toward Catalan and resistance to Catalan normalization efforts. As such, favoring transparency when discursively constructing the linguistic situation in language policy may in fact help normalization efforts.

Multilingualism in Catalonia, however, is not simply limited to Catalan and Spanish. Beyond clearer acknowledgment of Spanish, language policy discourse needs to elaborate on the languages that have a role in contributing to social cohesion in Catalonia within the framework of multilingualism. As demonstrated in this study, immigrant populations often live multilingual lives that involve the use of Spanish, Catalan, one or more HL(s) and additional languages such as English and French, and thus play a vital role in the shaping of multilingual and multicultural societies. Yet their multilingualism is nearly invisible in policy discourse, where Catalan is established as the key player in contributing to social cohesion and the center of the multilingual framework. To a limited degree, other officially recognized languages, such as Aranese and Catalan Sign Language, are acknowledged. However, language policy generally fails to spotlight the role of other widely spoken languages in Catalonia, which raises the questions: (1) what does it mean to be an officially recognized language in Catalonia? and (2) how do other widely spoken, yet unrecognized languages fit into the collective Catalan identity? English, for example, is manifestly present and highly valued among many of the informants in this study. To some extent, English is included in language planning in higher education, where the Catalan government has proposed that university graduates demonstrate intermediate-level proficiency in a language that is part of the European Union's Common European Framework of Reference for Languages, which can include – but is not limited to – English (Soler & Gallego-Balsà, 2019). However, such language planning does not extend to many first-generation immigrants who have received their education in the countries of origin.

As another example, Arabic has a long history in Spain, and in fact predates the development of modern Spanish, Catalan, Aranese and Catalan Sign Language, which has resulted in significant lexical contributions to Spanish (and to a lesser extent, Catalan and Aranese). More importantly, Arabic has remained a stable language in Spain (including in Catalonia) more recently, owing to the generations of immigrants – primarily from Morocco – who have maintained use of the language even outside of the home environment. Given its significant interaction with Spanish and Catalan culture, and the fact that the number of Arabic speakers even outnumbers those of some of official languages of Catalonia, including Aranese (Institut d'Estadística de Catalunya, 2018), such a significant presence may be an indicator that Arabic merits similar recognition in Catalonia, or more broadly in Spain. However, bearing in mind that such measures would require a significant leap from the status quo, a less dramatic yet still significant step in language policy development would be to offer more profound and critical reflection on the status of different languages in Catalonia. As shown in this study, HLs such as Arabic are valorized differently from Spanish and Catalan – both among immigrant and TL communities – and therefore carry different degrees of linguistic capital. These variances may thus inform the extent to which different languages are collectively tolerated, accepted and/or integrated within Catalan society. That being the case, discourse in language policy that addresses such differences (and often imbalances) may serve to foster greater inclusivity in terms of how multilingualism and multiculturalism are understood and manifested in Catalonia.

Final Remarks

Like any scholarly work examining an ongoing and unresolved situation, this study cannot offer a definitive conclusion; neither can the findings be reduced to generalizations about the experiences of immigrants or of Muslim women in Catalonia. Instead, I would propose that this work highlights some key elements that must be centered in the study of language and identity. First and foremost, intersectionality is an integral element in not only understanding identity, but in elucidating how identity interacts with language. As shown throughout this book, informants' intersectional identities as Muslim women appeared to play a profound role in their linguistic behavior. Specifically, these identities are shaped by macro social structures that are constructed by both the TL and heritage communities, such as members of the former assuming foreignness in informants and thus lacking knowledge of Catalan; or in the case of the latter, maintaining interactional norms that are rooted in the gendered, religious sociolinguistic structures from their countries of origin.

While this study certainly supports findings from previous works that I cited in Chapters 2 and 3, my work lends a new perspective in focusing on Muslim women, illustrating that linguistic behavior – particularly among immigrant populations – may be far more nuanced than what previous work suggests. Besides ethnic/geographic backgrounds, there are a multitude of elements that construct the sociolinguistic structures ingrained in immigrants upon their arrival in a new society, all of which are social, political, historical and/or cultural constructions that play a significant role in the ease with which immigrants may acculturate in a new society. This is further complicated by the reality that acculturation is also a function of various factors coming out of the TL community, including the distinctive statuses of different languages in a multilingual society like Catalonia, the TL community's attitudes toward different immigrant groups (which are often disparate and shaped by xenophobia and/or racism), to name a few. Taking into account the many complexities that shape an individual's transition into a new society, it is unsurprising that acculturation – as shown throughout this book – is a transgenerational process. While this study focused on first- and second-generation immigrants and highlights the different experience of each generation, acculturation certainly does not stop with the second-generation and is perhaps even a process that does not have a distinct endpoint. What is clear from this study, however, is that both immigrant and TL communities play important roles in what acculturation looks like.

Individuals and communities, however, are not the only key players in shaping the extent to which immigrants are able/wish to integrate into a society. As demonstrated throughout this book, and particularly in this final chapter, language policy in a multilingual society like Catalonia also plays an integral role in how immigrants may engage with and valorize different languages used in any given community. Both quantitative and qualitative data from this study demonstrated in particular the high status, yet decentered presence of Catalan in favor of Spanish and HLs, suggesting that language policy aiming to establish Catalan as a vehicular language has accomplished this goal only partially and that further reevaluation of existing policies are perhaps required if one of the central goals of the Catalan government is to promote social cohesion through linguistic practices. Specifically, policy and planning need to offer greater consideration for the immigrant population in Catalonia, and the measures that may better serve them in terms of truly integrating into Catalan society; that is, by sharing this responsibility with the TL community while also recognizing that multilingualism involving Spanish, Catalan and HLs is a reality for most immigrants.

Ultimately, it is crucial to understand the acculturation experiences of Muslim women on their own terms. In furthering sociolinguists' understanding of how this population's linguistic behavior interacts with transient and intersectional identities that evolve throughout the acculturation process, this book serves as not only a contribution to the fields of sociolinguistics and gender studies, but it is also hoped that this work inspires additional scholarship on this timely topic, and further dialogue on the pivotal relationship between language and identity for immigrant populations.

Appendix A: Questionnaire

Cuestionario

Información general:

1. Fecha:
2. Género:
3. País de origen/nacimiento:
4. Edad:
5. Etnicidad/herencia:
6. Estado civil:
7. Número de hijos:
8. Lengua(s) materna(s):
9. Otras lenguas que habla:
10. Nivel más alto de educación completada:
11. Años de educación formal en español y/o catalán: español: _____ catalán: _____
12. Ocupación actual:
13. ¿En qué otros países has vivido/visitado, y por cuánto tiempo?

Trasfondo de lengua:

1. ¿Qué lengua hablas con más frecuencia ahora? Puedes nombrar más de una.
2. ¿Qué lengua se usa con más frecuencia en tu comunidad? Puedes nombrar más de una.
3. ¿Quién es la persona principal que te crió?
4. ¿Habló tu lengua nativa contigo la persona que te crió?
5. Si dices sí, ¿cuánto habló contigo? ___ un poco ___ mucho
6. ¿Con qué lengua te sientes más cómoda?

Opiniones: Indica la respuesta que te describe mejor.

1. Mi cultura materna/de herencia puede sobrevivir sin la lengua materna/de herencia.
    a. Totalmente de acuerdo

b. De acuerdo
   c. Ni de acuerdo ni en desacuerdo
   d. En desacuerdo
   e. Totalmente en desacuerdo
2. Mantener mi lengua materna/de herencia es importante para mí.
   a. Totalmente de acuerdo
   b. De acuerdo
   c. Ni de acuerdo ni en desacuerdo
   d. En desacuerdo
   e. Totalmente en desacuerdo
3. Mi lengua materna/de herencia es una parte importante de mi identidad.
   a. Totalmente de acuerdo
   b. De acuerdo
   c. Ni de acuerdo ni en desacuerdo
   d. En desacuerdo
   e. Totalmente en desacuerdo
4. Estoy satisfecha con mis habilidades en mi lengua materna/lengua de herencia.
   a. Totalmente de acuerdo
   b. De acuerdo
   c. Ni de acuerdo ni en desacuerdo
   d. En desacuerdo
   e. Totalmente en desacuerdo
5. Mi etnicidad/herencia tiene un papel importante en mi vida personal.
   a. Totalmente de acuerdo
   b. De acuerdo
   c. Ni de acuerdo ni en desacuerdo
   d. En desacuerdo
   e. Totalmente en desacuerdo
6. Me gustan las tradiciones y costumbres de mi cultura de herencia.
   a. Totalmente de acuerdo
   b. De acuerdo
   c. Ni de acuerdo ni en desacuerdo
   d. En desacuerdo
   e. Totalmente en desacuerdo
7. Siento mucho cariño por la cultura catalana.
   a. Totalmente de acuerdo
   b. De acuerdo
   c. Ni de acuerdo ni en desacuerdo
   d. En desacuerdo
   e. Totalmente en desacuerdo
8. Me gustan las tradiciones y costumbres españoles.
   a. Totalmente de acuerdo

    b. De acuerdo
    c. Ni de acuerdo ni en desacuerdo
    d. En desacuerdo
    e. Totalmente en desacuerdo
9. Estoy satisfecha con mis habilidades en español.
    a. Totalmente de acuerdo
    b. De acuerdo
    c. Ni de acuerdo ni en desacuerdo
    d. En desacuerdo
    e. Totalmente en desacuerdo
10. Estoy satisfecha con mis habilidades en catalán.
    a. Totalmente de acuerdo
    b. De acuerdo
    c. Ni de acuerdo ni en desacuerdo
    d. En desacuerdo
    e. Totalmente en desacuerdo
11. Me gusta estar con gente que son de etnicidades diferentes de la mía.
    a. Totalmente de acuerdo
    b. De acuerdo
    c. Ni de acuerdo ni en desacuerdo
    d. En desacuerdo
    e. Totalmente en desacuerdo
12. Si tengo hijos, es importante que sepan mi lengua de herencia.
    a. Totalmente de acuerdo
    b. De acuerdo
    c. Ni de acuerdo ni en desacuerdo
    d. En desacuerdo
    e. Totalmente en desacuerdo
13. Si tengo hijos, es importante que sepan español.
    a. Totalmente de acuerdo
    b. De acuerdo
    c. Ni de acuerdo ni en desacuerdo
    d. En desacuerdo
    e. Totalmente en desacuerdo
14. Si tengo hijos, es importante que sepan catalán.
    f. Totalmente de acuerdo
    g. De acuerdo
    h. Ni de acuerdo ni en desacuerdo
    i. En desacuerdo
    j. Totalmente en desacuerdo
15. Cuando hablo con otra persona bilingüe, a veces alterno entre lenguas.
    a. Totalmente de acuerdo
    b. De acuerdo

c. Ni de acuerdo ni en desacuerdo
   d. En desacuerdo
   e. Totalmente en desacuerdo
16. Me gustaría aprender más sobre mi etnicidad/cultura de herencia.
   a. Totalmente de acuerdo
   b. De acuerdo
   c. Ni de acuerdo ni en desacuerdo
   d. En desacuerdo
   e. Totalmente en desacuerdo
17. Pienso que la alternancia entre lenguas en una conversación es una manera aceptable para comunicarse.
   a. Totalmente de acuerdo
   b. De acuerdo
   c. Ni de acuerdo ni en desacuerdo
   d. En desacuerdo
   e. Totalmente en desacuerdo
18. Me gusta estar con gente de la misma etnicidad como yo.
   a. Totalmente de acuerdo
   b. De acuerdo
   c. Ni de acuerdo ni en desacuerdo
   d. En desacuerdo
   e. Totalmente en desacuerdo

Indica la lengua que completa mejor las siguientes oraciones.
1. La lengua que me gusta hablar más es:
              español ____ catalán ____ lengua de herencia ____
2. La lengua que me conecta más con mi cultura es:
              español ____ catalán ____ lengua de herencia ____
3. Veo películas y programas de tele en:
              español ____ catalán ____ lengua de herencia ____
4. Escucho la radio/música en:
              español ____ catalán ____ lengua de herencia ____
5. Leo sobretodo en:
              español ____ catalán ____ lengua de herencia ____
6. Uso medios sociales (Facebook, Twitter, etc.) en:
              español ____ catalán ____ lengua de herencia ____
7. La lengua más difícil de aprender es:
              español ____ catalán ____ lengua de herencia ____
8. La lengua que es más útil para mi vida profesional es:
              español ____ catalán ____ lengua de herencia ____
9. La lengua que es más útil en mi vida diaria es:
              español ____ catalán ____ lengua de herencia ____
10. Escribo correos electrónicos sobretodo en:
              español ____ catalán ____ lengua de herencia ____

11. La lengua que uso con mi familia/entre amigos es:
    español ____ catalán ____ lengua de herencia ____
12. Cuando mando mensajes de SMS a alguien, normalmente los mando en:
    español ____ catalán ____ lengua de herencia ____
13. Cuando hablo con gente que no conozco, hablo:
    español ____ catalán ____ lengua de herencia ____
14. La lengua que más me gustaría dominar es:
    español ____ catalán ____ lengua de herencia ____
15. Si estoy en un restaurante, generalmente hablo con los empleados en:
    español ____ catalán ____ lengua de herencia ____
16. Si estoy en la oficina del médico, generalmente hablo con los empleados en:
    español ____ catalán ____ lengua de herencia ____
17. Si estoy en un supermercado, generalmente hablo con los empleados en:
    español ____ catalán ____ lengua de herencia ____

Indica qué hablante asocias más con las siguientes descripciones:

1. Moderno: español/catalán ____ lengua de herencia ____
2. Mentalidad abierta: español/catalán ____ lengua de herencia ____
3. Culto: español/catalán ____ lengua de herencia ____
4. Sociable: español/ catalán ____ lengua de herencia ____
5. Simpático: español/catalán ____ lengua de herencia ____
6. Rico: español/catalán ____ lengua de herencia ____
7. Religioso: español/catalán ____ lengua de herencia ____
8. Alfabetizado: español/catalán ____ lengua de herencia ____
9. Internacional/global: español/catalán ____ lengua de herencia ____
10. Prestigioso: español/catalán ____ lengua de herencia ____
11. Puro: español/catalán ____ lengua de herencia ____
12. Informal: español/catalán ____ lengua de herencia ____
13. Bello: español/catalán ____ lengua de herencia ____
14. Práctico: español/catalán ____ lengua de herencia ____
15. Poderoso: español/catalán ____ lengua de herencia ____
16. Formal: español/catalán ____ lengua de herencia ____
17. Autoritario: español/catalán ____ lengua de herencia ____
18. Emocional: español/catalán ____ lengua de herencia ____

Questionnaire

General information:

1. Date:
2. Gender:
3. Country of origin/birth:

4. Age:
5. Ethnic origin:
6. Marital status:
7. Number of children:
8. Native language(s):
9. Other languages that you speak:
10. Highest level of completed education:
11. Years of formal education in Spanish and/or Catalan: Spanish: _____ Catalan _____
12. Current occupation:
13. Which other countries have you visited/lived in and for how long?

Language background:

1. What language do you speak most often now? You may list more than one.
2. What language is most commonly used in your community? You may list more than one.
3. Who was the main person or people who raised you?
4. Did the person/people who raised you speak your native language with you?
5. If yes, how much did they speak with you? (a little, a lot, etc.)
6. What language do you feel most comfortable communicating in?

Opinions: Indicate the degree to which you agree with the following statements.

1. My native/heritage culture can survive without the native/heritage language(s).
   a. Totally agree
   b. Agree
   c. Neither agree nor disagree
   d. Disagree
   e. Totally disagree
2. Maintaining my heritage/native language(s) is important to me.
   a. Totally agree
   b. Agree
   c. Neither agree nor disagree
   d. Disagree
   e. Totally disagree
3. My native/heritage language(s) is/are an important part of my identity.
   a. Totally agree
   b. Agree
   c. Neither agree nor disagree

d. Disagree
   e. Totally disagree
4. I am satisfied with my abilities in my native language/heritage language.
   a. Totally agree
   b. Agree
   c. Neither agree nor disagree
   d. Disagree
   e. Totally disagree
5. My ethnicity/heritage plays an important role in my personal life.
   a. Totally agree
   b. Agree
   c. Neither agree nor disagree
   d. Disagree
   e. Totally disagree
6. I like my heritage culture's traditions and customs.
   a. Totally agree
   b. Agree
   c. Neither agree nor disagree
   d. Disagree
   e. Totally disagree
7. I feel a strong attachment to Catalan culture.
   a. Totally agree
   b. Agree
   c. Neither agree nor disagree
   d. Disagree
   e. Totally disagree
8. I like Spanish traditions and customs
   a. Totally agree
   b. Agree
   c. Neither agree nor disagree
   d. Disagree
   e. Totally disagree
9. I am satisfied with my abilities in Spanish.
   a. Totally agree
   b. Agree
   c. Neither agree nor disagree
   d. Disagree
   e. Totally disagree
10. I am satisfied with my abilities in Catalan.
    a. Totally agree
    b. Agree
    c. Neither agree nor disagree
    d. Disagree
    e. Totally disagree

11. I enjoy being around people who are from different ethnic backgrounds than me.
    a. Totally agree
    b. Agree
    c. Neither agree nor disagree
    d. Disagree
    e. Totally disagree
12. It is important to me that (if) I have children, they know my heritage language.
    a. Totally agree
    b. Agree
    c. Neither agree nor disagree
    d. Disagree
    e. Totally disagree
13. It is important to me that (if) I have children, they know Spanish.
    a. Totally agree
    b. Agree
    c. Neither agree nor disagree
    d. Disagree
    e. Totally disagree
14. It is important to me that (if) I have children, they know Catalan.
    a. Totally agree
    b. Agree
    c. Neither agree nor disagree
    d. Disagree
    e. Totally disagree
15. When speaking to another bilingual person, I sometimes switch between languages.
    a. Totally agree
    b. Agree
    c. Neither agree nor disagree
    d. Disagree
    e. Totally disagree
16. I am interested in learning more about my ethnic background/heritage culture.
    a. Totally agree
    b. Agree
    c. Neither agree nor disagree
    d. Disagree
    e. Totally disagree
17. I think that switching back and forth between languages in a conversation is an acceptable way to communicate.
    a. Totally agree
    b. Agree
    c. Neither agree nor disagree

d. Disagree
   e. Totally disagree
18. I enjoy being around people from the same ethnic group as me.
   a. Totally agree
   b. Agree
   c. Neither agree nor disagree
   d. Disagree
   e. Totally disagree

Indicate the language that best completes the following sentences.
1. The language that I like to speak the most is:
   Spanish ____ Catalan ____ Heritage language ____
2. The language that connects me the most to my culture is:
   Spanish ____ Catalan ____ Heritage language ____
3. I mostly watch TV and movies in:
   Spanish ____ Catalan ____ Heritage language ____
4. I mostly listen to the radio/music in:
   Spanish ____ Catalan ____ Heritage language ____
5. I mostly read in:
   Spanish ____ Catalan ____ Heritage language ____
6. I use social media (Facebook, Twitter, etc.) in:
   Spanish ____ Catalan ____ Heritage language ____
7. The most difficult language to learn is:
   Spanish ____ Catalan ____ Heritage language ____
8. The language that is most useful to my professional life is:
   Spanish ____ Catalan ____ Heritage language ____
9. The language that is most useful to my daily life is:
   Spanish ____ Catalan ____ Heritage language ____
10. I write emails mostly in:
   Spanish ____ Catalan ____ Heritage language ____
11. The language I use among family and friends is:
   Spanish ____ Catalan ____ Heritage language ____
12. When I text someone, I usually text them in:
   Spanish ____ Catalan ____ Heritage language ____
13. When I speak to people I don't know, I speak:
   Spanish ____ Catalan ____ Heritage language ____
14. I am most motivated to master:
   Spanish ____ Catalan ____ Heritage language ____
15. If at a restaurant, I speak to the staff in:
   Spanish ____ Catalan ____ Heritage language ____
16. If at the doctor's office, I speak to the staff in:
   Spanish ____ Catalan ____ Heritage language ____
17. If at a grocery store, I speak to the staff in:
   Spanish ____ Catalan ____ Heritage language ____

Indicate which speaker you associate the most with the following descriptions:

1. Modern: Spanish/Catalan ____ Heritage language ____
2. Open-minded: Spanish/Catalan ____ Heritage language ____
3. Educated: Spanish/Catalan ____ Heritage language ____
4. Sociable: Spanish/Catalan ____ Heritage language ____
5. Friendly: Spanish/Catalan ____ Heritage language ____
6. Wealthy: Spanish/Catalan ____ Heritage language ____
7. Religious: Spanish/Catalan ____ Heritage language ____
8. Literate: Spanish/Catalan ____ Heritage language ____
9. International/global: Spanish/Catalan ____ Heritage language ____
10. Prestigious: Spanish/Catalan ____ Heritage language ____
11. Pure: Spanish/Catalan ____ Heritage language ____
12. Informal: Spanish/Catalan ____ Heritage language ____
13. Beautiful: Spanish/Catalan ____ Heritage language ____
14. Practical: Spanish/Catalan ____ Heritage language ____
15. Powerful: Spanish/Catalan ____ Heritage language ____
16. Formal: Spanish/Catalan ____ Heritage language ____
17. Authoritative: Spanish/Catalan ____ Heritage language ____
18. Emotional: Spanish/Catalan ____ Heritage language ____

Appendix B: Interview Questions

Preguntas de entrevista

1. (**Trasfondo**) ¿Dónde naciste y en qué otros lugares has vivido?
2. (**Identidad como minoridad**) Como una minoridad, ¿sientes una conexión a la vida aquí? ¿Sientes que encajas aquí? ¿Por qué sí o no?
3. (**Uso de lengua**) Pensando de las lenguas que sabes, ¿con qué frecuencia usas cada, y con quién?
4. (**Competencia**) ¿Cómo describirías tus habilidades en cada lengua? ¿Tienes dificultades para comunicarte en estas lenguas?
5. (**Mantenimiento de lengua/cultura de herencia**) ¿Piensas que hay una presencia de tu lengua/cultura de herencia aquí? ¿Piensas que aumenta o disminuye con el tiempo? Estás satisfecha con el estatus actual (ej: en tu familia o comunidad), o deseas que sea diferente de alguna manera?
6. (**Cambio de preferencias**) ¿Piensas que la manera en que hablas, o que tus preferencias lingüísticas han cambiado con el tiempo? ¿Cómo?
7. (**Prestigio**) Pensando de las lenguas que oyes en Barcelona, ¿cómo evaluarías cada lengua en cuanto a su prestigio, y por qué?
8. (**Género**) Depende de si hablas con un hombre o mujer, ¿varía tu estilo de habla, o la lengua que escoges? ¿Cómo? ¿Ha cambiado esta tendencia con el tiempo?
9. (**Cambio de código**) ¿Puedes pensar de una ocasión cuando habías alternado entre lenguas mientras estabas conversando con alguien? ¿Qué te hace alternar entre lenguas?

Interview Questions

1. (**Background**) Where were you born and what places have you lived?
2. (**Identity as a minority**) As a minority, do you feel connected to life here? Do you feel that you belong? Why or why not?

3. (**Language use**) Thinking of the languages that you know, how often do you use each of them and with whom?

4. (**Competence**) How would you describe your abilities in each language? Do you ever have any difficulties when communicating in any of these languages?

5. (**Heritage language/culture maintenance**) Do you think that there's much of a presence of your heritage language/culture here? Do you think it's increasing or decreasing with time, and how so? Are you happy with its current status (in your family, in your community), or do you wish things were different in any way?

6. (**Change in preferences**) Do you think that the way you speak or that your language preferences have changed over time? In what ways?

7. (**Prestige**) Thinking of all the languages you hear in Barcelona – regardless of whether or not you know them – how would you rank each of them in terms of prestige, and why?

8. (**Gender**) Does your manner of speaking or the language you choose to use vary at all depending on whether you're speaking to a man or woman? How so? Has this tendency changed over time?

9. (**Code-switching**) Can you think of any times where you had switched between languages while conversing with someone? What makes you switch languages?

References

Ajuntament de Mataró (2019) Estudi de la Població. See https://www.mataro.cat/ca/actualitat/publicacions/estudi-de-la-poblacio-de-mataro/estudi-de-la-poblacio-mataro-1-de-gener-de-2019/estudi_poblacio_mataro_1_gener_2019.pdf (accessed 2 July 2021).
Ali, F. (2020) Multilingualism and acculturation in Catalonia: An analysis of Muslim immigrant women. *Cuadernos de Lingüística Hispánica* 36, 181–209.
Ali, F. (2021) At the intersection of language, gender, and religion: Self-reported linguistic ideologies and practices of Muslim women in Barcelona. *Sociolinguistic Studies* 15 (2/3), 223–245.
Ali, F. (in press) Constructing identity through code choice and code-switching: Evidence from multilingual Muslim women in Barcelona. *Revista Española de Lingüística Aplicada* 36 (2).
Ali, F. and Ready, C. (2021) Integration or assimilation? A comparative intertextual analysis of language policy in Madrid and Catalonia. *International Journal of Language and Law* 10, 24–47.
Ansah, G.N. (2018) Acculturation and integration: Language dynamics in the rural north-urban south mobility situation in Ghana. *Legon Journal of the Humanities* 29 (1), 53–72.
Astor, A. (2020) Religion and counter-state nationalism in Catalonia. *Social Compass* 67 (2), 159–176.
Atkins, C.P. (1993) Do employment recruiters discriminate on the basis of nonstandard dialect? *Journal of Employment Counseling* 30, 108–118.
Atkinson, D. (2018) Catalan and Spanish in an independent Catalonia: Linguistic authority and officiality. *Language in Society* 47 (5), 763–785.
Austin, J.L. (1962) *How To Do Things With Words*. Cambridge, MA: Harvard University Press.
Badosa Roldós, A. (2020) The mirror effect: Identity and minorisation among the Quechuas and Amazighs in Catalonia. *The SOAS Journal of Postgraduate Research* 12, 4–19.
Balfour, S. and Quiroga, A. (2007) *The Reinvention of Spain: Nation and Identity Since Democracy*. Oxford: Oxford University Press.
Benítez Fernández, M. (2019) Levelling in progress: A case study of young people speaking Moroccan Arabic in Zaragoza, Spain. *Sociolinguistic Studies* 12 (2), 165–183.
Bentahila, A. (1983) *Language Attitudes among Arabic-French Bilinguals in Morocco*. Clevedon: Multilingual Matters.
Billings, A. (2005) Beyond the Ebonics debate: Attitudes about black and standard American English. *Journal of Black Studies* 36 (1), 68–81.
Block, D. and Corona, V. (2019) Critical LPP and the intersection of class, race and language policy and practice in twenty first century Catalonia. *Language Policy* 21 (4), 1–21.
Branchadell, A. (2015) Language education for adult migrants in Catalonia: Nation-state ambitions without nation-state resources. In J. Simpson and A. Whiteside (eds) *Adult Language Education and Migration* (pp. 82–93). New York: Routledge.
Bucholtz, M. and Hall, K. (2005) Identity and interaction: A sociocultural linguistic approach. *Discourse Studies* 7 (4/5), 585–614.

Butler, J. (1990) *Gender Trouble: Feminism and the Subversion of Identity.* New York: Routledge.
Butler, J. (1993) *Bodies That Matter: On the Discursive Limits of 'Sex.'* New York: Routledge.
Carner-Ribalta, J. (1995) *The Catalan Nation and its People.* Houston, TX: American Institute for Catalan Studies.
Chakrani, B. (2011) Covert language attitudes: A new outlook on the sociolinguistic space of Morocco. In E.G. Bokamba, R.K. Shosted and B.T. Ayalew (eds) *Selected Proceedings of the 40th Annual Conference on African Linguistics* (pp. 168–177). Somerville, MA: Cascadilla Proceedings Project.
Constitution of Spain (1978) See http://www.senado.es/constitu_i/indices/consti_ing.pdf (accessed 23 June 2021).
Court of Justice of the European Union (2021) Press release no 128/21: Judgment in joined cases C-804/18 and C-341/19 WABE and MH Müller Handel. See https://curia.europa.eu/jcms/upload/docs/application/pdf/2021-07/cp210128en.pdf (accessed 17 July 2021).
Craig, H. (2016) *African American English and the Achievement Gap: The Role of Dialectal Code Switching.* New York: Routledge.
Crameri, K. (2014) *Goodbye, Spain? The Question of Independence for Catalonia.* Brighton: Sussex Academic Press.
Crenshaw, K. (1989) Demarginalizing the intersection of race and sex: A Black feminist critique of antidiscrimination doctrine, feminist theory and antiracist politics. *University of Chicago Legal Forum* 1 (8), 138–167.
Cortès-Colomé, M., Barrieras, M. and Comellas, P. (2016) Changes in immigrant individuals' language attitudes through contact with Catalan: The mirror effect. *Language Awareness* 25 (4), 272–289.
Darvin, R. and Norton, B. (2014) Social class, identity, and migrant students. *Journal of Language, Identity, and Education* 13, 111–117.
De Fina, A. (2015) Narrative and identities. In A. De Fina and A. Georgakopoulou (eds) *The Handbook of Narrative Analysis* (pp. 351–368). Malden, MA: Wiley Blackwell.
Deaux, K. (2006) *To Be an Immigrant.* New York: Russell Sage Foundation.
Departament de Justícia (2019) Islam. See http://justicia.gencat.cat/web/.content/afers-religiosos/documents/Mapa_2014/2014_Fitxa_Islam.pdf (accessed 25 June 2021).
Doss, R.C. and Gross, A.M. (1994) The effects of Black English and code-switching on intraracial perceptions. *Journal of Black Psychology* 20 (3), 282–293.
Doughty, C.J. and Long, M.H. (eds) (2003) *The Handbook of Second Language Acquisition.* New York: Blackwell.
Dwyer, C. (2000) Negotiating diasporic identities: Young British South Asian Muslim women. *Women's Studies International Forum* 23 (4), 475–486.
Estors Sastre, L. (2014) Les Actituds lingüístiques segons l'origen dels aprenents de català com a llengua d'acollida. *Treballs de Sociolingüística Catalana* 24, 153–171.
Fader, A. (2001) Literacy, bilingualism and gender in a Hasidic community. *Linguistics and Education* 12 (3), 261–283.
Fader, A. (2006) Learning faith: Language socialization in a Hasidic community. *Language in Society* 35 (2), 207–229.
Fader, A. (2007) Redeeming sacred sparks: Syncretism and gendered language shift among Hasidic Jews in New York. *Journal of Linguistic Anthropology* 17 (1), 1–23.
Fader, A. (2009) *Mitzvah Girls: Bringing Up the Next Generation of Hasidic Jews in Brooklyn.* Princeton, NJ: Princeton University Press.
Freed, A. (1996) Language and gender research in an experimental setting. In V. Bergvall, J. Bing and A. Freed (eds) *Rethinking Language and Gender Research: Theory and Practice* (pp. 54–76). London: Longman.
Fukuda, M. (2017) Language use in the context of double minority: The case of Japanese-Catalan/Spanish families in Catalonia. *International Journal of Multilingualism* 14 (4), 401–418.

Fukuda, M. (2020) Transmission of Japanese as a heritage language in the bilingual polity of Catalonia: A case study. *Journal of Asian Pacific Communication*. Advance online publication.

Furseth, I. (2011) The hijab: Boundary work and identity negotiations among immigrant Muslim women in the Los Angeles area. *Review of Religious Research* 52 (4), 365–385.

Gardner, R.C. and Lambert, W.E. (1972) *Attitudes and Motivation in Second Language Learning*. Rowley, MA: Newbury House.

Garner, S. and Selod, S. (2015) The racialization of Muslims: Empirical studies of Islamophobia. *Critical Sociology* 41 (1), 9–19.

Geeslin, K.L. with Long, A.Y. (2014) Social approaches to second language acquisition (Ch. 4). In *Sociolinguistics and Second Language Acquisition: Learning to Use Language in Context* (pp. 101–132). New York, NY: Routledge.

Generalitat de Catalunya (1983) Llei de normalització lingüística a Catalunya. See https://llengua.gencat.cat/web/.content/documents/legislacio/llei_de_politica_linguistica/arxius/lleinl83.pdf (accessed 23 June 2021).

Generalitat de Catalunya (2004) Pla per a la llengua i la cohesió social. See http://www.xtec.cat/serveis/eap/e3900133/pdf/cohesio.pdf (accessed 23 June 2021).

Generalitat de Catalunya (2017a) Pla de ciutadania i de les migracions, 2017–2020. See https://treballiaferssocials.gencat.cat/web/.content/01departament/08publicacions/ambits_tematics/immigracio/Plans_i_programes/06plainmigracio_cat_2017_2020/Pla_inmigracioue_CAT_OK.pdf (accessed 23 June 2021).

Generalitat de Catalunya (2017b) October 1 referendum results. See https://govern.cat/govern/docs/2017/10/06/17/33/f5784e70-2ab7-4b66-b439-9c644af14cc0.pdf (accessed 27 June 2021).

Generalitat of Catalunya (2019a) Foreign Population by Countries. *Institute of Statistics of Catalonia*. See http://www.idescat.cat/poblacioestrangera/?b=12 (accessed 23 June 2021).

Generalitat of Catalunya (2019b) Informe de política lingüística. See https://llengua.gencat.cat/web/.content/documents/informepl/arxius/IPL-2019.pdf (accessed 23 June 2021).

Goble, R. (2016) Linguistic insecurity and lack of entitlement to Spanish among third-generation Mexican Americans in narrative accounts. *Heritage Language Journal* 13 (1), 29–54.

Gore, S. (2002) The Catalan language and immigrants from outside the European Union. *International Journal of Iberian Studies* 15 (2), 91–102.

Hajar, A. (2017) Identity, investment and language learning strategies of two Syrian students in Syria and Britain. *Language, Culture and Curriculum* 30 (3), 250–264.

Hammer, K. (2017) Language through a prism: Patterns of L2 internalisation and use in acculturated bilinguals. *Journal of Pragmatics* 117, 72–87.

Hoffmann, C. (2000) Balancing language planning and language rights: Catalonia's uneasy juggling act. *Journal of Multilingual and Multicultural Development* 21 (5), 425–441.

Holmes, J. (1993) Immigrant women and language maintenance in Australia and New Zealand. *International Journal of Applied Linguistics* 3 (2), 159–179.

Holstein, J. and Gubrium, J. (eds) (2003) *Inside Interviewing: New Lenses, New Concerns*. Thousand Oaks, CA: Sage Publications.

Huguet, À. and Janés, J. (2008) Mother tongue as a determining variable in language attitudes. The case of immigrant Latin American students in Spain. *International Journal of Bilingual Education and Bilingualism* 8 (4), 247–260.

Ianos, M., Caballé, E., Petreñas, C. and Huguet, Á. (2019) Language attitudes of young Romanians in Catalonia (Spain): The role of heritage language maintenance programs. *Multilingua* 38, 335–355.

Iikkanen, P. (2019) Migrant women, work, and investment in language learning: Two success stories. *Applied Linguistics Review* 1. Ahead of print.

Inda, J.X. (2000) Performativity, materiality, and the racial body. *Latino Studies Journal* 11 (3), 74–99.
Institut d'Estadística de Catalunya (2018) Usos lingüístics de la població. Llengua inicial, d'identificació i habitual. See https://www.idescat.cat/indicadors/?id=anuals&n=10364 (accessed 23 July 2021).
Kamada, L.D. (2010) *Hybrid Identities and Adolescent Girls: Being 'Half' in Japan*. Bristol: Multilingual Matters.
Kang, A. (2004) Constructing ethnic identity through discourse: Self-categorization among Korean American camp counselors. *Pragmatics* 14 (2/3), 217–233.
Khan, K. and Gallego Balsà, L. (2021) Racialized trajectories to Catalan higher education: Language, anti-racism and the 'Politics of Listening'. *Applied Linguistics* 42 (6), 1083–1096.
Killian, C. (2003) The other side of the veil: North African women in France respond to the headscarf affair. *Gender and Society* 17 (4), 567–590.
Killian, C. and Johnson, C. (2006) 'I'm Not an Immigrant!': Resistance, redefinition, and the role of resources in identity work. *Social Psychology Quarterly* 69 (1), 60–80.
Korteweg, A. (2008) The Sharia debate in Ontario: Gender, Islam, and representations of Muslim women's agency. *Gender and Society* 22 (4), 434–454.
Korteweg, A. (2017) The failures of 'immigrant integration': The gendered racialized production of non-belonging. *Migration Studies* 5 (3), 428–444.
Lakoff, R. (1973) Language and woman's place. *Language in Society* 2 (1), 45–80.
Lambert, W., Hodgson, R., Gardner, R. and Fillenbaum, S. (1960) Evaluational reactions to spoken languages. *Journal of Abnormal and Social Psychology* 60, 44–51.
Lanz, T., Daussà, E. and Pera-Ros, R. (2020) Two-way integration of heritage and minoritized speakers: Voices from Catalonia. In U. Hoinkes and M. Meyer (eds) *Der Einfluss der Migration auf Sprach- und Kulturräume [The Impact of Migration on Language and Culture Areas]* (pp. 179–208). Hamburg: Peter Lang.
Levon, E. (2015) Integrating intersectionality in language, gender, and sexuality research. *Language and Linguistics Compass* 9 (7), 295–308.
Levon, E. and Mendes, R.B. (eds) (2016) *Language, Sexuality, and Power: Studies in Intersectional Sociolinguistics*. Oxford: Oxford University Press.
Marshall, S. (2007) New Latino diaspora and new zones of language contact: A social constructionist analysis of Spanish speaking Latin Americans in Catalonia. In J. Holmquist, A. Lorenzino and L. Sayahi (eds) *Selected Proceedings of the Third Workshop on Spanish Sociolinguistics* (pp. 150–161). Somerville, MA: Cascadilla Proceedings Project.
Massey, D. and Sánchez, M. (2010) *Brokered Boundaries: Creating Immigrant Identity in Anti-Immigrant Times*. New York: Russell Sage Foundation.
Menard-Warwick, J. (2009) *Gendered Identities and Immigrant Language Learning*. Bristol: Multilingual Matters.
Mijares Molina, L. (2006) *Aprendiendo a ser marroquíes. Inmigración, diversidad lingüística y escuela*. Madrid: Ediciones de Oriente y del Mediterráneo.
Mohamed, S., González, C. and Muntendam, A. (2019) Arabic-Spanish language contact in Puerto Rico: A case of glottal stop epenthesis. *Languages* 4 (4), 93.
Mora, A., Trejo, P. and Roux, R. (2016) The complexities of being and becoming language teachers: Issues of identity and investment. *Language and Intercultural Communication* 16 (2), 182–198.
Moreno-Fernández, F. (2009) Integración sociolingüística en contextos de inmigración: marco epistemológico para su estudio en España. *Lengua y migración* 1 (1), 121–156.
Moscoso García, F. (2013) El programa hispano-marroquí de enseñanza de Lengua Árabe y Cultura Marroquí (LACM) sometido a revisión. Arabe marroquí y amazige, lenguas nativas (L1). *Anaquel de Estudios Árabes* 24, 119–136.

Moustaoui Srhir, A. (2013) Nueva economía y dinámicas de cambio sociolingüístico en el paisaje lingüístico de Madrid: el caso del árabe. *Revista Internacional de Lingüística Iberoamericana* 1 (21–XI), 89–108.

Moustaoui Srhir, A. (2016) Tú serás el responsable ante Dios el día del juicio si no le enseñas árabe [a tu hijo o hija]: lengua árabe, identidad y vitalidad etnolingüística en un grupo de marroquíes en Madrid. *Lengua y migración* 8 (1), 51–79.

Moustaoui Srhir, A. (2018) Recontextualización sociolingüística y superdiversidad. El árabe en el paisaje lingüístico del barrio de Lavapiés en Madrid. *Lingue e Linguaggi* 25, 197–225.

Moustaoui Srhir, A. (2020) Making children multilingual: Language policy and parental agency in transnational and multilingual Moroccan families in Spain. *Journal of Multilingual and Multicultural Development* 41 (1), 108–120.

Moustaoui Srhir, A., Vázquez, G.P. and Varela, L.Z. (2019) Procesos de agentividad y nuevos repertorios translingüísticos de los estudiantes de origen magrebí en Galicia. *Al-Andalus Magreb* 26, 07-1.

Muslims for American Progress (2018) An impact report of Muslim contributions to New York City. See https://www.ispu.org/wp-content/uploads/2018/08/MAP-NY-Key-Findings-Web.pdf (accessed 28 July 2021).

Newman, M. and Trenchs-Parera, M. (2015) Language policies, ideologies and attitudes in Catalonia. Part 1: Reversing language shift in the twentieth century. *Language and Linguistic Compass* 9 (7), 285–294.

Norton, B. (2013) Identity and second language acquisition. In C.A. Chapelle (ed.) *The Encyclopedia of Applied Linguistics* (pp. 1–8). Blackwell Publishing Ltd.

Norton, B. (2000) *Identity and Language Learning: Gender, Ethnicity, and Educational Change* (1st edn). Harlow: Longman.

Observatorio Andalusí (2019) Informe anual 2019. See https://ucide.org/wp-content/uploads/2021/04/ia2019.pdf (accessed 28 June 2021).

Parlament de Catalunya (2006) Statute of Autonomy of Catalonia. See https://web.gencat.cat/en/generalitat/estatut/estatut2006/titol_1/ (accessed 13 July 2021).

Parlament de Catalunya (2010) Llei d'acollída de les persones immigrades i de les retornades a Catalunya. See https://www.parlament.cat/document/nom/TL111.pdf (accessed 23 June 2021).

Park, M. (2011) Identity and agency among heritage language learners. In K.A. Davis (ed.) *Critical Qualitative Research in Second Language Studies: Agency and Advocacy* (pp. 171–207). Charlotte, NC: Information Age Publishing.

Pauwels, A. (1997) The role of gender in immigrant language maintenance in Australia. In W. Wolck and A. Houwer (eds) *Recent Studies in Contact Linguistics* (pp. 276–286). Bonn: Dümmler.

Perocco, F. (2018) Anti-migrant Islamophobia in Europe. Social roots, mechanisms and actors. *REMHU: Revista Interdisciplinar da Mobilidade Humana* 26 (53), 25–40.

Pew Research Center (2011) The future of the global Muslim population: Muslim-majority countries. See https://www.pewforum.org/2011/01/27/future-of-the-global-muslim-population-muslim-majority/ (accessed 5 June 2021).

Pew Research Center (2018) New estimates show U.S. Muslim population continues to grow. See https://www.pewresearch.org/fact-tank/2018/01/03/new-estimates-show-u-s-muslim-population-continues-to-grow/ (accessed 28 June 2021).

Plann, S. (2009) Arabic: Another 'other Spanish language'? *International Journal of Multilingualism* 6 (4), 369–385.

Polkinghorne, D.E. (1995) Narrative configuration in qualitative analysis. *Qualitative Studies in Education* 8, 5–23.

Predelli, L. (2004) Interpreting gender in Islam: A case study of immigrant Muslim women in Oslo, Norway. *Gender and Society* 18 (4), 473–493.

Pujolar, J. (2007) African women in Catalan language courses: Struggles over class, gender and ethnicity in advanced liberalism. In B. McElhinny (ed.) *Words, Worlds, and Material Girls* (pp. 305–348). New York: De Gruyter Mouton.

Pujolar, J. (2010) Immigration and language education in Catalonia: Between national and social agendas. *Linguistics and Education* 21, 229–243.

Pujolar, J. and Gonzàlez, I. (2013) Linguistic 'Mudes' and the de-ethnicization of language choice in Catalonia. *International Journal of Bilingual Education and Bilingualism* 16 (2), 138–152.

Ready, C. (2021) 'Yo me siento andalusí': El marco espaciotemporal en la construcción de identidad de inmigrantes marroquíes en Granada, España. *Lengua y migración* 13 (1), 7–32.

Rice, C., Harrison, E. and Friedman, M. (2019) Doing justice to intersectionality in research. *Cultural Studies ↔ Critical Methodologies* 19 (6), 409–420.

Rida, A. and Milton, M. (2001) The non-joiners: Why migrant Muslim women aren't accessing English language classes. *Prospect* 16 (1), 35–62.

Rodríguez-García, D., Solana, M., Ortiz, A. and Ballestín, B. (2021) Blurring of colour lines? Ethnoracially mixed youth in Spain navigating identity. *Journal of Ethnic and Migration Studies* 47 (4), 838–860.

Roller, E. (2002) When does language become exclusivist? Linguistic politics in Catalonia. *National Identities* 4 (3), 273–289.

Sadiqi, F. (2009) Language, gender, and power in Morocco. In H. Herzog and A. Braude (eds) *Gendering Religion and Politics* (pp. 259–275). New York: Palgrave Macmillan.

Sánchez-Muñoz, A. (2016) Heritage language healing? Learners' attitudes and damage control in a heritage language classroom. In D. Pascual y Cabo (ed.) *Advances in Spanish as a Heritage Language* (pp. 205–218). Philadelphia: John Benjamins.

Schumann, H. (1978) The acculturation model for second-language acquisition. In R.C. Gingras (ed.) *Second Language Acquisition and Foreign Language Teaching* (pp. 27–50). Washington, DC: Center for Applied Linguistics.

Schumann, J. (1986) Research on the acculturation model for second language acquisition. *Journal of Multilingual and Multicultural Development* 7, 379–392.

Selod, S. (2018) Gendered racialization: Muslim American men and women's encounters with racialized surveillance. *Ethnic and Racial Studies* 42 (4), 552–569.

Siguán, M. (1992) *España plurilingüe*. Online: Alianza Editorial.

Silverstein, M. (1979) Language structure and linguistic ideology. In P.R. Clyne, W.F. Hanks and C.L. Hofbauer (eds) *The Elements: A Parasession on Linguistic Units and Levels* (pp. 193–248). Chicago, IL: Chicago Linguistic Society.

Skilton-Sylvester, E. (2002) Should I stay or should I go? Investigating Cambodian women's participation and investment in adult ESL programs. *Adult Education Quarterly* 53 (1), 9–26.

Soler, J. and Gallego-Balsà, L. (2019) *The Sociolinguistics of Higher Education: Language Policy and Internationalisation in Catalonia*. Cham: Palgrave.

Stewart, I., Pinter, Y. and Eisenstein, J. (2018) Sí o no, ¿que penses? Catalonian independence and linguistic identity on social media. In M. Walker, H. Ji and A. Stent (eds) *Proceedings of the 2018 Conference of the North American Chapter of the Association for Computational Linguistics: Human Language Technologies, Volume 2 (Short Papers)* (pp. 136–141). New Orleans, Louisiana.

Trenchs-Parera, M. and Newman, M. (2009) Diversity of language ideologies in two generations of Spanish-speaking youth of immigrant origin in Catalonia. *Journal of Multilingual and Multicultural Development* 30 (6), 509–524.

Tsalikis, J., DeShields Jr, O.W., and LaTour, M.S. (1991) The role of accent on the credibility and effectiveness of the international business person: The case of Guatemala. *The Journal of Personal Selling & Sales Management* 11 (1), 31–41.

Turell, M.T. (ed.) (2000) *Multilingualism in Spain: Sociolinguistic and Psycholinguistic Aspects of Linguistic Minority Groups*. Clevedon: Multilingual Matters.

Varro, G. (1992) Les 'langues immigrées' face à l'école française. *Language Problems & Language Planning* 16 (2), 137–162.

Vasilopoulos, G. (2015) Language learner investment and identity negotiation in the Korean EFL context. *Journal of Language, Identity & Education* 14 (2), 61–79.

Vila i Moreno, F.X. and Galindo Solé, M. (2012) Sobre la història i l'extensió de la norma de convergència lingüística a Catalunya. *Institut d'Estudis Catalans*.

Woolard, K. (1989) *Double Talk: Bilingualism and the Politics of Ethnicity in Catalonia*. Stanford, CA: Stanford University Press.

Zentella, A. (1987) Language and female identity in the Puerto Rican community. In J. Penfield (ed.) *Women & Language in Transition* (pp. 167–179). Albany, NY: State University of New York Press.

Index

Accommodation 5, 37, 40, 67, 129
Acculturation
   Acculturation Model (see also
     Schumann, J.) 4–6, 28–33,
     38–41, 43–45
Ali, F. 42, 50
Ansah, C. 41
Arabic language 7–8, 22–27, 32, 50,
   58, 65, 69, 76, 82, 91, 96–97,
   131, 142
Aranese 12–13, 17, 142
Assimilation 4, 19, 24–25, 30, 39,
   43–44, 102, 108, 127–128
Atkins, C.P. 98
Atkinson, D. 20
Attitudes (see also 'language attitudes')
   20, 23, 35–41, 52–55, 62–65,
   69–70, 77–79, 92–94, 96–97,
   104, 110–124, 126–127, 132,
   137–138, 141
Astor, A. 20, 131
Austin, J.L. 29

Badosa Roldós, A. 23
Balfour, S. 14
Barcelona 1–5, 12–13, 47, 49, 132
Belonging 5, 8, 18, 57–59, 67, 70, 92,
   100, 109, 127–128
Benítez Fernández, M. 26
Bentahila, A. 115, 118, 120
Berber 22, 50, 69–70, 100
Billings, A. 98
Block, D. 17, 37
Branchadell, A. 19
Bucholtz, M. 28
Butler, J. 28–30, 123, 130

Carner–Ribalta, J. 14
Catalan language 5, 12–27, 35–38,
   50–68, 70, 76–78, 83, 90–99,
   102–103, 104–124, 126–129,
   131, 135–143
Catalan government (see also
   Generalitat de Catalunya) 13,
   17–18, 27, 137, 141–144
Catalan Sign Language 12–14, 17, 138
Catalonia 4–5, 11–27, 35–38, 47, 60,
   66, 90, 109, 121–124, 126, 128,
   131–144
Chakrani, B. 115, 118, 120
Code-switching 31, 56, 98
Constitution of Spain 16
Craig, H. 98
Crameri, K. 19–20
Crenshaw, K. 31–32
Cortès-Colomé, M. 37–38, 64,
   121, 126

Darvin, R. 28, 42
Deaux, K. 44
De Fina, A. 54
Departament de Justícia 22
Domains of use 92, 105–110
Doss, C. 98
Doughty, C.J. 40
Dwyer, C. 33

Education 18–19, 34, 51, 54–55, 62,
   90–92, 107, 109, 118–119, 124,
   126, 137, 139–140, 142
Employment 21, 96, 105, 108, 119
English 3, 12, 34, 50, 53–54, 59–62,
   66–67, 77, 105, 133, 142
Estors Sastre, L. 38
Ethnicity 50, 72, 113–114
European Union 20, 34, 142

Fader, A. 34
Family 6–7, 22, 25–26, 68, 74, 80,
   82–83, 86, 108, 122

Children 7, 17, 22, 34, 51, 54–55, 108, 110, 112, 118
    Parents 80, 82, 84, 90, 91
Franco, Francisco 14–15, 64, 136
Freed, A. 30
French language 33, 50
Fukuda, M. 22, 43

Gallego-Balsà, L. 142
Gardner, R.C. 40
Geeslin, K.L. 40
Generalitat de Catalunya (see also *Catalan government*) 13, 16, 18–19, 49, 140–141
Gender 3–7, 9, 28–35, 42–49, 54–55, 58, 71–73, 78, 79, 88–89, 108, 123, 129–132, 134
Generation
    First-generation 22, 43, 51, 53–54, 57–78, 83–84, 102, 104–122, 126–127, 129–130, 137
    Generation 1.5 51, 56, 90
    Second-generation 35, 43, 51, 53–54, 79–103, 105–122, 126–127, 129–130, 136–138, 143
Goble, R. 43
Gore, S. 21, 36, 38, 121, 126

Hajar, A. 42
Hammer, K. 41
Heritage
    Heritage communities 25, 127, 129
    Heritage speakers 43, 48
Hijab 49, 68, 77, 94–97, 101, 121, 123, 129–130
Hoffman, C. 17
Holmes, J. 31
Holstein, J. 55
Huguet, À. 121

Ianos, M. 23
Identity
    Gendered identity (see *Gender*)
    Heritage identity (see *Heritage*)
    Religious identity 2–4, 6–10, 20, 22, 24–27, 31–34, 46–49, 55, 58, 63, 68, 71–75, 78–79, 81–82, 85–86, 94–96, 101–102, 115–116, 122–123, 129–131, 134, 139
    Immigrant identity 4–5, 43–45
Ideologies 8, 11, 14–15, 17, 19–20, 25, 30–31, 35–37, 43–45, 55, 68, 102, 128, 132, 135–141
Iikkanen, P. 42
Immigrant 4–6, 9–10, 12, 18–27, 30–49, 51, 57–124, 125–135, 138–144
    Immigrant identity (see *Identity*)
Immigration (see also *migration*) 14–15, 21, 26, 44–35
Inda, J.X. 28, 30, 123, 130,
Informe de política lingüística 13–14, 20, 22
Integration 4, 18–19, 24, 33, 38–39, 41, 43–44, 61, 77, 96, 98, 102, 128–129, 133–134, 140
Intersectionality 5–6, 9–10, 28, 31–32, 43–46, 78, 125, 129–131, 143–144
Investment (see also *Norton, B.*) 28, 32, 38–43, 70, 109, 126, 133
Islam (see also *Muslim*) 6–8, 22–24, 31–33, 48–49, 68, 72, 74–75, 78, 82, 95

Kamada, L. 42
Kang, A. 28
Killian, C. 33, 44
Korteweg, A. 31, 44

Lakoff, R. 29–31
Language attitudes 37–38, 63, 110–124, 132, 144
Language learning 32, 34, 38, 40–45, 60, 64–65, 76–77, 128, 132, 137
Language maintenance 13, 19–27, 31, 35, 108, 112–113, 119, 136, 138
Language planning 17, 137, 141–142
Language policy 11–27, 47, 77, 101–103, 128, 135–144
Language use 4–6, 11–12, 17, 27–30, 34–35, 51–55, 60, 67, 80, 94, 100, 104–109, 120–123, 128–129, 132
Lanz, T. 43
Levon, E. 32
Llei de normalització lingüística (see also *Llei de política lingüística* and *Linguistic Normalization Act*)
Llei de política lingüística 16

Likert scale 52, 104, 110–114, 118–119, 121–122
Linguistic normalization 8, 16–17, 139
Linguistic Normalization Act (see also *Llei de política lingüística* and *Llei de normalizació lingüístic*) 16

Marshall, S. 121
Massey, D. 123
Mataró 47, 84
Menard-Warwick, J. 32, 42
Migrant (see *immigrant*)
Migration (see *immigration*)
Mijares Molina, L. 23–24
Mohamed, S. 24
Mora, A. 42
Moreno-Fernández, F. 21–22
Moroccan 1, 21–27, 33, 38, 47, 56–57, 69–70, 73–76, 80–83, 91, 97–98, 100–101
Mosques 7, 33, 48–49, 75
Moustaoui Srhir, A. 24–25, 122
Multiculturalism 24, 54, 95, 100–103, 140, 142–143
Multilingualism 11–12, 24–26, 54, 70, 99–100, 119, 122, 125, 134, 140–144
Muslim (see also *Islam*)
Muslim speech communities 6–7

Narrative analysis 54
Newman, M. 17–18, 35–36, 47, 121, 139
Norton, B. 28, 31–32, 40–42

Parlament de Catalunya 124
Park, M. 43, 54
Pauwels, A. 31
Performativity 29–30, 123, 129–130
Perocco, F. 8
Pew Research Center 2, 22, 32
Pla de ciutadania i de les migracions 18, 140
Pla per a la llengua i la cohesió social 18, 141
Plann, S. 26
Polkinghorne, D.E. 54
Positionality, researcher 47–48
Predelli, L. 33
Prestige (see also *status*) 14, 26, 57, 60–62, 98, 109, 115, 118, 126, 133, 139

Pujolar, J. 17, 37, 119, 121
Punjabi language 50–52

Racism 68, 74, 86–87, 92–93, 143
Ready, C. 19, 25–26
Religion (see *identity*)
Rice, C. 32
Rida, A. 34, 139
Roller, E. 17

Sadiqi, F. 33
Sánchez-Muñoz, A. 30, 43, 123, 130
Schumann, J. 36, 38–41
Selod, S. 8
Siguán, M. 14
Silverstein, M. 55
Skilton-Sylvester, E. 42
Social cohesion 18, 103, 140–142
Soler, J. 142
Solidarity 2, 4, 115–120, 122–123, 136
Spain 2, 5, 12–16, 20–21, 23–27, 45–46, 50–51, 62–64, 72–73, 77, 95–96, 100–101, 131, 142
Spanish language 4–5, 9–10, 12–17, 20–22, 24–26, 31, 35–38, 50–56, 58–62, 64–67, 70–71, 73–74, 77, 79, 83–84, 86, 88, 91, 93–102, 104–112, 115–127, 129–133, 135–138, 141–142, 144
Status (see *prestige*)
Stewart, I. 20
Statute of Autonomy 12, 17, 124

Trenchs-Parera, M. 17–18, 35–36, 47, 121, 139
Tsalikis, J. 53
Turell, M.T. 12

Urdu language 3, 48, 50–54, 56, 59–60, 62, 65, 70–71, 80–81, 92–93, 133

Varro, G. 24
Vasilopoulos, G. 42
Vila i Moreno, F.X. 37

Woolard, K. 14, 21, 35, 37

Xenophobia 69–70, 87–88, 94, 143

Zentella, A. 30–31